The Politics of Memory

The Politics of Memory

Urban Cultural Heritage in Brazil

Andreza Aruska de Souza Santos

ROWMAN &
LITTLEFIELD
INTERNATIONAL
London • New York

Published by Rowman & Littlefield International Ltd.
6 Tinworth Street, London, SE11 5AL, UK
www.rowmaninternational.com

Rowman & Littlefield International Ltd. is an affiliate of Rowman & Littlefield

4501 Forbes Boulevard, Suite 200, Lanham, Maryland 20706, USA
With additional offices in Boulder, New York, Toronto (Canada), and Plymouth (UK)
www.rowman.com

British Library Cataloguing in Publication Data
A catalogue record for this book is available from the British Library

ISBN: HB 978-1-78661-121-5

Library of Congress Cataloging-in-Publication Data

Library of Congress Control Number: 2019952188

ISBN: 978-1-78661-121-5 (cloth)
ISBN: 978-1-5381-4813-6 (pbk)
ISBN: 978-1-78661-122-2 (electronic)

For Alex.

Contents

Acknowledgements

This research started and finished with many cups of coffee shared across different houses in Ouro Preto. My debt to those who opened their homes to share their stories, memories, and annoyances with me will last forever. My special thanks to Celestina and Valeria Toffolo for being my hosts and my home away from home. To all Council members, my thanks for letting me be part of the meetings and for the friendship we established. To all functionaries in the Secretariat of Culture and Patrimony, my eternal thanks. I also want to thank the architects of the Institute for Historic and Artistic Patrimony in Brasília and Ouro Preto. The municipal archive in Ouro Preto was an open door to delve into the city's history, and I thank the functionaries working there.

I made friends during interviews, and I met friends of friends, to all of those I met in Ouro Preto, thank you, I will always return for more conversations. I also interacted with professors and students of the Federal University of Ouro Preto and visited the University of Brasília to exchange theoretical ideas with former professors, those interactions were extremely valuable to me.

Intellectually, I owe to Mark Harris for his precious contribution in every stage of this research. Not only his guidance but also his example in being a professor with a genuine passion for social interactions made me navigate the ethnographic world with a sense of contemplation. Peter Gow and his expertise on Brazil and anthropological writing as well as Angela Torresan, who examined this work when it was a dissertation, made my own ideas clearer to me. I am also in debt to several colleagues who offered feedback to the early stages of this research. There were those that could help me find the right tone to best represent a version of the stories I heard in Ouro Preto: Margaret Loney, who read this work from beginning to the end, has my especial thanks. Jessica Volz, Courtney Stafford-Walter, and Alex Mielke, thank you very much for suggesting edits and creatively exploring with me the world of Brazilian expressions.

I wrote this book while based at the Latin American Centre (LAC) at the University of Oxford. To my LAC colleagues Tim Power, Eduardo Posada-Carbo, David Doyle, Leigh Payne, and Diego Sanchez-Ancochea, many thanks for supporting me with the encouragement I needed. I also wish to thank Elizabeth Ewart, Elisabeth Hsu, and Ramon Sarró, who were fundamental during my arrival in Oxford. To Michael Keith, who shares with me a passion for the study of cities, whether in Brazil, in South Africa, or in India, many thanks for the support and inspiration in the many conversations and workshops we organised together. To Monique Marks, my special thanks for having inspired me to follow ethnographic investigations during my days as a young exchange student in Durban. The impact Monique has had on my writing is a reflection of the inspirational academic she is.

I would have never survived the research leading up to this book without the support from my family. To my wonderful sisters, mum, dad and niece, words cannot tell how much this is all because of you.

Alex, thank you for reading my work, for keeping me company, for guessing my thoughts when I could not express them. You know this work and me better than anyone else, and I thank you for your patience and love. This book is for you.

Andreza Aruska de Souza Santos,
Oxford, 2019

List of Graphs, Images, Map, and Tables

GRAPHS

IMAGES

MAP

TABLES

Preface

When I tell people that I was born in the city of Brasília, they look at me with intrigued faces as if a generation already born and raised there could not yet exist. Indeed it is due to my upbringing in Brasília that I am interested in the study of cities, what they represent, and their limitations in materialising social transformations. Being a *Brasiliense* in Ouro Preto was, however, challenging. Not only was I alien to the colonial town in the view of most people I met there but also to the life in a small city. Even then, I was never an outsider in Ouro Preto, due to a coincidence of elements I do not control. I accidentally learned the *mineiro* accent, and my social background opened many doors – allowing me to navigate not only amongst wealthy students, as I was coming from an elite university, but also amongst modest residents with whom I could share stories of a childhood in unpaved streets and the stories of migration I learned from my grandparents. I met people from all segments of society, and this privilege, which those I interviewed did not have, was mainly due to the hybridity of my upbringing and adaptation to other contexts beyond Brasília, in Hamburg, Freiburg, Durban, Delhi, Vienna, St. Andrews, Leipzig, São Paulo, or Oxford. Each city where I lived taught me something about city planning, preservation, and changes that I could apply to my own life as a native or a migrant.

Establishing friendships in Ouro Preto, however, at times put me in conflict, knowing the views of people who were directly opposing each other. Conflicts are engraved in the coming pages, and mine is an exercise in making sense of conflicts in a scholarly way, while at the same time respecting the friendship and privacy of individuals, even when they are public images. I recognise that as an anthropologist, a political scientist, a friend, the challenge to write about a city where everyone knows everyone else is tremendous. When I presented my work in two workshops in Ouro Preto in 2017 and 2018, I was fortunate to receive the feedback and approval from those I care most about here, the *Ouropretanos*. With *Ouropretanos* I share the passion to learn more about their city, the fictional and the everyday Ouro Preto.

Introduction

Who decides which stories about a city are remembered? How do interpretations of the past shape a city's present and future? In this book, I discuss notions of power and national identity by examining how nation states negotiate the preservation of urban spaces and how a city interprets, resists, and consents to the functions and meanings that it has inherited and that it reinvents for itself. Looking at the Brazilian city of Ouro Preto, which is hailed as a National Monument (1930) and as one of the first generations of UNESCO World Heritage Sites (1980), I provide a detailed analysis of the expectations, results, and subsequent conflicts in the preservation and management of Ouro Preto's urban heritage. In the process, I attend to the hierarchies of educational attainment, geographic dynamics, racial tensions, and socio-economic disparities that the city embodies. Drawing on recent scholarship concerning the narratives and aesthetics of public objects, I show that there is no possible consensus among residents and experts regarding the role of cultural heritage and its management. There are multiple and often competing views, needs, and desires among the types of people who use the city – permanent residents, politicians, students, and tourists. These differences naturally impact perceptions of history, aesthetics, and preservation. Preserving the sensorial and visual aesthetic of Ouro Preto as a heritage site also competes with the call to foster an inclusive urban infrastructure that adequately satisfies the needs of contemporary everyday living. In this puzzling and often paradoxical context, where everyone and everything are interconnected, I discuss the importance of a perspective that empowers diverse voices, as preservation requires widespread participation to reach flexible compromises.

The temporal pendulum upon which urban heritage swings – the preservation of the past for the benefit of the future – affects poor and wealthy residents differently. In the case of the conservation of nature, concerns about the 'end of the world' compete with those about the end of the month (Stiglitz 2019). However, the power struggles over the forms, functions, and memories of a city do not appear in public spheres as much as they do in everyday narratives. Despite the existence of participatory spheres of governance, of which Ouro Preto's City Council for the Preservation of Cultural and Natural Heritage (COMPATRI, or simply 'the Council' in this book) provides a prime example, attendance at such meetings is limited, and not all participants feel at liberty to openly voice their concerns. On the one hand, participation takes place in cities confined to a central-planning model, which led to the preservation of places such as Ouro Preto and the construction of Brasília and other cities in the twentieth century, on the other hand, not all citizens are adequately organised and informed to navigate in the participatory planning wave of the 2000s (Caldeira and Holston 2015: 2004). The imbalanced power play involving politicians, the private sector, and citizens can be observed in meetings where participants often remain silent about the views of the city that they share in private, or they publicly give their consent on issues despite voicing their fervent disagreement elsewhere. This ethnography is an attempt to understand the nuances of silence and consent that surface in participatory meetings concerning heritage. It further aims to identify the political weapons over city uses and interpretations happening beyond the public realm.

By looking at participatory practices in contemporary Ouro Preto, it is possible to evaluate common criticisms directed at many preserved sites in Brazil, where the process of preservation was imbued with personal relationships and state-centred momentum that did not address the needs of those most affected by such initiatives. When state-led preserved cities did not foster the socio-economic transformations envisioned when those preservation efforts were conceived, this top-down model buckled, giving way to participatory models. Participation over city making, however, can be either a 'means of deflecting pressing political and social concerns given its preoccupation with the . . . medium rather than the message' (Ellin 1996: 137) or a genuine opportunity for residents to direct the scope of preservation efforts in their vicinity. At such a crossroads, my discussion turns to addressing mechanisms that determine whether a heritage site turns into a mummification of the past, lifelessly displaying long-gone splendour, or becomes a living treasure for the heirs of today.

In Ouro Preto, power struggles have been materialised in architecture throughout the city's history. The construction and preservation of Brazilian Baroque architecture offered a cultural synthesis of art, religion, and creativity (Underwood 2001: 528). For that reason, Brazilian Baroque was selected as a visual metaphor for Brazilian national history at the dawn of Getúlio Vargas's government (1930–1945). As president, Vargas was concerned with the formation of national unity. In a country with a large number of former slaves and slave owners, Europeans, mixed-race Brazilian-born nationals, and indigenous communities, the focus on a common enemy – the colonisers – had much to offer in the search for a national identity (Chasteen 2003: xviii). Ouro Preto and its plots for independence supplied national heroes that became eternalised in stone, mortar, and plaster, giving a concrete image to the country (see image I.1). While preserved sections of the city provide a visual narrative of aesthetic tastes and manifestations of defiance against the crown, the houses erected on the slopes of hills have their own story to tell. When looking at houses on the outskirts and at mines, a nuanced and complex social history emerges that is at once multi-ethnic and supra-national, filled with religious syncretism, class divisions, and forms of resistance. The 'non-historic' city is thus a site where the 'difficult heritage' of Brazil is celebrated (Macdonald 2015). Tangible memories of slavery and socio-economic divisions, which can disturb a sense of national unity, can also serve as locations

Image I.1. Ouro Preto, Museum Casa dos Contos, 2013. ***Source*****: Personal collection.**

around which to resist a polarised view of the colonised and the colonisers, thus giving space to slaves' accounts and the complexity of mining economies. A story of power through architecture in Ouro Preto thus challenges an investigation of politics limited to political parties or public spheres of participation. At the same time, it challenges the understanding of city history limited to the borders of preservation. Dwelling places of the past and present, together with the city's infrastructure, represent forms of assimilation and resistance, inclusion and exclusion.

CULTURAL HERITAGE, CITIES, AND CITIZENSHIP

My research on Ouro Preto is part of the broad anthropological literature on cultural heritage, cities, citizenship, and the dynamics among these factors that fuel discussions about the preservation of cultural and natural heritage sites all over the world. The singularity and irreplaceability of natural landmarks and man-made monuments have inspired the preservation of select locations on a global scale. The ambition to hail sites as places of universal value and to protect them for generations to come gave rise to the title of Human Patrimony, initiated by UNESCO in 1972 (Canclini 2012: 69). Under this designation, monuments, entire cityscapes, and, more recently, forms of intangible heritage are preserved because of their exceptional value to humanity.

While many places seek the World Heritage status to boost tourism and attract special attention, the restrictions that accompany such a designation can stifle growth and intensify political divisions. The classification and maintenance of locations as cultural heritage sites can lead to tensions between dynamic social contexts and established cityscapes. Maintaining a city as a monument can also mean that it can no longer grow or change. A shared acceptance of aesthetic values or historic interpretations is not only rare but also contingent on social dynamics (Canclini 2012: 71). To understand the definition of norms, values, maintenance, or change in a preserved location is to understand the disputes over dominance between groups (or hegemonic narratives) across time and space. By looking at Ouro Preto across different moments in history, it becomes possible to locate the events inscribed in the city's monuments, as well as those left off the record. Cultural heritage thus becomes a reading of power structures and nationalistic narratives materialised in the city through positive and negative space. One of the difficulties inherent in the concept of 'world heritage' is that the call to immortalise select moments in history comes at the cost of forgetting others. Herzfeld (2010: 262) discusses a Eurocentric view of heritage, which relates to the predominant presence of European cities in the list of World Heritage Sites and contextualises the fundamental idea of heritage, which is grounded in 'Western notions of inheritance and kinship' and the Latin root of the word 'patrimony'.[1] One may then wonder about countries or small communities, with their different ways of thinking about kinship, inheritance, and materiality, and how or why they represent those aspects as cultural heritage. Why would societies, especially in the developing world, strive to be included in a list of tangible cultural heritage sites, when such a designation comes at a local cost, often inciting conflicts and negatively impacting progress with addressing housing and infrastructure demands?

One answer to this comes from urban anthropology, where authors have been aware that 'political authority took shape in stone', as Metcalf (1989: xi) discusses it in the context of British architecture in colonial India. City structures can create a semblance of order, while non-material approaches can internalise such an appearance and homogenise perceptions (Mitchell 1991). In Brazil, city preservation and planning have been used to foster specific social values, such as development, national worth, and independence. Far from being merely a tool to maintain something of outstanding historical value, preserving a site as a form of heritage can become a mechanism to reinforce, alter, or create social values, which represents a reoccurring theme in this book.

My discussion engages with the premise that governments often look for a particular cultural order, materialised and preserved through cultural heritage, to give them inertia and to justify their continuation (Borneman 1992: 5). All too often, however, this international or national order of things may be incompatible with subnational dynamics (ibid.: 5), such as urban growth, technological changes, and ageing populations. Cultural interpretations, too, are subject to change. In Ouro Preto, the colonial architecture, wrought with historical significance, remains nationally and internationally acclaimed. In the city itself, however, there are ambiguities regarding what people make of their urban environment. Residents at times mirror and perpetuate the national values ascribed to their city, feeling a sense of pride about its unique architecture and history of insurgency against the Portuguese. Yet their own stories and narratives often diverge from this unilateral and romanticised account. The past that residents communicate is not only one of heroism but also of economic injustices spanning colonial and postcolonial times. Permanent residents and visitors 'endow with meaning what [t]he[y] see' (Lynch 1960: 6). On the other hand, meaning – the significance and purpose of cultural heritage – is not only learned from normative, government-led accounts but is also contextually based.

The national development agenda, leading to city planning and preservation in Brazil, necessarily factors in employment, housing, social inclusion and exclusion, and other aspects that are representative of everyday interactions with the city. Modernist city planning – which gave rise to Brasília and other cities – and city preservation – of which Ouro Preto supplies a prime example – are interrelated projects. While Brasília offered the world a paragon of modernist architecture, under the same doctrine of impacting social transformation through state-centred planning (Holston 2010: 101), cities were also preserved (Chuva 2003: 320). Such top-down models did not seek popular consultation, building new cities or constructing a narrative for old ones offered residents and visitors de-contextualised experiences.

Like city planning that excludes, a selective version of history can also alienate the urban experience. A general dissatisfaction with modernist architecture is usually associated with cities whose cultures resist such an aesthetic ethos. This perception can also stem from a sense of nostalgia that eschews the complexities of a modern architectural city and the lifestyle that it supports by creating a yearning for the simpler life that preserved cities intrinsically symbolise. Ouro Preto is one of these 'cities of the past' that was ironically preserved at the dawn of modernist city planning. However, residents do not feel a sense of belonging to it, instead, they want what modernist cities purportedly offer: paved roads and modern conveniences. Thus, when Brazil and other countries look for historic and cultural models for destitute city centres in large capitals, Ouro Preto emerges as a relevant example. Nonetheless, historicism in urbanism can not be a romantic answer to contemporary cities unless an analysis of how socio-economic contexts influences in the formation of memories is carefully conducted. The search for 'historic' centres, consistent with the national and international interest in historicising, romanticising, and restoring rather than building cities from scratch (Ellin 1996: 13, 18), needs to be juxtaposed alongside ethnographic accounts of everyday life in places such as Ouro Preto, Toledo, Cuzco, and Athens. These are locations where a hierarchy of time and space can prevent people from freely navigating through neighbourhoods and stories.

Regardless of being a city tasked with creating national values and telling a story, Ouro Preto has multiple roles: It is a space of permanent residency, tourism, higher education, and mining. The uses of the city vary depending on the day of the week and the time of the day. With respect to places like Ouro Preto, city theorists have moved away from quantitative or vocational definitions and have offered alternative lenses through which one can 'read' a city. Cities have been discussed as a person (Sennett 1996; Reed 2002), in terms of images (Lynch 1960; Olson 1994; Conley and Augé 2002), and in the light of colonial and postcolonial theories (Metcalf 1989; Mitchell 1991; Rabinow 1989; Rama 1996) and kinship (Borneman

1992). My analysis fittingly starts with the following reflections by Carvalho (2013):

> In the city as organism, what is the lifeblood? People, cars, capital, dreams? Who diagnoses 'ailments' and administers a 'cure'? In the city as text, who reads, what gets to be read, how do we agree upon a 'language'? And in the city as Mystic Writing Pad or palimpsest, what does it mean for things past to resurface? How do we listen to a 'trace'? Which practices persist because they adapt, and which vanish because they cannot change?
>
> (Carvalho 2013: 6)

Communicated perceptions of the city are inherently subjective and, in turn, controversial. That is not to say that we should not attempt to author our own understanding of urban environments, as much of current anthropology looks at cities as the place where the ethnographer may live permanently and not provisionally. In ethnographic city reflections, contradictions and irregularities are as telling as are consistencies. Ouro Preto's preserved cityscape surprised me with its intertwined priorities of permanence and mutability. It is my objective to explore these themes throughout the scope of this book.

Latour and Yaneva (2008: 8) state that for buildings that look 'desperately static', we need the opposite of a camera (that converts moments into material) because we need to convert materials into moments and, in turn, memories. The necessary device, they clarify, is theory (ibid.: 81) or, more specifically, anthropological theory. Anthropological theory allows buildings to be brought to life, to breach with a strict object-subject dualism by assessing the creative dimension that underlies the creation of every building, including the endurance or ageing of materials, as well as the contested interpretations and uses of edifices (ibid.: 86). Investigating adaptation to the city's associated narratives as well as contested interpretations and functions of man-made spaces alerts any hasty scholar on cultural heritage to the fact that though conservation is a biased process (Herzfeld 2010: 259), inhabitants seem to navigate with open eyes and minds. When it comes to the preservation of their city: Some may profit from their 'historic' residences, turning them into guesthouses (ibid.: 260); others may feel uncomfortable praying in a local church when it becomes a tourist destination that charges admission. Such churches, villages, or cities may only stand still when deemed of historic or aesthetic value.

With this approach, I move beyond the apparent opposition between a static meaning of preserved history and an open-ended, fluid existence – the city as a place where life happens. Cultural heritage is a means through which to understand the complexity of experiences in a city that is simultaneously permanent and in flux. I make it my task to guide the reader through Ouro Preto as a city marked by multiple dimensions of such contradictions.

GETTING TO OURO PRETO AND *OUROPRETANOS*

As a native Brazilian who grew up in Brasília, a city designated as a UNESCO World Heritage Site within three decades of its construction, the idea of a town that is prevented from growing and adapting to its citizens' needs has puzzled me as a resident and as a scholar. What I have learned through my own (De Souza Santos 2013) and others' work on Brasília is that in preserving buildings, 'the spirit of Brasília' – a spirit of innovation, improvisation, and experimentalism – is adrift (Holston 2010: I). Ironically, the city that inspired new visions for Brazil now prevents future generations from rethinking or modifying their surrounding urban space. Nevertheless, my own experiences in the city also show that *Brasilienses,* when excluded from housing in the central Plano Piloto, will not necessarily turn against campaigns to preserve the city. The symbolism of Brasília's monumental buildings, the openness of the esplanade, and the dream of equality materialised in the visual sameness of the residential blocks foster a sense of pride among residents and visitors. The discrepancies between the ideals of the plan and the undesirable aspects of the resulting reality, from urban sprawl to violence, cannot be reduced to a dualistic narrative in everyday experiences. Thus, when opting to study Ouro Preto, I started with my own experiences while living there. I decided to investigate preserved cityscapes out of a personal interest in how and why cities diverge from the stated intentions of urban planning and preservation. In a country countering the violence in urban centres with nostalgia, could Ouro Preto's vernacular architecture and centralised cultural dynamism offer a model for emulation to other urban spaces in Brazil? If so, how could I present an ethnography of a living city that neither fails nor succeeds in fulfilling static plans because it is always in transition with new citizens, new demands, and new problems? How could I, at the same time, be critical of the inequality that persists in urban spaces in Brazil?

When I moved to Ouro Preto in March 2013, I spent my first two months there in a centrally located bed and breakfast. This living situation enabled me to interact with other guests and the staff while collecting insights about the significance of Ouro Preto to Brazilians and visitors from other parts of the world. I then lived with two *Ouropretano* families, one in a lower-middle-class suburb and the other in the city centre. My first contacts with *Ouropretanos* were through hospitality staff and tour guides. Because my informants were also my friends and hosts in this context, they placed considerable trust in me when letting me into their private and professional lives. While I didn't change any identifying information in this book, I am respectful of the trusting nature of our relationship. The perspectives that I cite are my interpretation of my informants' opinions and memories, as collected during my fieldwork in 2013 and my yearly visits thereafter. In the following, I explain my methodology for ascertaining answers to my research questions and the choices that I made when including or excluding certain information in this book. I am grateful to those individuals who enabled me to study their observations about the city and its status as a heritage site.

I followed the work of the City Council for the Preservation of Cultural and Natural Heritage, or the Council, as I refer to it in this book, throughout 2013. This group, formed by politicians, technicians, and community leaders – almost all of them residents of Ouro Preto – was the institution that made the majority of the decisions concerning the reach and maintenance of cultural heritage in the city. The Council generally convened once a month and presented a controversial agenda for the preservation of tangible cultural heritage, which is the focus of my research. By following these meetings and interviewing members, I could form an understanding of the everyday challenges involved in maintaining preserved sites. My analysis considers the human dimension of preservation by evaluating the impact of preservation on residents and on those who participate in the shaping of preservation policies. As part of my ethnographic responsibility, I avoid identifying the arguments of specific individuals out of respect for their right to privacy. Moreover, I am more interested in synthesising and contextualising what lies behind discussions and hesitations in public political meetings than in ascribing statements to particular individuals. It is with this same rationale that I have, in limited instances, anonymised names in interviews with permanent residents. When information could be deemed contentious or embarrassing, I followed in the footsteps of other ethnographers by not including such data (Goldman 2013: 25).

By exploring the Council's work, this book contributes to the study of participatory practices in Brazil by considering small municipalities. Most existing studies have looked at participation in larger cities, such as Rio de Janeiro, São Paulo, Belo Horizonte, and Porto Alegre (Avritzer 2006, 2010, 2012b; Holston 2008), or investigated pioneering practices, including participatory budgeting (Avritzer 2006, 2012a), participatory master plans (Avritzer 2010), and health councils (Cornwall 2008; Cornwall and Shankland 2013; Guareschi and Jovchelovitch 2004). Syndicalism and neighbourhood associations grounded urban social movements and local participatory practices. A defining difference in the case of smaller municipalities is that participation did not emerge from a 'strong presence of social movements' (Koster and Nuijten 2012: 183). Rather, local governments promoted it as a condition for accessing public funds (Koster and Nuijten 2012: 176).

Looking at participation in places like Ouro Preto, where everyone knows everybody else and kinship and friendship ties impact on employment opportunities, an ethnography of political meetings readily infiltrates into everyday talk and the domestic sphere. My analysis thus extends to everyday perspectives, practices, and scepticisms in Ouro Preto and how they support or resist preservation and participation. While 'patrimony' and 'citizenship' frequently appear together in city laws and reports in Ouro Preto, what is far more telling is the (lack of) power held by public spheres of local participation and how different ways of living and voicing city experiences assemble in state-sponsored meetings.

LOCATING OURO PRETO IN BRAZIL

Located in the southeast region of Brazil in the state of Minas Gerais, Ouro Preto was founded in 1698 in connection with the search for gold, which was, in turn, accompanied by slavery. When gold exploration ceased in the second half of the 1700s, Ouro Preto's population decreased, only to experience greater depopulation after its status as the capital of Minas Gerais shifted to another city, Belo Horizonte, in 1897.

While Ouro Preto now has nearly the same number of inhabitants that it had during the peak of gold extraction, the distribution of people in the territory is discernibly dissimilar. Most colonial cities in Brazil internalised the social hierarchy, integrating it in their organisation of domestic interiors. At that time, population density was centralised (Gledhill 2013: 123). Today, class differentiation in Ouro Preto is instead visible in segregated sections of the city, with socio-economic resources decreasing further away from the city centre.

As of the last census available in 2010, Ouro Preto had 70,281 inhabitants (IBGE 2010) distributed over thirteen districts: Ouro Preto (the main urban area with approximately 60% of the population) and twelve adjoining districts (see Map I.1). In this book, I embrace widely held definitions and, with few exceptions, refer to Ouro Preto as the main urban area and not as the totality of districts.

Ouro Preto also absorbs a considerable amount of temporary residents. Students number around 15,000; they often come from other areas and move elsewhere upon completing their studies. In addition, the city attracts approximately 500,000 visitors a year.[2] In terms of territorial size, Ouro Preto covers 1,245,865 km^2. By way of comparison, the city of São Paulo, while having only marginally more territory (1,521,101 km^2), sustains a population density that is 130 times that of Ouro Preto's (IBGE 2010).

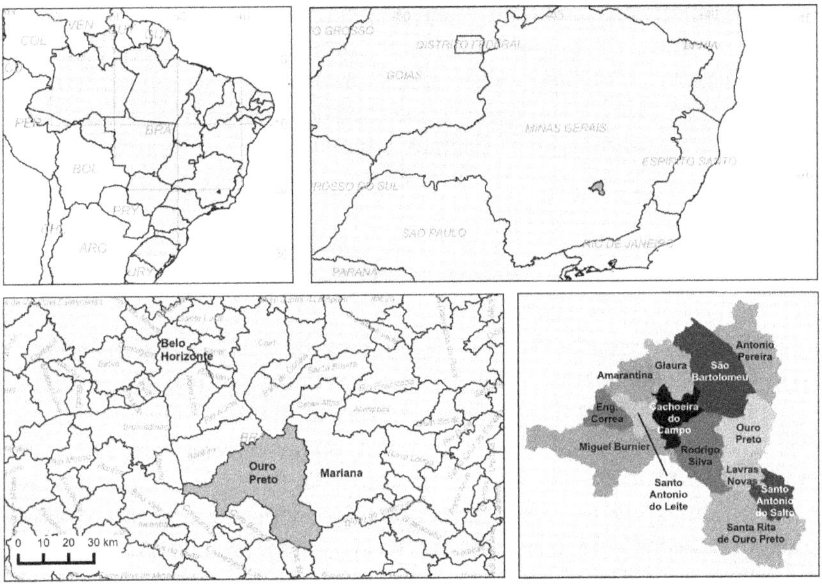

Map I.1. Ouro Preto (clockwise: Ouro Preto in Brazil; in the state of Minas Gerais; Ouro Preto as composed by thirteen districts; a close-up of Ouro Preto in relation to the neighbouring cities of Mariana and Belo Horizonte). ***Source*****: Prefeitura Municipal de Ouro Preto (n.d.), with adaptation.**

In Ouro Preto, industrial activities, especially mining, serve as the economic engine in terms of taxes. Unlike tourism, which is a superior source of job creation, even if it has a minimal impact on public revenues, mining offers high royalties to the municipality. Such contrasting aspects of population density and economics are materialised in houses, which were constructed during periods of high tourism and then sold or left unkempt when economic shocks affected the tourism industry. Similarly, mining created new neighbourhoods in times of expansion and work-related migration. In Ouro Preto, mining is widely credited as a driving force behind both the Baroque and the *Barraco*, the sheds on the outskirts that house temporary workers. The volatility of the economy and the housing market contrasts with other aspects of a static central cityscape. One of the defining contradictions of preserved city spaces is that permanent residents tend to live in temporary arrangements – in houses on the outskirts that are threatened by landslides or demolition – while temporary residents, including students and tourists, live in preserved areas. Such a construct of dwelling places brings both an idea of transience – because of eviction or short-term contracts – and permanence, in giving materiality to a narrative of colonisers against colonised. Contrary to what was planned with city preservation, colonisers were not overcome by way of independence but rather they prosper through a system of dominance from those coming from elsewhere, a truth that assumes contemporary contours in everyday narratives.

BOOK OUTLINE

The first chapter opens with an exploration of the ideas behind the preservation of Ouro Preto, as well as the social and economic expectations that exist in a city suffering from depopulation. I bring to the forefront a debate about cities and their contested ability to control social experiences. The second chapter turns to discussing the dynamics of Ouro Preto's colonial spaces, where buildings are preserved in conjunction with a system of organising the world between colonisers and colonised. A dichotomous interpretation of colonial society in Brazil erased and underplayed ethnic differences and economic complexities while overlooking elitist interests in colonial wars. The dearth of spaces through which to depict the multiplicity of ethnicities and interests at stake allows contemporary interpretations of a seemingly polarised history to resurface in the relationship between students and permanent residents.

How can we preserve a city that, instead of celebrating the end of colonialism, perpetuates a narrative of others and ourselves? I consider answers to such a dilemma in chapter 3. Gold mines offer a physical and social sphere in which social fractures can mend. In contemporary times, many descendants of slaves work as guides in old mines and emphasise the presence of their ancestors' spirits and stories. When slavery is remembered through spiritual accounts, there is a shift in power, enabling previously oppressed groups to achieve a degree of unfettered control. On a physical level, mines connect the outskirts to the centre; the wealth unearthed in the subterranean periphery gives materiality to urban architecture. However, as visiting mines is not a common activity in Ouro Preto, much of the history of slavery in the city remains off the record. While society in Ouro Preto remains highly divided and the city continues to be narrated through a dualist history of conflicts, participation emerges as a means by which to mediate the horizons of the past, present, and future to reach flexible compromises.

By way of extension, the fourth chapter examines dynamics of participation in Brazil and in other developing countries, taking into account how participation affects different populations of participants. In a city where everyone knows everybody else and there is a strong level of informality in the economy, participants in the Council feel the need to avoid conflict, even if the subject of heritage remains highly contentious. Heritage decision-making that passes from the government and into the hands of the people has the potential to produce more diplomatic outcomes. When looking at participatory meetings in chapters 5 and 6, I investigate whether the power of participation could extend beyond the legitimization of preservation and how participants could also be considered in outcomes. In chapter 5, I evaluate the use of asphalt in Ouro Preto and the circumstances that prompted the prefecture to improve mobility by paving previously cobblestoned streets with asphalt. This process laid bare the clashing priorities of cultural heritage and infrastructure. My analysis explores the surfaces on which people and vehicles move across the city and how those materials carry with them promises of social inclusion and exclusion. Should a road leading to a historic monument simulate the experience of another time? Where are the borders of a preserved site to be drawn? I discuss the role of participation as a ruling alternative to the lack of an established approach to managing the use of asphalt in and around a heritage site.

The sixth and final chapter wraps up a discussion about heritage and participation through the lens of one of Ouro Preto's most evocative districts, Miguel Burnier. Miguel Burnier is characterised by a village atop mineral deposits. Though the expansion of mining activities competes with the inhabitability of the region, mining generates the few jobs in the area, as well as the resources needed to maintain monuments. Heritage preservation, mining exploration, and residency in the area were discussed in Council meetings. A synthesis of these discussions invites the reader to imagine the origins of Ouro Preto – a city living two parallel realities – with mines below the surface producing the resources needed to sustain the architectonic wealth above. Mining cities including Ouro Preto, Potosi, and Guanajuato share an architecture that expresses the geography of colonial exploitation. Nonetheless, mining remains a profitable and often desirable activity, leading one to wonder whether the preservation of heritage and mining can coexist in harmony. How can participatory meetings allow for a convergence of interests with respect to the past, present, and future? My discussion extends to the material effects of time (Harms 2011: 93) for different participants.

My chief objective in the pages of this book is to address the politics of material memory in urban spaces from top-down and governed perspectives. In a country where slavery, the awareness of indigenous groups, and memories of military dictatorship remain largely off the record, this book is an attempt to discuss the process and enduring consequences of social remembering and forgetting. It is also an investigation of colonial and post-colonial structures. The focus on colonial plots for independence, which is key in the preservation of Ouro Preto, provides an opportunity to look away from the internal divides among indigenous groups, slaves, Brazilian-born elites, and other subgroups of the colonised. Discussing how colonial times are represented and narrated in Brazil's most iconic preserved site gives us a chance to contextualise euphemisms and silences that polarise and oversimplify the society of the past and present into either victims or perpetrators (Macdonald 2015), natives or outsiders. This ultimately denies history of individual subjectivities, contrary to what is expected in the creation of an inclusive identity.

Chapter 1

Expressing the Nation through Planning and Architecture

Locating National Memories

The history of Ouro Preto evolved from a colonial city built on gold production into a robust political centre that, in the late 1800s, ultimately relinquished its status as the capital of Minas Gerais. As Flávio, a member of the Council,[1] a former vice-mayor, and a former member of the local parliament, contends, the impetus for moving the political administration of Minas Gerais from Ouro Preto to another city was to project the notion that the political system itself had changed:

> *The discovery of gold in Ouro Preto, I don't know if you know the story, the men came here from São Paulo looking for gold . . . and from 1696 to 1698 began to inhabit Ouro Preto. There were many different camps (arraiais). Two of the most important ones were Antônio Dias and Pilar. When the Crown saw that the camps were growing too much, they came here and established a local administration . . . between the two main camps. This didn't take place until 1711. So the Crown appeared in town and the 'Imperial City of Vila Rica'*[2] *came into being. The history of Ouro Preto starts here. There was gold . . . but the gold ran out one day. As the gold ran out, the political importance remained because Ouro Preto was the capital of Minas Gerais for almost one hundred years. When the republican years started [November 15, 1889] its first act was to show that there was a new administration, and one of the resolutions was to change the capitals. . . . This had a strong effect here because this was the 'Imperial City of Ouro Preto', and the idea of Dom Pedro was very strong here. . . . So in 1889 rumours about changing the capital from Ouro Preto began.*
>
> (Flávio, May 8, 2013)

Throughout Latin America, colonial rule and plots for independence have manifested themselves in material forms. In Brazil, sweeping urban changes occurred when the country became a republic in 1889. The early twentieth century witnessed a strong push for urbanisation, economic diversification, and industrialisation. During that period, the construction of entirely new cities and buildings started as a response to rural-to-urban migration and reinforced the perception that a new political order had come to power. Despite this momentum, the city of Ouro Preto remained largely unspoiled from an architectural vantage point. Nonetheless, existing buildings had to assume new narratives and functions. The future of Ouro Preto was liberated within the façades of its imperial history. Perceptions of the buildings' colonial elements shifted in the 1930s as the new administration under President Getúlio Vargas redefined this 'imperial town' as a material expression of an independent and republican Brazil.

In light of the challenges of shifting established perceptions, this chapter will examine the process of redefining Ouro Preto's architecture and the controversies associated with these changes. I begin by exploring the centrality of architecture and planning in colonial and postcolonial cities in Latin America. A contemplation of Ouro Preto's cityscape will provide a point of entry for discussing Brazil's material forms of national identity and the limits of such symbolism in the face of socio-economic manifestations trapped in time and in space. To acquire an understanding of the limits of national expression on a local scale, I refer to my documented conversations with locals who are also contributors to the preservation of Ouro Preto. I highlight how Ouro Preto faces a tension between preservation, which caters to the ideals of the economic and intellectual elite and the more immediate priorities of the city's residents, who yearn for new houses and modern amenities. Ouro Preto is thus a lens through which one can read Brazil's development in early twentieth century as the image of new urban and political possibilities expressed through architectural symbolism but not necessarily through a new socio-economic order.

In the case of Ouro Preto, there is a gap between normative narratives expressing a nationalistic past and their possibility to foster specific experiences of national identity and belonging among today's residents. When residents of Ouro Preto discuss the city's history and their place in it, their narratives point to a system of exploitation and segregation that has persisted since colonial times; the language of independence and liberation does not enter into their stories. Cultural heritage is thus arbitrated by perceptions of continuous inequality and imageries of national independence. As Rama (1996: 72) puts it, 'A dream of the past, a dream of the future – and only words and images to steer the dreaming'.

PLOTS, PUNISHMENT, AND PATRIOTISM

Ouro Preto is a prime example of Brazilian Baroque architecture. According to Rama (1996: 2), Baroque architecture is the result of European absolutism in the seventeenth and eighteenth centuries, which fused religious exuberance with the political administration's projections of power, as was the case in Vila Rica, which became Ouro Preto. This absolutism was expressed in a radial city (ibid.: 5), where buildings of political and religious importance emanated from the city centre. The radial cities typically found in the Portuguese colonies, in contrast to the Spanish ones, usually have a less defined contour and multiple centres. Ouro Preto's hilly topography and rapid growth did not favour the implementation of a well-defined plan preceding habitation and the political administration operated within the existing framework (Castriota 2009: 131–135). Nevertheless, later, urban planning included the construction of various churches working as urban centres for religion, recreation, and art, while the main square remained a centre for political administration.

The Governor's Palace and one of the most important churches for politicians and the mercantile aristocracy were built in the main square, and residences for affluent families surrounded these core edifices. The radial layout of Vila Rica made hierarchies of political and religious orders visible. Administrative power reverberated in labyrinthine rings encircling the highest concentrations of churches and sites of political control.

Administrative authority, however, did not arise out of a socio-economic vacuum. Rama (1996: 12) reminds us that mining towns were locations of 'conspicuous consumption' and that the thirst for commodities and economic ostentation engendered a town of black slaves, traders, artisans, slave and mine owners, religious leaders, and politicians. Maxwell (1973) offers a telling portrait of society in Minas Gerais:

> A complicated mosaic of groups and races, of new white immigrants and second and third generation native Americans, of new slaves and native born captives not to mention the ubiquitous Açorians. Race consciousness was a powerful, even a predominant element in social relationships. African influence was powerful, especially in the subcultures of fetishism, folklore, and dance. Moreover, the *pardo* offspring of the early miscegenation had rapidly ascended into municipal and judicial office.
>
> (Maxwell 1973: 92)

The diversity of groups and interests and above all the greed in a land of gold (and soon enough the collapse of gold production) led to upheavals that defied the architectural illusion of political and religious control. Anti-colonial rebellions in Vila Rica illustrate why the city, after losing its gold and its residents, fuelled the national pride thirst.

The *Inconfidência Mineira*, Minas Gerais Conspiracy (1789) was a plot hatched and led by Vila Rica's most affluent men, most of whom wanted an independent Brazil. Although the plot failed, the conspiracy endowed the country with a national hero who would resurface when the political system changed in 1822.

The decline in gold production in the second half of the eighteenth century, coupled with the Crown's insistence on taxing the now less wealthy local elite, inspired conspirators (Brazilian-born wealthy intellectuals) to time their coup d'état at the moment of the feared tax collection, or *derrama*, in mid-February 1789 (Maxwell 1973: 116). Confident that residents would be outraged by the exploitative taxes, the conspirators hoped that the bourgeoisie, together with the rest of Brazil, would rise with them in their quest for independence. However, as Maxwell (1973: 152) writes, 'Greed was greater than nationalism'. It was easy for the administration to buy the betrayal of information in exchange for debt forgiveness amongst those who were worried about their own debts. The conspiracy was uncovered, the *derrama* did not take place, and Brazil remained a colony. Despite this immediate outcome, the movement inspired substantial change throughout Brazil. Other independence movements followed, carrying with them Vila Rica's new conceptions of nationalism, adding to those anti-slavery movements and increasingly complex notions of social justice (ibid.: 218). One of the most important legacies of the movement was the death of its scapegoat and martyr Silva Xavier, or Tiradentes, as he was known because of his part-time job of extracting teeth.

Unlike his co-conspirators, Tiradentes lacked a formal European education. He was not a man of property and did not have an influential family. He was the one claiming 'sole responsibility for the plot' (Maxwell 1973: 192). He was 'no angel': 'Yet in a history singularly lacking in noble men, Joaquim José da Silva Xavier remains an exception' (ibid.: 199). Being the least economically fortunate of those involved in the rebellion, Tiradentes assumed leadership of the conspiracy and was put to death on April 21, 1792, while the others faced exile (ibid.: 199). Colonial forces hanged him; his dismembered body was exhibited on the road between Rio de Janeiro and Vila Rica. He was, for good reason, a martyr-to-be for a future independent Brazil.

A monument immortalizing Tiradentes was erected in Ouro Preto to commemorate the 100th anniversary of his death (See Images 1.1a, 1.1b and 1.2). Law 3, passed on September 25, 1891,[3] authorised the government to build a marble column topped with a statue of Tiradentes in the centre of Independence Square, now known as Tiradentes Square. It was there that his head was displayed after the failure of the Inconfidência. A local newspaper from

Image 1.1a. Tiradentes Square without the Tiradentes monument. *Source*: Riedel 1868–1869.

Image 1.1b. Tiradentes Square with the Tiradentes monument, 2013. *Source*: Personal collection.

Image 1.2. Tiradentes statue, 2013. ***Source*****: Personal collection.**

April 21, 1892 conveys the sentiment towards Tiradentes and the monument in his name:

> *And therefore today's date constitutes for us a sacred day; because Tiradentes is a saint, sanctified by the great pontiff – the people.*
>
> (*Jornal Minas Geraes*, April 21, 1892: 4, my translation)

And so a square that was once the epicentre of colonial power – and home to the Governor's Palace, the jail, and one of the most exclusive religious brotherhoods – became a square synonymous with independence. Nonetheless, the symbolism of Tiradentes and the Inconfidência Mineira were not enough to prevent the demographic haemorrhage that followed when Belo Horizonte became the new capital of Minas Gerais in 1897.

CAPITAL CHANGES

> Belo Horizonte December 12, 1897: today, with all solemnity, the city of Minas is inaugurated. The president of the State signed the decree

> declaring the change in capitals on a grandstand specially prepared for that purpose. The crowd was considerable, and so were the ecstatic cheers.
>
> (*Jornal do Brasil*, December 13, 1897, my translation)

As if in a fever, people welcomed their new capital, Belo Horizonte – a city that owed its name to both the horizon created by the natural landscape as well as to the horizon of organisation, development, and exemplar planning (Zweig 1942: 238–239). Meanwhile, the houses and furniture left behind in the government buildings in Ouro Preto began to gather dust. Political speeches and propositions in the Ouro Preto House of Representatives (*Câmara de Vereadores*) demonstrate the concern for a city that had lost 40 per cent of its population in the three decades between 1890 and 1920 (Marques 2013: 251). The minutes from meetings that took place between 1901 and 1905 detail proposals for reducing housing taxes, as a number of houses were left deserted amid rising public debts. Many properties required immediate attention to prevent their complete self-destruction.[4] Flávio observed to me that

> *Nobody believed this would happen one day . . . but things went ahead, and in 1897 the capital moved away to the city of Belo Horizonte. I did research on it, Andreza. I listened to people's stories . . . everybody thought that Ouro Preto would die. There were only bureaucrats here; there was no industry, there was nothing. . . . Some people say residents left the keys in the door and left because the city would die . . . some say more than half of Ouro Preto got on the train and left. This was a break in the history of Ouro Preto; from day to night our history broke apart in terms of families, in terms of behaviour, in terms of employment, in terms of economy, in terms of culture, society, community . . . until some modernists came here in 1926 . . . and said, 'This is cultural heritage; this is a national reference. Our history is here'.*
>
> (Flávio, May 8, 2013)

Flávio continued the conversation about the history of Ouro Preto, and before he spoke about the rediscovery of Ouro Preto as what he referred to as a 'place of national memory', he examined how the city became meaningless – economically, politically, and demographically. Ouro Preto, previously named Vila Rica – the Rich Village of Brazil – used to be one of the 'wealthiest and most famous towns during the eighteenth century, . . . at the time when New York, Rio de Janeiro, and Buenos Aires were still insignificant settlements' (Zweig 1942: 233). Population decline was prominent in the early 1900s. No new houses were constructed, and no attempts were made to remodel old residences (graph 1.1). Despite the visible wear of time's passage, Ouro Preto preserved its potential to serve as an architectural expression of colonial times. This connotation did not compete with nationalistic interests, for Ouro Preto's colonial architecture was intrinsically linked to struggles for independence.

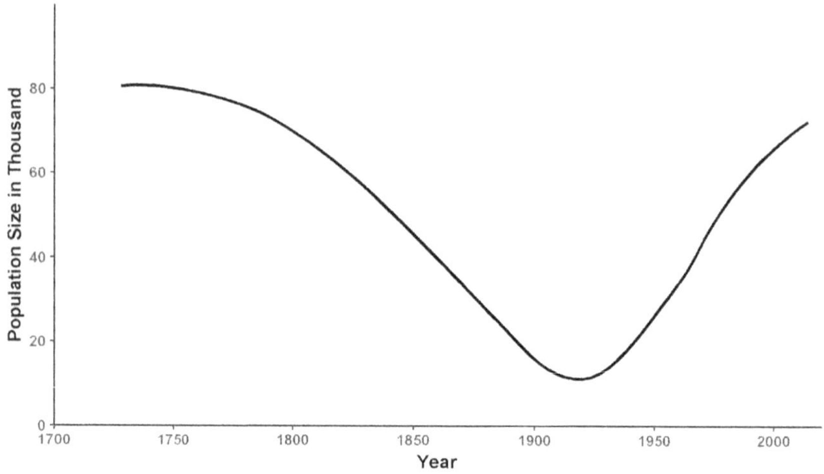

Graph 1.1. Ouro Preto's population, graph by the author. *Sources*: Batista da Costa 2011: 33; Castriota 2009: 137; IBGE 2010; Martins de Araujo 2013: 14; Maxwell 1973: 263.

NATIONAL MEMORY AND NEW NARRATIVES FOR OLD CONSTRUCTIONS

While the city's history and heroes were at the heart of laments when Ouro Preto relinquished its standing as the capital of Minas Gerais, nostalgia would soon facilitate the designation of Ouro Preto as a national cultural heritage site – a location perceived to be of national value. The new status of the old city produced a distinctive story of the past for the city and brought hope that it would enjoy a different future.

> It was here, on these high rocks,
> That seem to interrupt the horizon
> That the thought dawned radiant
> Of the freedom that the Messiah preached
> It was here! Says the gale;
> It was here! Says the old monument;
> It was here! Says everything with sentiment,
> Telling the stories of the past days.
> Save! Legendary and unharmed city!
> (Pires, June 30, 1902, my translation)[5]

The creation of national memory was an important political tool in the early twentieth century. The 1930s in Brazil constituted a period associated with the search for a brand of national unity that would conquer the powers of regional oligarchies. During Vargas's fifteen-year term (1930–1945) including during his dictatorship (1937–1945 *Ditadura do Estado Novo*), he created a 'state-sponsored citizenship' (Holston 2008: 186) through 'new rituals of national identification' (ibid.: 191) that included aspects ranging from labour laws to media and the arts. Tangible cultural heritage integrates sentimentality and edification in a way that exerts national control. Chuva (2009: 31) reminds us that efforts to produce a national history focussed on tangible representations of Brazil. Around 40 per cent of all monuments preserved in Brazil up until the 2000s were initially protected during Vargas's first term of political power (1930–1945; ibid.: 31). Architectural projects, such as the building of a modernist edifice to serve the Ministry of Education, translated his pioneering intentions into the language of three dimensions (ibid.: 202). The network of primarily Minas Gerais-born intellectuals working under Vargas's mandate exercised their authority in designating which places and monuments should become part of the national patrimony.

As a natural consequence, Brazilian nationalism found a home in Minas Gerais' colonial Baroque architecture. In the case of Ouro Preto, retrospectively historicising sites and events of national interest meant focussing on conspiracies against Portuguese rule. This placed Ouro Preto at the centre of preservation efforts and as the site of the *Inconfidência Mineira.* The city where the decapitated head of Tiradentes had been displayed became a fitting location for the celebration of independence, as the following decree signed by Vargas attests:

> Decree N. 22.928–12 July 1933.
>
> Hails the city of Ouro Preto as a national monument.
>
> . . .
>
> Considering that it is a duty of the Public Administration to defend the artistic patrimony of the nation and that the places where great historical events took place are part of a people's tradition;
>
> *Considering that the city of Ouro Preto, the former capital of the State of Minas Gerais, was a theatre of events of great historical relevance to the formation of our nationality and that it possesses old monuments, edifices, and temples of colonial architecture, veritable pieces of art that deserve protection and conservation;*
>
> Resolves:
>
> Article 1. The City of Ouro Preto is hailed as a National Monument without charge to the Federal Union.
>
> Article 2. The monuments . . . that constitute the historical and artistic patrimony of the City of Ouro Preto are under the watch and protection of the Government of Minas Gerais and of the Municipality of Ouro Preto. . . .
>
> Rio de Janeiro, 12 July 1933, 112th Independence and 45th Republic

Getúlio Vargas
Washington F. Pires
(Decree 22.928, July 12, 1933, my translation with emphasis added)

Hailing colonial towns as an expression of Brazilian nationalism was especially remarkable at the time because it refashioned colonial materials as symbolic forms that were connotative of independence. The *paulistas* (or *bandeirantes*) – the Brazilian-born men who explored the hinterlands (*sertões*) of Brazil in the late 1600s – were contrasted with 'the invaders from the coast', the Portuguese (Zweig 1942: 59). The gold that the *paulistas* discovered made Brazil the most precious gem in the Portuguese crown. The *paulistas* soon became the enemies when they claimed control of the lands. The *paulistas* (or *bandeirantes*) and Portuguese (*emboabas*) sparked a conflict in 1708–1709, known as the War of the Emboabas (Fausto 1999: 51). Depending on how you look at it, this was either one of the first Brazilian uprisings against the Portuguese rule or a war marked by a similar thirst for control and affluence through the collection of taxes and the possession of gold mines and slaves (Romeiro 2008). Despite different possible interpretations of the War of the Emboabas, the Minas Gerais intellectuals who were part of Vargas's government were associated with the *bandeirantes*, who secured a more favourable account in a history that became increasingly polarised between the colonisers and the colonised (Chuva 2009: 101), when they rediscovered Ouro Preto.

Nevertheless, the idea that cities can operate as living museums[6] does not explain how urban heritage can conjure up a consensus regarding historical perceptions. Clearly, the material world is subject to plural interpretations: It has different meanings for different people and is further shaped by contextual influences, whether they are temporal, economic, or political. If places and monuments tell a story, who is the author and who is the editor – the architect who creates the vision or the observer who makes sense of it? Finally, if interpretations change, how can materials be physically unchanged? I engage with these questions, first addressing the issues of authorship and selective memory. Chuva (2009) refers to those presiding over the selection of Brazil's material patrimony in the 1930s and 1940s as 'architects of memory'. While these 'architects of memory' were not architects by profession, they had the power to reconstruct buildings along metaphorical lines.

EDITORS OF HISTORY

Brazil's 'architects of memory' resurrected a past of national heroes. Their studies were published in bulletins and magazines with the objective of informing the population about the values that dictated the process of historicising monuments. One such publication, the magazine *Revista do Patrimônio*, was printed uninterruptedly from 1937 until 1947; it documented a period that was pivotal in the protection and regulation of Brazilian patrimony. Most articles published during this decade focussed on Minas Gerais in general and Ouro Preto in particular (IPHAN, n.d.). They presented biographical accounts of select artists and placed particular emphasis on the sculptor and architect Antonio Francisco Lisboa (known as Aleijadinho, or Little Cripple) and his prolific production in Ouro Preto (Chuva 2009: 253). The magazines also focussed on *Inconfidentes*, as well as on the Baroque style in general, collecting information on cathedrals, chapels, and paintings. When perusing the dense issues of this magazine, the development of a historical approach that supported the protection of buildings and monuments associated with a national patrimony rises into view. Brazilian Baroque, of which Minas Gerais provides a prime example, exhibited 'original and intrinsic breadth' (Avila 2001: 116) in being popularised by an isolated society that used local materials to depict foreign aesthetic influences (Castriota 2009: 138).

'Architects of memory' are thus editors of history. A historic and artistic past is not invented, in the sense of being off the record, but is certainly imaginative in regard to what is selected to be recounted, forgotten, or preserved. Such degree of openness in the process of choosing and compiling Brazil's national patrimony was possible through Decree 25, passed on November 30, 1937, which organised the protection of historic and artistic patrimony. The law classified goods of public interest as those associated with memorable historical facts relating to the nation or sites of 'notable expression', whether natural or man-made. This national law was attuned to international movements, such as the Conference of Athens in 1931,[7] which also supported the national focus on historic and artistic monuments in the formation of a national past. The Conference prompted the reconstruction of monuments after World War I in a way that made their historic and artistic features accurately visible (Choay 2011: 156–157).

The law's openness to interpretation allowed for the subjective selection of forms and images worthy of preservation and placed implicit emphasis on an underlying narrative capable of justifying these determinations. This explains why historians and writers also played a fundamental role in the process (Chuva 2009: 198). As Rama puts it in the context of other countries in Latin America,

> The written word designed the foundations of national identity and constructed a version of it in people's minds, all in the service of a particular political project.
>
> (Rama 1996: 70)

Those written practices, however, reinforced a 'standard of art and architecture dominated by Minas Gerais's colonial production' that oriented (and still orients) patrimonial practices in the country (Chuva 2009: 63).

As Brazilian Baroque gained notoriety, preservation efforts primarily took place in regions where that style was prominent. Historical and artistic definitions became increasingly intertwined. More than 60 per cent of the seventy-seven urban sites now protected by the Institute for Historic and Artistic Patrimony (IPHAN)[8] are located in the southeast and northeast regions, which are places representative of a colonial past (IPHAN 2015). The repercussions of these choices are noticeable throughout Brazil. For example, Gilberto Velho (2006) recounts his experience in the Historic and Artistic Patrimonial Council in 1984, when the Afro-Brazilian candomblé tradition was subject to protection for the first time. When Brazil's intangible heritage surfaces in a place that lacks 'artistic' architecture, perceptions of the importance of such customs are far from unified.

In this manner, periodicals were used to broadcast and consolidate a national memory that gave precedence to certain inclusions over others. Baroque colonial cities were recognised as 'theatres of events of great historical relevance in the formation of our nationality' (Decree 22.928, 1933). The meaning of historic and artistic patrimony was thus connected with a national image. Historic and artistic can then assume a contemporaneous façade, if the same formula – importance in the formation of Brazil's nationality – is met. For example, in the same 1930s and 1940s Baroque movement, modernist lines from 1950s and 1960s were preserved almost concomitantly to their constructions. Both Brazilian Baroque and modernist constructions served the nation through the provision of national symbolism (Chuva 2009: 100). Underwood (2001) explains the connection between the two styles as a 'spiritual quest for identity rooted in an aesthetic exploration of the tropical landscape and the colonial Baroque condition':

> Architecture, the monumental extension of the flesh of the body into the flesh of the world, has been for Niemeyer a means to incorporate (literally and metaphysically) a vision of the Brazilian soul and achieve a sense of cultural identity. . . . His work is thus important for understanding Modern Brazilian art because it has forged a conceptual and historical link between the colonial Baroque and Modernism.
>
> (Underwood 2001: 526)

One example of the intersection of Baroque and modernist architecture in the search for a Brazilian national identity is the modernist hotel in Ouro Preto's colonial city centre. Tourists visiting Ouro Preto during the golden age of Brazilian preservation efforts saw it as 'the Toledo, the Venice, the Salzburg, the Aigues-Mortes of Brazil' (Zweig 1942: 243). The construction of a new hotel to accommodate the influx of tourists in Ouro Preto was a necessity, as the following extract from a 1935 newspaper article demonstrates:

> Among all of the pressing needs in our land, the most urgent is the construction of a hotel that satisfies the exigencies of our progress and the intensity of the tourism that grows by the day.
>
> (*Jornal Voz de Ouro Preto*, November 10, 1935, my translation)

The construction of the Grande Hotel de Ouro Preto (Image 1.3), designed by Oscar Niemeyer, the future mastermind behind the city of Brasília, crowned years of intense investment in the city's cultural heritage, including the opening of the city's largest museum (Museu da Inconfidência), the conservation of residential buildings, and the safeguarding of churches. The hotel was formally opened in 1945 and featured gardens conceived by Burle Marx (Prefeitura Municipial de Ouro Preto 2012b).[9]

Image 1.3. Grande Hotel de Ouro Preto (with plain façade and straight rooflines, in contrast with a typical colonial roof), 2013. *Source*: Personal collection.

Even though the hotel's construction was linked to the tourism that the city's architectural past generated, the building, with its modernist elements, stands out from its colonial neighbours. As much as the hotel and surging tourism awakened hopes of economic development and progress, the non-traditional design provoked suspicion and controversy among locals. The architect Lucio Costa viewed the structure as 'beautiful and genuine' (Chuva 2009: 209), and preservationists saw it as harmonious given its compliance with the principles of a 'good architecture' (Leonidio 2007: 203). Such interpretations of Brazilian creativity hoped, above all, to give materiality to progress.

FROM BAROQUE TO BRASÍLIA

Brasília was inaugurated on April 21, 1960 the anniversary of the death of Tiradentes. This date was not a coincidence, for it had been decreed in Law 3273, which was passed on October 1, 1957 (Kubitschek 2010: 108).[10] The narratives embedded in Brasília's modernist architecture, often associated with innovation, were also underpinned by the push to give materiality to ideas of national development. There was no better day for the birth of Brasília and for the reinforcement of nationalistic imagery than the anniversary of the death of the martyr of Brazilian independence.

A few years later, however, Lucio Costa, Brasília's urban planner, was forced to defend his project. A city once described as a meta-synthesis for Brazilian citizenship that would unify the country with roads bridging one side to the other (Kubitschek 2010: 101) became famous for its socio-spatial divide (Holston 2010). Despite the visual sameness of the city's residential blocks, the fact that they served only a minority of the population while the rest lived in underdeveloped satellite cities meant that to defend the preservation of Brasília required a defence of the city's intentions and innovations despite a reality of the coexistence of architecture and 'anti-architecture' – 'the facilities and relative well-being of one part, and the difficulties and the chronic uneasiness of the majority' (Costa 1990: 4, my translation).[11]

Notwithstanding Brasília's increasing urban sprawl in the form of unplanned satellite cities lacking almost every urban amenity, from asphalt to hospitals, Costa (1990: 2, my translation) asserts that the city attests to Brazil's 'lively and latent strength . . . a rational gesture of courage in the direction of a definitive Brazil'. UNESCO's recognition of the city's artistic elements in 1987 confirms, as Costa similarly maintains, that the right choices were indeed made.

The building of a distinctive modern façade in the middle of the preserved colonial layout of Ouro Preto and the preservation of Brasília show that the definitions of historic and artistic were wrapped in ideals of nationality. However, when writing about the colonisation of Egypt, Mitchell (1991: ix) asserts that colonialism is not restricted to 'the establishing of a European presence but also to the spread of a political order that inscribes in the social world a new conception of space'. In his evaluation of cities in Latin America over colonial and early postcolonial periods, Rama (1996: 1) maintains that Latin American cities have expressed a 'rationalizing view of an urban future'. In this manner, Brasília or Ouro Preto may be analysed as controversial manifestations of colonial continuity because of an imposed material order that served a political interest, despite a narrative of independence. Brasília's city planners aspired to cultivate socio-economic fairness but refused to change the original design in the face of unintended urban sprawl. While in Ouro Preto preservation bolstered tourism in a way that excluded local residents. In the related laws, local residents are mentioned only in passages discussing fines. One of the laws that aimed at preserving the façades of Ouro Preto's buildings is translated here. In Decree 13, passed on September 19, 1931, the mayor at the time emphasised the importance of preserving colonial buildings for tourists:

> *Considering that a great interest from the tourists* that frequently come to visit the city and its surroundings springs from the colonial expression of its edifices, its buildings, its squares; *considering that the buildings that destroy the colonial appearance, painfully damage the sensibility of tourists*, I decree:
>
> 1. The construction of buildings and edifices that do not harmonise with the colonial style of the city is not permitted within the urban perimeter.
> 2. Existing buildings in the urban perimeter that do not adhere to the Article above should be modified only on the façades when they need to be repaired.
>
> (Decree 13, September 19, 1931, my translation and emphasis)

A little less than a year later, through Decree 25 on September 3, 1932,[12] the same mayor detailed how restoration efforts and even the cleaning of buildings had to avoid altering the façades of colonial buildings. Fines were imposed for any violations, indicating that residents could not run the risk to 'painfully damage the sensibility of tourists' (Decree 13, September 19, 1931) without punishment.

The imagery of Brazilian nationalism in Ouro Preto is thus ambivalent: Through the preservation of forms that recall a heroic past, an undemocratic process of urban living is perpetuated. The question of which symbolic meanings are factually created when places are preserved is something I grapple with throughout this book as I engage with ethnographic material that suggests how residents interpret Brazil through the lens of preserved spaces. I also analyse how an imposed narrative of national meaning is slowly replaced by one of political participation in city planning. How can reinforced socio-economic inequality possibly correct myopic political decisions? How do changes in the governance of Ouro Preto's cultural heritage impact the visual presentation of continuity? As Abram and Weszkalnys (2013: 14) assert, 'The temporality invoked by planning may thus be inherently irregular, and its outcomes continually deferred'. The contentious and deferred results of Ouro Preto's preservation efforts impose on the city's present and future.

DEMOGRAPHIC GROWTH AND CITY PRESERVATION

In 1933, the mayor writes a decree that establishes the importance of Ouro Preto . . . then Getúlio Vargas preserves it as national patrimony and from there onwards that was the way; they rescued Ouro Preto, but that rescue is not yet economic . . . it did not generate employment, and Ouro Preto continued more or less unstable, until the aluminium business began. Already in the 1940s . . . what is today Novelis [an aluminium company] had started . . . and that was the economic pillar of Ouro Preto for many decades, but Ouro Preto was still very small. Until the 1970s, when Novelis experienced a period of very intense growth, and a lot of people came here . . . a man would come, register at the company, and would fence off a piece of land on the hill, and the prefecture would find a way for the man to build his house there. So the periphery you see today in Ouro Preto – 'the other Ouro Preto' – is from that time more or less. And that brought some problems, an urban sprawl without any planning . . . and problems with people who have no connection to Ouro Preto and its significance as cultural patrimony.

(Flávio, May 8, 2013)

The preservation of Ouro Preto raised expectations for the economy, primarily through tourism and university life, but, as Flávio emphasises, an economic solution did not automatically accompany the city's designation as an embodiment of national patrimony. When Zweig (1942) recounts his visit to Ouro Preto around 1940, it is possible to imagine that the city was small and fiscally weak. His observations of the once economically and politically important city direct attention to houses that look visibly tired:

> Their paint is old and grey, peeling off, and wrinkled like the face of an old man. . . . Late in the evening one has a ghostly feeling that the people one sees are still those of the past, or their shadows. One is surprised sometimes to hear the church bells strike the hours, for why count them when time itself stands still?
>
> (Zweig 1942: 242)

Despite the city's severe economic decline, its ghostly houses were meant to showcase legendary heroism, and the construction of the modernist hotel opened the door to notions of a vibrant future. Nevertheless, the idea of heroes, heritage, and tourism as stimulants of economic growth or repopulation was deferred. When the city's economic and demographic development ultimately took place, it was not a direct result of preservation efforts. Instead, as Flávio explained, the aluminium industry brought in migrant workers and, in turn, prompted chaotic construction on the city's periphery.

One way to identify concerns regarding the changes affecting Ouro Preto is to read UNESCO reports from 1990, 1993, 2003, and 2004. In 1980, the World Heritage Committee decided that the historic town of Ouro Preto, along with other places of similar importance, such as the historic centre of Rome, would be added to the World Heritage Sites list. Ever since then, State of Conservation Reports have been produced. The 1990 Report articulates that the number of people living in Ouro Preto had grown and expressed concern because the permanent character of the city layout (protected locally,[13] nationally,[14] and also internationally[15]) could not accommodate new residents who, as a result, built new neighbourhoods on hillsides, despite the risk of landslides. To address this trend, UNESCO suggested shoring up sloped areas because of the dangers of heavy rainfall (UNESCO 1990). Ouro Preto was preserved as artistic and historical evidence, and its whole setting – including the landscape that encircles it – is important. New houses in surrounding areas 'distort the original urban landscape' (UNESCO 2003) and can physically endanger monuments.

While the lack of housing is a pressing issue affecting many people's lives, it is the national importance of Ouro Preto that takes precedence. João Carlos, the head of the IPHAN office in Ouro Preto, explained to me during a recorded interview that the controversies relating to population growth and city preservation now invite society to direct the course of preservation efforts:

> *A great deal of the preservation of cultural patrimony was deeply connected to periods of economic decay. Now imagine me as the head of an office in a super-active economy, in a society where everybody wants asphalt, in a society where everybody wants bathrooms with tiles, where everybody wants a second floor, nobody wants walls of wattle and daub, everybody wants modern living, you know; everybody wants solar heating, and at the same time I have to preserve this city that is here, and I have to take it to the 21st century, you see. There is a failure in the Brazilian architectural discourse. It does not give me an answer. Therefore, I have to discuss it with society.*
>
> (João Carlos, August 22, 2013)

When a city such as Ouro Preto faces material concerns – narrow streets for vehicles and homeowners who want to renovate buildings to accommodate new needs – architecture needs to offer answers. Before it can provide creative solutions to accommodate an eighteenth-century city in the twenty-first century, it has to find a narrative that rationalises change or that justifies maintenance. João supports the notion that such a discussion should be inclusive.

Whether participation is a way to allow for the enforcement of preservation norms or a chance to modify the city according to multi-layered claims is a consideration that shapes my analyses. Inviting society to define patrimonial parameters is already very different from earlier practices in Ouro Preto that empowered select intellectuals and a body of technical experts living in Brazil's big cities, such as Rio de Janeiro, Brasília, and Belo Horizonte. This methodology detached preservation institutions from local concerns. As Flávio pointed out, in addition to a perception of distance, there was also a conflict where residents did not know what they could do in the city or how to find out information because

> *The mayor administers the city but not entirely because he has a parallel duty with IPHAN, which is a national organisation, and that led to conflicts. It always led to problems because how can the city grow? I will expand my house (fazer um puxadinho), I will build a second floor, but how will I do that? Whom do I ask for authorisation? Is it to the prefecture or to IPHAN? In reality, it should be both of them, but they did not talk to each other. And the prefecture always took the position of 'washing its hands' [to not assume responsibility] 'Ah, let the patrimony people [IPHAN] say no because I depend on people's vote, I am not the one who will say no, this patrimony . . . this evil patrimony, this patrimony that belongs to rich people from Belo Horizonte, from Brasília, they are not letting you build your house'. That went on for many years, generated problems for the city, unplanned growth, and infrastructure deficit.*
>
> (Flávio, May 8, 2013)

As Flávio explained, the development of national policies resulted in local effects (mainly economic costs) to the prefecture or civil society in maintaining or restoring buildings. The decree hailing Ouro Preto as a national monument reveals that no charge to the Federal Union resulted from that decision; the guardianship of the city was a municipal and regional obligation. This indicates that though heritage decisions were made in geographically removed spaces, the costs – economic and political – were localised. Another reason for the unpopularity of these policies has to do with the fact that this was also the first occurrence in Brazil for ownership rights to be limited (Chuva 2009: 147). Therefore, as innovative and restrictive, protection policies were contested amongst those whom they directly affected. Disputes in Ouro Preto grew when the city experienced economic and demographic growth unrelated to the preservation of its historic and artistic symbolism.

PROTECTED MATERIALS IN CHANGING TIMES

In Ouro Preto new houses were built when industries began to expand their operations. Residents needed to build houses so that they could stop paying rent, provide for growing families, and commute to work at the aluminium companies around Ouro Preto. The divorce between national and local interests took place in a dualism between a cultural and touristic city centre and the 'non-cultural' and 'non-historic' outskirts. According to Flávio, the political disputes in Ouro Preto reflect the conflicts regarding city growth along the periphery and city preservation in the city centre:

> *We had two Ouro Pretos, the Ouro Preto of the centre, and the Ouro Preto of the periphery. The Ouro Preto of the rich and the Ouro Preto of the poor. The Ouro Preto of the guy that worked . . . and the Ouro Preto of the tourist. So the elections began to articulate that, the man who is the mayor today for example, Zé Leandro, he called the other one, Ângelo [his opponent], 'the tourist'. Ângelo was a mayor three times and has a strong cultural identity. . . . Today he is the president of the Brazilian Institute of Museums. So these two men since the 1980s polarise politics in Ouro Preto in speeches about the good against the evil, the tourist against the native, progress against preservation, the truck against the carriage . . . the Baroque against the 'barraco' (shack).*
>
> (Flávio, May 8, 2013)

Numbers reveal the intense demographic growth of Ouro Preto's urban areas. In the 1960s, the city had a total of 28,229 inhabitants, and by 1980, that number had increased to 48,088 (Batista da Costa 2011: 331). Following this trend of exponential growth, in 2010 Brazil census, the estimated population was 70,281 (IBGE 2010). Unsurprisingly, the preserved urban centre of Ouro Preto could not accommodate new families. Most new residents were used to houses that were not static monuments but rather dwelling places, or 'an inseparable part of life that grows, flourishes, decays and is reborn', as they are in other developing countries (Mitchell 1991: 53). Flávio recounted that most newcomers erected new houses in nearby areas and commuted to the city centre for banking, shopping, and other activities at the core of daily life. Central areas remained largely unchanged, catering to a population that could adapt to stiff regulations and cope with rising prices impacted by the influx of temporary residents and tourists. The accompanying images (Images 1.4a and 1.4b) depict the maintenance of central areas.[16]

However, images 1.5a and 1.5b show the Pilar neighbourhood, part of Ouro Preto's central area, and on the hill in the background is a contemporary housing space. Neighbourhoods in areas outside the protected perimeter

Image 1.4a. São Francisco Church in Ouro Preto's city centre, 1880. ***Source*****: Ferrez 1880.**

are often visible from protected areas, which, in turn, distorts the colonial characteristic of Ouro Preto without necessarily being illegal, as the regulations in the non-protected perimeters follow different guidelines.[17] The reach of the colonial city is thus a subject of debate, as it can either be interpreted as a geographic boundary or as a visible horizon.

Neighbourhoods growing in the outskirts of the city are also a result of university expansion. The School of Pharmacy (1839) and the School of Mining (1876) unsuccessfully invested in attracting students to Ouro Preto, which was not as big of a draw as were larger cities. The schools enjoyed significant growth only after a new road was built in 1953 connecting Belo Horizonte to the old capital (Martins de Araujo 2013: 41) and when the two schools merged in 1969, creating the Federal University of Ouro Preto (UFOP). The growth in Ouro Preto's student population coincides with industrial activities also expanding, but the students were the main group to enjoy central housing. Some public buildings that accommodated administrative staff when Ouro Preto was the capital of Minas Gerais were transformed into University buildings. Similarly, private houses that used to lodge public servants were made into halls for new students. The population of students in Ouro Preto has continued to rise, with the majority

Image 1.4b. São Francisco Church in Ouro Preto's city centre, 2013. *Source*: Personal collection.

Image 1.5a. Pilar area, 1936. *Source*: Fontana 1936.

Image 1.5b. Pilar area and contemporary neighbourhoods in the background, 2013. *Source*: Personal collection.

of students coming from nearby cities or from the southeast region of Brazil. Central houses were unable to accommodate the growing numbers of students, which in 2013 represented 20 per cent of Ouro Preto's total population.[18] Some neighbourhoods have expanded to accommodate these temporary residents, partly because of the economic advantages that they bring (Image 1.6).

Most urban amenities are concentrated in the preserved city centre, which, as has been discussed, was mainly occupied by wealthier residents, students, and tourists. The zone signifies a place of work and subsequently of income to those living in more rural regions. It also features resources for the restoration and maintenance of public areas and private properties, making the gap between central (colonial) and peripheral (contemporary) regions increasingly apparent. When Ouro Preto attracts resources through designated programmes, such as Monumenta[19] (starting in 2000) and PAC Cidades Históricas[20] (2009 and 2013), the controversy relating to city borders comes to light. President Dilma Rousseff's speech when launching *PAC Cidades Históricas* in the city of São João Del Rei (Minas Gerais) and the conversation with the head of the local IPHAN

Image 1.6. Transformation of houses into residential blocks in Bauxita, near the main university campus, 2013. ***Source*****: Personal collection.**

office in Ouro Preto typify the disengagement between national aspirations and local views:

> This event is for me a celebration of our culture, to the memory of our people. . . . Therefore I am very happy to be here today, in this beautiful region of my country, to put into practice the PAC Historic Cities, which will support the restoration and recovery of edifices, public squares, and public spaces of great historic relevance to all of Brazil. . . . In the old streets of our historic cities, the monuments, the churches are locations where the founders went and where our origins are, the core of our nationality.
>
> (Rousseff 2013, my translation)[21]

Resources for historic cities are associated with the maintenance and restoration of monuments of national importance. However, surrounding areas modify the centre indirectly through new buildings visible from the centre, and the appeal of those areas to also feature in programmes for historic cities has gained traction, as João Carlos explains:

> *You know, I am very concerned . . . that they are investing 36 million Reais on edifices. You know I think we should have at least 10 million Reais for public transport, street improvements, if we will make underground cabling or not, if we will create new public squares, if we will no longer use certain roads . . . this discussion can no longer be postponed, it is no longer the discussion of buildings and their façades, if Ouro Preto is white or not, you see. That is why I tell you, I can no longer do this as the head of the IPHAN office. Firstly, I do not have enough staff for that, [secondly] for public policies the prefecture has to participate with me, you know, I can be discussing, I can be an instrument for discussion . . . an instrument for policies, techniques . . . of discussion with society.*
>
> (João Carlos, August 22, 2013)

The irony of the situation is that the colonial city depends on what it excludes. On a practical level, the city relies on resources from industrial activities housed in the outskirts; meanwhile, many residents living in the periphery depend on a historic city centre for jobs relating to tourism and conservation. Preserved colonial heritage sites are also valuable because they are rare. Ouro Preto's town centre is one of the few in Brazil to have maintained a colonial layout. Most cities have only individual buildings or small areas designated as worthy of preservation. New buildings providing direct and indirect economic support are simultaneously a symbolic threat to central Ouro Preto. In his writings about Rio, Carvalho (2013: 12) claims that it is a 'porous' city rather than a 'divided' one, as the city is interrelated in its many areas 'like the different sides of a coin', despite excessive social inequality. In

Ouro Preto, the described interdependency among different areas and social groups is similar to Rio's porosity, however that does not reduce the vigilance with which borders are preserved.

Due to complex contextual factors, the definition of cultural heritage invites answers that address economic, political, technical, and social facets. The political basis that gave rise to a preservation agenda primarily addressed cities that were suffering from urban decay and depopulation. The impulse to define structures as nationally symbolic and therefore worthy of preservation faced severe opposition when the economic and demographic situations of cities including Ouro Preto changed. Today, preserved cities are coming to terms with their own mortality, pressing for the strictures of heritage to be redefined by those whom it should serve.

CONCLUSION

Ouro Preto's first settlements in the late 1600s inaugurated a period marked by the rush for gold and the power disputes that it instigated. The central administration radiated rigorous control, reinforced by the support of the Church. Looking at the central square, it is possible to see not only how urban planning and architecture was chief in colonial administration but also how it remained key in independence projects. When times changed, from colonial to independent Brazil, Ouro Preto's main square did not change in its material elements, but immaterially it was named differently, becoming Independence Square, and currently, Tiradentes Square. The site is an enduring centre for the government, for national symbolism, for tourism, and for education. A centre for colonial administration, for Minas Gerais's administration, for national symbolism, and presently for tourism and education, the Tiradentes Square shows the different meanings and functions that the same urban space can have if buildings are to remain. The square thus becomes an optimal framework for evaluating change in the context of a city that seeks to remain visibly unaltered.

Different narratives for Ouro Preto's main square exemplify the fact that the network of intellectuals determining sites of national interest during Vargas's rule served as authors as much as they were editors of national memory. Another push in favour of heritage liberty came from the demographic development of certain colonial cities emptied after decades of economic decline. In times of low population density, specific regulations concerning materials, forms, and fines were enough to guarantee the maintenance of certain buildings. Nevertheless, in cities such as Ouro Preto, as the population curve ascended, the relationship between residents, the prefecture, and preservation organisations (such as IPHAN) had intricate arrangements that are central to the following chapters. While the prefecture often benefited from the expansion of mining and facilitated city growth counter to preservation efforts, it also had the responsibility to maintain preserved areas. The prefecture often delegated preservation responsibilities to IPHAN, making the relationship between that organisation and the city's residents a strained one. Students and tourists who can afford to reside in central areas have become unpopular amongst long-term residents, who feel excluded from heritage sites to which they should instead be privileged. Finally, stiff urban regulation is not always politically effective, especially when those who directly benefit from it, namely tourists, do not vote in local elections. Elections in Ouro Preto thus present a dichotomy expressed as preservation versus development, rich versus poor, centre versus periphery. This dichotomy begins to break down when the city's economy is taken into account, as the peripheral region pays most of the taxes (because minerals are extracted there) and also houses most of the workforce that supports the city centre and the tourism sector.

In the midst of this complex urban reality defined by a historic and artistic perimeter embodying socio-economic fissures, the Municipal Council on the Preservation of Cultural and Natural Patrimony (the Council) is an idealised sphere where society – politicians, technicians, and community leaders – can discuss and direct cultural heritage in town. In early preservation efforts, the 'power of the pen' to define heritage often enjoyed a certain distance from conflict. Not only were intellectuals and technicians largely based in political capitals, but they hid behind a technical language with words such as 'genuine', 'authentic', and 'national', pedagogically explained in written sources that sought to support a heroic past (or utopian future). When the Council brings together local technicians, politicians, and community leaders, one thing those representatives will not have is the comfort of ruling from afar. Meetings are open to the public and concerned with present-day (and controversial) topics that technical or legal clarifications cannot resolve.

Before analysing how the Council directs the future of heritage in its meetings, I address the notion of heritage from the perspective of Ouro Preto's residents. Material expressions can forge memories (Connerton 1989, Halbwachs 1992). However, narratives about the past are present-based and people's experience in time and space may resist homogeneous versions of the past (Jovchelovitch 2012). I will hone in on this assertion by contemplating how different groups of people (e.g., residents, students, and tour guides) make sense of Ouro Preto's monuments, which stand as symbols that are subject to local interpretations and conditioned perceptions. By doing so, I discuss how symbols face multiple interpretations, challenging buildings and architects to endure in their representative roles.

Chapter 2

Fault Lines in a Fragmented City

In this chapter, I discuss how permanent residents and students in Ouro Preto perceive and communicate socio-spatial relationships in the city. Discussing social and spatial interactions reinforces aspects already examined in chapter 1, namely that Ouro Preto's inhabitants do not experience the housing, cultural, or economic opportunities of the preserved cityscape evenly. More importantly for this book, this inequality means that not all residents perceive the city in terms of national heroism or shared identity. Rather, to some residents, preserved downtown areas express ongoing social inequalities through materials and commemorative celebrations.

How cultural heritage privileges some people and ideas over others in Ouro Preto is a question that occupied me throughout my fieldwork. To start this chapter, just as I finished the previous one, I bring to the forefront the Tiradentes Square, a central location to relate Ouro Preto to a Brazilian heroic history. On one side of the square, the building that used to be the jail and the House of Representatives in colonial days became the Museum of Inconfidência, where the remains of the heroes of that conspiracy rest in a mausoleum. On the other side, the old Governor's Palace (that lost function when political authority shifted to Belo Horizonte) is now a university building and hosts a museum for science and technology. In the centre of the square, facing the Museum of Inconfidência, a statue of Tiradentes was erected, as detailed previously. However, when looking at the square, residents do not always relate it to Independence and heroism, as the editors of history anticipated. Rather, the square is often used to portray a continuation of colonial circumstances. Tiradentes's statue reminds some residents that those in wealthier positions have always dominated the city and that someone who disputes power relations faces personal costs. Moreover, the buildings on each side cater mainly for outsiders; the museum is chiefly visited by tourists, and the university is an institution with few local students.

With Brazil being a society so strongly divided and spatially segregated, authors such as DaMatta (1991b: 113) argue that it is not surprising that the country is known for its festivities, a potential opportunity to bridge social divides. In Ouro Preto, people share the use of the city centre in commemorative events, celebrating the city and its heritage in open festivals. However, many inhabitants tell stories of events, meant to bring together different socio-economic groups, as places of social fragmentation. This chapter showcases how segregation arises at such celebrations.

Because of segregating experiences in the city, Ouro Preto is mainly presented in terms of groups. Amongst permanent residents prevails a perception of economic and housing privileges for 'those coming from elsewhere' (*quem vem de fora* – tourists and students) leading to the socio-spatial exclusion of *Ouropretanos*. Marginalised residents have reasons to cooperate in a network of daily relationships that involve informal jobs and provisional housing. However, the instability that affects some residents also leads to interim competition within as well as interactions between groups. Having to share a common space while at times having diverging or overlapping interests, how do the different populaces of the city navigate perceived fault lines?

The challenge for those involved in urban preservation includes maintaining the city, yet having to take into consideration the diverse oppositions and collaborations between individuals that occur in response to preserved sites or beyond historic and aesthetic appraisals. To take into account improvised houses even though it is the regularity of the landscape that calls attention, and to consider the temporality of social relationships when residents' narratives describe regularity, is the focus of this chapter. Moreover, I discuss how interpretations over the city's past and present between different groups of city users can affect heritage policies and preservation goals.

A TALE OF TWO CITIES: STUDENTS AND RESIDENTS

Everyday accounts about Ouro Preto are usually centred on inhabitants' disputes. As Angela, a resident in the city centre of Ouro Preto explained, the city has an enduring legacy as a place that excludes its own citizens and privileges impermanent residents and visitors. Angela offered me a remarkable story about the conflict between students and residents in town and how this difficult relationship was exacerbated by the commemoration of the anniversary of the School of Mining. As a writer and storyteller, Angela delved into residents' accounts about the city to find inspiration for her book about the treasures, ghosts, and folklore of Ouro Preto (Xavier 2009). This book is filled with the events surrounding disputes between Ouro Preto's groups: colonisers and the colonised, slaves and foremen and the feeling that these groups did not cease to exist but remain in the city shaping the 'energy of the place' (*a energia da cidade*, in Portuguese). Angela illustrates this through the conflicts of some permanent residents who live close to student halls (*Repúblicas*)[1] and are faced with loud student parties, often feeling disrespected by those temporary house occupants. She explained:

> *From what I read, from what the elderly have told me, before, imagine the situation in the city, the capital changed in the Republican years, in 1897. The capital left. The population too, the majority left. Everybody who had a business left to live in Belo Horizonte, everybody who was connected to public administration . . . you see, 'Ah we will live in the new capital, an entirely neoclassic city, beautiful, let's leave this thing here where so much disgrace took place: slaves, death, Tiradentes, a colonial place that represents a lot of things we want to forget. . .'. Everybody left. Those who didn't were those who had no money to leave. . . . And who came here? The people from the districts. . . . So, as the population who re-populated Ouro Preto came after 1897. . . from that date onwards it is another history and today we have the third generation of adults from those who came after the change of capitals. So the university, it inherited what? It got the Government Palace and installed the School of Mining. It got the headquarters where the Legislative Assembly was and installed the School of Pharmacy, and the best houses in the city became student halls. So they [the university] ruled the city. . . . The university grew too much, but I moved to live here, I am not from here, I am from the West of Minas, but I really like antiques and ended up coming here to work in schools. . . . I came here and was crazy for this city, in love . . . and I realised that Ouro Preto had three separated nuclei; one is the university, the professors and students have a world apart. The artists, today this part no longer exists, there is a bit, before there were many artists, people connected to culture, historical patrimony, the museum, visual arts, who spent seasons in Ouro Preto, like the university. And there is the Ouro Preto population that I met because I married an Ouropretano and that is why I wrote that book because I wanted to pay a tribute to the people of Ouro Preto. A city that has such a sizeable university, that has various multinationals and mining companies that explore this region . . . and the museums are all administered by people who are not from here; Ouropretanos are usually secretaries, porters, you see. These people are a fantastic people. I wanted to write a book about Ouro Preto's struggle. . . . This is a very strange place. There are a lot of people from elsewhere here and the people from Ouro Preto have a dispute, envy and they want you to get nowhere too, instead of getting together and trying to do something together, they want you to go wrong. 'I cannot do it so you cannot do it either', something like that.*
>
> (Angela, November 4, 2013)

As Angela explained, the conflict between students and residents is not a recent one; it dates back to the change of capitals, even before the creation of the Federal University of Ouro Preto (UFOP), when students from the School of Mining and School of Pharmacy occupied the main central buildings while non-students – who were also migrating to a vacant town – were prevented from taking up those central houses. This notorious privilege of students echoes conflicts in the city's past. The historical injustice suffered by the city at the hands of those coming from elsewhere was often brought up throughout my fieldwork, indicated by the use of the terms *forasteiros* or *emboabas* (colonisers), or 'those coming from elsewhere', as opposed to *nativos* (natives of Ouro Preto) or *moradores* (residents). Natives are not necessarily born in Ouro Preto but are economically unprivileged. Residents speak of how the city favours students in housing and job opportunities. However, these accusations and their correlations with the past also invite reflection. As Angela described, Ouro Preto is 'a very strange place', where residents do not get together to combat the oppression they describe. Rather, they 'have a dispute, envy and they want you to get nowhere too', as she phrased it, illustrating it with an incident that happened to a downtown family some time ago. In the example, though it centres on a dispute between students and residents, it also brings to the fore a lack of collective action from residents:

> *They [the family] were always struggling because of noise. It was impossible to sleep, these Repúblicas here they put everything on at the loudest volume . . . and they had kids, very small when they moved here, who would say, 'mum how will we sleep with this noise?' It was impossible, something absurd. In the university traditions (trotes, in Portuguese) they made people walk around naked while others made noise with pots on the window up to midnight, 1 am, any day of the week, you see, there was no respect. They started to have conflicts . . . and the husband would go to public telephones to call the police . . . but when the police left the noise would come back. It was something absurd. This family travelled on the Doze, October 12, when they celebrate the anniversary of the School of Mining [Angela begins to speak quietly as if telling a secret] and when they came home you would not believe it; what they did to their house; they wrote on the garage: 'native asshole' . . . [and she returns to her normal voice] they sued students but nothing happened, students blamed a Bolivian fellow who had already left the country. . . . The husband refused to repaint the gate 'we will leave it, when the hangover is over they will see what they did'. . . . The prefecture told them to paint it white, but the gate remained that way. One of their kids was in the second year [at school] and the teacher asked the kids to paint a picture of their houses, he painted the house and on the gate, he wrote 'native asshole'. The teacher called the family to go to the school. They told the teacher 'he painted a picture of our house, pass by and you will see'. . . .*

So there is a relationship of arrogance, you see, oppression of the people of the city. . . . But everybody is afraid to talk . . . or call the police. . . . To me the change of capital and the population that came here [explains the oppression], some even became rich in Ouro Preto, but they came here very humble and oppressed, you see. Who were the most important people? The people from the university. . . .

I personally believe that in a place where so many terrible tragedies happened there is bad energy that remains because there are many stories, I have to believe that.

(Angela, November 4, 2013)

The conversation with Angela revealed how fragmented the city is: an artistic community (that no longer features in most narratives), a student group, and permanent residents. The conflicts that arise between students and residents, however, do not always lead to cooperation within each individual group. From the perspective of a resident, Angela explained that economically oppressed, envious of those in better positions, and afraid of disputes, residents have coped with students' abusive behaviour alone and have not responded as a group. The 'energy' that endures in Ouro Preto is then that of conflicts between city dwellers, mainly perceived as part of groups (with students and permanent residents recognised as the main groups) as well as that of the envy, betrayal, and fear within such groups. Events such as *Doze* exemplify such a situation in Angela's recollections of local stories, where residents had to cope with abuses, and students looked down on residents referring to 'natives' as a form of insult. When examining my field notes from October 12, 2013, similar to Angela's account, I took note of an event that brought together students from Ouro Preto and other cities, while isolating non-student local residents who could not cross the threshold.

THE *DOZE* IN 2013

Each year October 12 is celebrated in Ouro Preto as it marks the founding of the School of Mining on October 12, 1876. The event known as *Doze*, meaning the twelfth, is celebrated by almost every República in town. On October 12, 2013, already during the day, fireworks burst in the sky incessantly, streets were packed with cars, and music could be heard coming from all directions. The celebrations being held in various Repúblicas usually start early in the afternoon with a barbecue for current and former students, and the most established Repúblicas host parties that last all night long.

Gaining access to some of the Repúblicas is very challenging. The parties charge no entrance fee, but the most distinguished Repúblicas (usually larger and older) have security at the entrance as well as a student (usually a first-year student, called in town *bicho* – animal in English) deciding who enters. In my case, at the door of a well-established República, I was asked whom I knew in that hall. I said the name my friends had told me to say, but that person was a friend of a friend and I was not allowed inside. Like me, there were many people waiting outside who did not know insiders. At some point the door opened, a few people left and I made my way inside, not being seen by the *bicho* or security. The República was a mansion. There were maybe a few hundred people in a basement turned into a disco and around the same number of people in the backyard, where there was a band playing samba.

Various students and alumni attended the party, and usually former students subsidise drinks or a music group, which explains how the beverages and music are free to all guests. Some of the people inside the house were also visitors from other cities, and for commuters, there were mattresses for overnight stays. As I met people from other parts of Brazil in the house, I could not stop thinking about the first people I met outside, some were young residents who knew no students.

Despite its popularity and frequency, the traditional party is still unknown to those who have never entered a República and who are left to imagine (often negatively) what happens inside. Many permanent residents resent Repúblicas because they have to build their houses informally in the periphery, while students live and party in mansions located centrally. Those who live beside students, such as Angela described, hate such parties because they disturb the neighbourhood. Narratives of conflict over noise are present in discussions about *Doze* and about the students in general, marking students' behaviour as abusive.

The association of students with noise has even prompted the creation of a Municipal Law, *Silence Law*,[2] which was provoked by disruptions to the Easter celebrations in 2006. During that event, the religious procession was interrupted by the noise coming from a private students' party. Though the law now determinates parameters for sonic nuisance and sets fines for those who violate these limits, student festivities still lead to police interventions, and residents depart the town in anticipation of events such as *Doze*. However, events cannot always be anticipated.

One example of an unexpected event was a movie shot in Ouro Preto in October 2013. That occasion brought together fireworks, music, and people walking up and down the streets at night. The unexpectedly noisy night could not be blamed on any particular group, as no one had been informed. Apart from some cameras being set on a main street during the daytime, shops operated normally and the usual signs indicating an event failed to materialise on the streets. However, at night a band started to play while people danced and walked up and down the hill as if during carnival. Taken by surprise, residents arriving by car could not park or drive along that street. The shooting was part of a publicity campaign of a major international brand, but similar to any other noisy event, the residents automatically blamed the disrespect on the students, though no one really knew who were the actors who danced that night.

Students and permanent residents have different interests in terms of which things to celebrate, how, and where; and events in Ouro Preto such as *Doze*, Easter, or the occasional movie shooting demonstrate such differences. Conflicts between permanent residents and students, often narrated in terms of noise nuisance, are however mainly grounded in ideas of economic and spatial prerogatives.[3]

The university principal, Dr Marcone, explained to me that offering centrally located houses free of charge to students, in case the university owns the República (Image 2.1), increases the negative image of the institution amongst residents. However, he said, the university student body was changing, from students mainly from other cities to those from local areas. Until

Image 2.1. Housing in Ouro Preto, 2013. On the forefront is a República and on the background are residential houses, further out in the city and simpler. *Source*: Personal collection.

2005 only 10 per cent of all students at the Federal University of Ouro Preto were from Ouro Preto, and according to him, that number was close to 30 per cent at the time of our interview on September 30, 2013.

Although the number of local residents registered as students is increasing, the perception of the university as a space for privilege remains, and residents, mainly living on the periphery and working low-paid jobs, have little chance of becoming students.[4] Economically privileged students who come from elsewhere predominate in Ouro Preto, especially in prestigious courses such as engineering. For these students, in 2013, the university also offered some studentships,[5] including 900 rooms in Repúblicas that charge no accommodation fees.

Permanent residents have never approved the offer of centrally located historic houses to students and have voiced their discontent through noise complaints. Other negative stories associated with Repúblicas are frequent, such as drug abuse and sexual harassment. The consequence of the division between students and residents for cultural heritage is considerable. The conflict frames perceptions of colonial abuses as continuous and the use of expressions such as 'the energy of the city' illustrates that. The uses of central housing and the related soundscape of the town are at the core of complaints, hence adding pressure to the educational aspect of that heritage site.

STUDENTS' HOUSES

Ouro Preto has around 20 per cent of its population made up of university students, the majority of them coming from other cities, while 46 per cent of the residents of Ouro Preto have not completed more than eight years of education (Da Gama Cerqueira 2003). The great number of students who move from elsewhere to Ouro Preto for higher education is not new. Already in the 1980s, the University held entrance exams in Belo Horizonte to avoid the chaotic traffic brought by too many travellers in the small historic city (Imprensa Universitaria da UFOP 1982). The university has continually expanded since its creation in 1969, and the high number of commuters arriving in the city for studies in the 1980s would not be out of date these days. UFOP students come especially from the southeast region of Brazil.

Camélia, who works for the Dean on Communitarian and Students' Affairs, explained that approximately 85 per cent of students come from other municipalities and will look for accommodation in town.[6] The options for students who will not live with their own families vary from university-organised houses and apartments (the university selects residents); Federal República (when the university owns the house and does not charge accommodation fees nor regulates the choice of occupants) or Private República (students will look for a house and share rental costs); and private accommodation (a more costly option). The choice of residence will result in different forms of being in the city. Repúblicas are at the centre of residents' complaints about noise, while other residences are not so noticeable. Camélia explained the popularity of Repúblicas, and students usually get to know each other through these shared houses and not through their classes. As an example, she mentioned the recent struggle to establish a student union. Finding a representative for the community of students proved difficult because Repúblicas have their own traditions and festivities, as well as closely bonded groups of current students and alumni. This also means that Repúblicas do not only separate the student population from permanent residents but also divide the community of students according to residence type.

There is, however, a reason to keep up the present system of Repúblicas, and Camélia offered Federal Repúblicas as an example. She explained that those houses are free to host festivities and select students because this system of self-management is successful in comparison with other properties, where the university regulates admission and needs to mediate internal conflicts, a problem that rarely occurs in Repúblicas. Finally, students meet the costs of house maintenance. Expensive to maintain, central houses hosting students are well kept. However, there was a need to review that system, because of abuses found in the process of selecting newcomers, who often go through a system of tests (*trotes*) before they become official residents in a República. 'The university had to interfere because people were avoiding going to Repúblicas. Frequently, new students were scared of those houses' (Camélia, September 30, 2013).

Understanding students' misgivings about joining Repúblicas is important, as it adds grey areas to the so far dual relationship between students and residents. The student community is not a cohesive group opposed to permanent residents but a diversified cluster.

Visiting one of the many Repúblicas in town, I spoke to some residents who organise tests for newcomers, a source of scepticism for both new students and permanent residents. These challenges, as described before, are usually loud, and neighbours of Repúblicas dislike them especially for that reason. New students fear their time as *bicho* (animal, as freshers are known) when they undergo the tests, a probation period of six to twelve months called *batalha* (struggle). During this time, they have to wait on others at parties. They may face *vento* (storm) when residents mess up their room by tying up clothes or turning the bed upside down. Some students are woken up with a bucket of cold water and do all household chores. If the newcomer is approved in the *batalha*, the house hosts a party for them and they receive a nickname. In 2012, during such a party, two *bichos* died from alcohol poisoning. This was also a year that sparked an increased politicisation in Repúblicas, which had to defend themselves in the form of student representatives and paid lawyers to explain the use of houses for parties and the process of selecting new students.

Victor, the President of the Association of Federal Repúblicas of Ouro Preto in 2013, explained that the deaths in 2012 laid bare the commonly held image of the parties and alcohol abuse associated with Repúblicas. Since the deaths, the university has begun to increasingly regulate the students' conduct, linking membership in a Federal República to academic performance. In addition, the university follows the process of *batalha* to ensure the candidates are not exploited. Finally, he explained that to reduce the negative perceptions of Repúblicas held by many people, students organise volunteer activities, such as visiting nursing homes and collecting food for donation. Those are attempts to demystify life in Repúblicas and promote changes as 'there is a myth about what happens to new students when they come to Federal Repúblicas. My mum didn't want me to come to Ouro Preto' (Victor, October 30, 2013). Similarly, for Octavio, the President of the Association of Private Repúblicas, to whom I spoke on November 4, 2013, the student life in Ouro Preto was negatively portrayed in the media, and the death of the students in 2012 added to that.[7]

Representatives like Victor and Octavio, however, argued that what is often left out when life in Repúblicas is assessed is the fact that they offer an opportunity not only to share bills but also to share university life. Victor, for example, mentioned that when the university assigns students to houses, they do not always get along, something Camélia also highlighted. Many people get jobs and internships in their future careers through the houses they lived in as students, as is the case in fraternities in Anglo-American universities. Nevertheless, because some of the challenges given to enter a house are still maintained, despite growing university regulation, new students are often wary about the house system. When I was talking to Octavio, for example, as he explained to me how *bichos* no longer have to do the heavy house chores (cleaning after a party, preparing shopping lists, doing house maintenance), he however asked a *bicho* to prepare a coffee for us. Octavio then explained that some situations remain the same, such as *bichos* picking up the phone if it rings, and the same when the bell rings, they are the ones who open the door.

The idea that *trotes* no longer exist in town, or at least not as it used to be, does not convince residents or students, and some students avoid Federal Repúblicas or start up their own Private Repúblicas as a result and develop different entrance rules, while others may give up on that system altogether and look for other housing options. In the case of Octavio's house, they are struggling to find new residents. Private Repúblicas such as his often compete against each other to find new students. When they are faced with high rent and fewer students to share costs, parties are viewed as an economic solution. Although parties have helped the houses meet living expenses, they also diminish the chances of finding new residents, as two students who moved from Repúblicas to university-administrated accommodations explained to me:

> *Sometimes there were no parties in my República, but there was one in the neighbouring ones, so for the four days I lived in a República there was a party every day and it was practically impossible to sleep. On the last day, there was a meeting and 'bicho' cannot participate in the meetings, so I came back from my classes and it rained that day and I was all wet and I was left outside until the end of the meeting. I said, this is not for me and looked for a house to rent.*
>
> (Isis, November 8, 2013)

Another student also talked about her attempt to live in Repúblicas:

> *It [batalha] was very psychological . . . like nobody would talk to you in the house or would be rude to you . . . it is really bad to arrive home and nobody looks at you. . . . It was to see if you can bear it, I did not find it too bad, for example, if one day you have a bad boss you already experienced that . . . you will not be so easily irritated . . . but as I had just left home and had never lived alone it was very difficult for me and I decided to leave. I tried four Federal Repúblicas I could not bear it. . . . I had to clean the house . . . search for house appliances online, I had to do all those things. . . . Nowadays it is very different, it [batalha] changed a lot.*
>
> (Jéssica, November 8, 2013)

Jéssica concluded by pointing out that she came to know Ouro Preto after she left Repúblicas, '[before leaving] I knew nothing, I had never visited a museum or anything . . . it is like a bubble and you are inside of it'.

The use of centrally located houses for student accommodation and celebrations leads to the local use of terms such as *forasteiros* (colonisers) to refer to students, who come from elsewhere, take advantage of local facilities for a short period of time, and do not sympathise with the place or the people (living in a bubble). For example, students pay fines and lawyers rather than follow noise restrictions. Even what students refer to as a positive aspect, creating networks of jobs and internships, is locally viewed as a perpetuation of privilege. Equally, charitable activities targeting local residents are not always positively perceived, not only it reinforces a hierarchy between students and residents, but also the recipients of those projects mention that when the classes are over activities stop.[8] Finally, because of the various parties thrown by students, there is little time left to join other activities in town, and many students reported never visiting museums or other local cultural events (a point I discuss in chapter 3). Local commerce complains as larger events such as *Doze*, which could increase local trade, extends to a point that beverages often have to come from neighbouring towns. Moreover, students host their guests, and hotel owners dispute their right to do so.

Nevertheless, for Marcelo, a resident living close to the main campus in Bauxita (see image 1.6),[9] a neighbourhood that hosts a growing number of students, the idea of a dualism between oppressed residents and abusive students does not exhaust local controversies. Residents also have beneficial relationships with students. Marcelo explained that some residents have rented their houses to students, charging a price much higher than what a family would pay, and have moved to a town with less real estate speculation.[10] Those residents, however, know that to meet costs, students would share that space with a number of others (up to forty) and organise socials, hence compromising public services in the area (sewage system as well as the Silence Law). Neighbours then either cope with crowded student houses nearby or offer to contribute to the rental fees so that a family can occupy the space. Adding to that, the university creates jobs for the city, a point that the principal clarified by stating that when there is a university vacation, the city is empty and local businesses lose income.[11]

This discussion allows for understanding the relationship between (and within) groups of students and permanent residents as neither absolutely negative nor positive, and these groups are not always polarised against each other, nor do they cooperate within each individual group. Thus, it is necessary to enquire what creates regular perceptions of separation between groups in a context where relationships unwrap fluid practices. Souza (2001: 54) states that it is important to look at which values are perceived as a privilege and why; in other words, to look at values as part of everyday life that define ideas and use of power.

Looking at Ouro Preto and preservation values associated with it, educational and cultural activities are pivotal in the city. Not only the preservation of the town offers a stimulus for education and cultural opportunities, but also refined cultural activities and formal education relate to ideals of middle class in Brazil (Owensby 1999). Focussing on the first half of the twentieth century, Owensby (1999) discusses the making of middle-class life in Brazil. The author explores meritocracy, professionalisation, and the obsession with a social hierarchy as part of middle-class standards. The years that Owensby (1999) analyses are important because they were the years of the preservation of Ouro Preto as a national monument. Thus the city, more than an image of Brazil, offered a self-image for the Brazilian middle class and the importance of educational and cultural urban centres. This image did not embrace residents living in the city then, mainly the poor and uneducated coming from the countryside, nor the ones of today, who do not always find a place at the university or agree with the status of the institution in town. However, residents do not feel solely frustrated with educational activities. As discussed earlier, some may enjoy financial benefits, and as I discuss in the following, wealthy permanent residents enjoy the offer of cultural events in the centre of town. Events such as the Jazz Festival give some insight. The Jazz Festival highlights more than the typical division between students and permanent residents; the event separated publics according to class.

CLASS PERCEPTION IN OURO PRETO

The 2013 Jazz Festival – *Tudo é Jazz* – started on a Friday in a local museum, with a reception for a select group of people. Unaware that the reception was exclusive, people hoping to attend the Festival waited by the door, where security guards checked names to allow for entrance. After the invitation-only reception, a music procession guided the crowd to a space in front of a church, and that public space again had a reserved area with chairs for government authorities, the sponsors of the event and their guests, and an open area for the general public.

The event was mainly popular amongst tourists and for those working at the prefecture and at the local art school (Art Foundation of Ouro Preto), or for some of the local restaurant and bar owners (the local upper class). There were only a couple of students, as it was also a weekend of graduation celebrations and most Repúblicas were hosting parties for students, former students, and families. On my walk home, I realised that while the Festival and some Repúblicas were packed with people, so was Rua Direita, the main street in town, crowded with its own public, mainly poor residents from the peripheries, *morros*, drinking at local bars.

The Jazz Festival on a Friday night was different from many other events in town because it physically separated parts of the public using guest lists, security guards, and a fenced-off area (Image 2.2a).[12] However, even without these instruments of division, clusters seemed to be separated in town: students at their parties (Image 2.2b), some residents in Rua Direita, and other residents attending concerts.

This separation of people into groups also occurs when other events take place in town. Even without physical barriers, people may be together in the city centre, but they do not mix, as Teko explained. Teko is a local hip-hop artist, broadcaster of a daily radio programme called *Fala Favela* (Speak up, Favela), and a resident of the outskirts, *morros*. He explained the dynamics of 'finding your place' (*achar o seu lugar*) in Ouro Preto to me:

> *Ouro Preto is like three cities. There is the city of Ouro Preto with the hills; if you get the flag* [see image 2.3] *of the city you will see that there are three hills there . . . one hill is ours, that is about the 'morros' where the working force*

Image 2.2a. The Jazz Festival (area with controlled access in front of the stage), September 14, 2013. *Source*: Personal collection.

Image 2.2b. Students in Repúblicas, next to Festival's venue, 2013. *Source*: Personal collection.

> *is [the Ouro Preto that was in Rua Direita]. There is the Ouro Preto city for tourists, that is the city of cultural heritage [the Ouro Preto that was at the Jazz Festival]. And there is also the Ouro Preto university town [the Ouro Preto that was in the Repúblicas]. So those are Ouro Pretos that do not mix together. . . . And the community takes more what belongs to it. Those events in the Tiradentes Square . . . they do not have a lot of attendance from the Ouropretano, there was the Mimo Festival,*[13] *there was the Jazz Festival, this weekend they are organising another event there, and so on, and the community does not participate. So what happens, people get to the centre, see what is happening on the square and go to Rua Direita. It has always been like that. . . . Because people do not see themselves, I don't know how to put it, they do not see themselves as part of that. . . .*
>
> *There are three cities, it seems each person is in his own place (cada um na sua). . . . From afar you see the houses are all the same, as if it was all the same.*
>
> (Teko, October 18, 2013)

But it is not all the same, and even in the selection of music style or music performers, differences become noticeable. For example, Teko asserts that 'everything is difficult when you live in Ouro Preto, when you are a resident of the city of Ouro Preto', and he mentions his hip-hop movement that tried to present at the Winter Festival in 2008. Teko explained that the community would be more likely to visit the centre for the Festival if a music style such as hip-hop, popular in the outskirts, was included in the programme, but he was told hip-hop did not suit the event. Later, Teko and his colleagues saw other rappers from elsewhere in the programme. 'It looks as if what is possible is possible, but you have to come from outside Ouro Preto', Teko said. Local hip-hop groups usually sing songs about an Ouro Preto that never changes.

Teko used the emblem of Ouro Preto (Image 2.3)[14] to depict three cities: the city of cultural heritage, the city of the working class who live on the slope of hills, and the city of students – three groups that may attend the same events without mixing. The use of the expression 'finding your place' (or 'know your place', 'putting one in one's place'), in the conversation with Teko, recalls the examination by Sheriff (2001: 69) when describing racial separation in Brazilian society. Though Teko did not mention aspects of race, this is not to be neglected, as it pervades social interactions. The hip-hop movement in Ouro Preto is mainly connected to the black community (FIROP – Forum for Racial Equality of Ouro Preto), and the residents celebrating in Rua Direita during events are often from the poorer, peripheral parts of the city and are commonly dark-skinned.

The separation between races in Brazil, however, is framed silently and through meta-discourse. Silence and euphemisms pertaining to racial

Image 2.3. Ouro Preto's emblem, or 'the three cities that get together but do not mix'.
***Source*: Prefeitura Municipal de Ouro Preto, 2019.**

prejudices prevail in ethnographies about urban Brazil (Sheriff 2001: 62), and in my case, this was no different. However, to understand the silence about race in Brazil, some elements need to be considered. For example, a light-skinned Brazilian living in a poor and black-dominated neighbourhood may be socially identified as black – not to be confused with a dark-skinned Brazilian living in an upper class, white-dominated neighbourhood. Context is a determining factor. Self-appearance (Sheriff 2001: 72–73), which is what some would call aesthetic racism (Souza 2010: 188) is also part of the discussion and connected to ways of dressing and hairstyles, which offer the possibility of altering colour and class perceptions in Brazilian society. A collective understanding of social location *meu lugar* (my place) is created in the face of a differentiating system that considers race, appearance, and economic class. Residents often respect social boundaries as a mechanism of defence from discrimination, anticipating responses to their dress code or race in events that are mainly white and wealthy (Schofield et al. 2016: 3057).

In sum, during the Jazz Festival, some residents may join together with tourists to enjoy the festivities; these are mainly restaurant and hotel owners who are not opposed to tourists in everyday accounts or in spatial dynamics. Residents, especially the upper class, can profit from tourists and, as discussed earlier, they privilege music, theatre, fine art, and other refined cultural activities to assert a hierarchical status (Owensby 1999). Residents who live on the slope of hills, 'the community' or the *morro*, do not have the same cultural opportunities in their neighbourhoods, and when they are in the city centre, whenever an event takes place, they are usually separated from students and from those that enjoy the events offered – 'the city of cultural heritage' – as Teko described 'they do not see themselves as part of that'. However, though Teko described three social groups in events, when he talks about the refusal to allow his hip-hop group presentation, he sees a separation between those coming from elsewhere against *Ouropretanos* as pivotal. City separations are therefore complex in definitions, as class separations at times may also be summarised in the separation between *Ouropretanos* and those coming from elsewhere.

Residents who may not 'find their place' in centrally located festivals do however find opportunities for work at city events and in hotels and restaurants, making their relationship with tourists and the upper class owners of hotels and restaurants one of social exclusion and economic dependency.

RESIDENTS WORKING IN THE TOURISM INDUSTRY

Ana works in a local hotel downtown and has lived in Ouro Preto almost all her life. Although because of this she knows about most of the events taking place in town, she does not attend any of them. According to her,

> *April 21 is terrible [the death anniversary of Tiradentes], you need a badge to walk in the city [areas with restricted access]. The people from Ouro Preto cannot even see the festivity, it complicates everybody's lives, it is very bad for the city.*
>
> (Ana, April 2013)

Because of these difficulties, many people in town refer to the festivities on April 21 or September 7 (Brazilian Independence Day) as 'Doctor April 21' or 'Doctor September 7', hinting at the celebrations' segregation and exclusivity. Such a way of communicating about events again emphasises how, despite efforts to promote cultural heritage in town, the format that is selected cements socio-economic divisions.

Ana adds that the city lacks leisure activities and that she would move out if she could. Before I could underline a list of leisure options, she continued: 'People do not get together even in leisure time, we [residents] do not feel comfortable in the middle of tourists'. Talking in terms of us (residents) and others (elite families, tourists, and students) was a strong feature in her narrative. She explained that residents could not visit a restaurant, as it would be too expensive. To Ana, 'those who come from other cities have more power here', and she mentions students' advantage of living in the city centre for free. In contrast, Ana's house is in the outskirts, an adjunct house built in a hurry on the top of her mother-in-law's house, known in Brazil as *puxadinho*. She also discusses the privilege of wealthier families who often come from other places in Brazil or from abroad to establish businesses in town. 'Some families have always had everything and that is perpetuated unless a [less privileged] person goes elsewhere, saves money and comes back'. Ana describes how people from Ouro Preto need to get out of town to make money, as Ouro Preto itself is a city of kinship and friendship opportunities (*apadrinhamento*), and 'those who command do so because they can; those who obey do so because they are sensible'.[15] People in Ouro Preto do not dispute with others in a privileged position: 'When the bus tariff rose recently nobody said a thing'.

Supporting Ana's statement, Martins, another long-term resident who works in a Bed & Breakfast downtown (she currently lives in a temporary government housing provision, having lost her previous house to a landslide), mentions the Tiradentes Square as a good frame for the city. The square has in its centre the building that used to be a Palace next to the one that was the jail. Despite being close together, they conveyed worlds apart. Just as the prison was geographically close to the palace but socially far, Martins and Ana work close to events, know them, and yet feel detached from them. Events in Ouro Preto have segregations that are unveiled across time, conversations, and observations of street dynamics. The calendar in Table 2.1 shows

Table 2.1: Main events in Ouro Preto

January	*February*	*March*	*April*
Religious celebrations to Nossa Senhora do Rosário	Carnival (one of the most well-known carnivals in Brazil, behind only Rio, Salvador, and Olinda)	Guava festival in the district of São Bartolomeu	Easter Processions Anniversary of Tiradentes's death on April 21 Anniversary of the founding of the Pharmacy school (April 4, 1839)
May	*June*	*July*	*August*
Religious celebrations (in town the month is known as Maria's Month)	Corpus Christi celebrations Cinema Festival	Ouro Preto's anniversary Winter Festival (music, dance, art, and workshops)	Religious fests in Ouro Preto's Districts MIMO festival (concerts, films, and workshops)
September	*October*	*November*	*December*
Nation's week (celebrations for the Independence of Brazil) Jazz, Museum, and Theatre Festivals	Anniversary of the founding of the School of Mining (October 12, 1876)	Aleijadinho's week (when awards are given to those engaged in preservation activities)	Religious festivities

some of the festivals that take place in town annually. Though there are many celebrations, those working in tourism talk about boredom, as they 'do not feel comfortable in the middle of tourists' and cannot afford restaurants or shops that cater mainly for 'those coming from elsewhere'. The city's status as cultural heritage, the increasing need to stage events to satisfy tourists, and the accompanying lack of opportunities to change the dynamics of space use amplify this feeling of detachment in the workforce in town.

The calendar excluded events that are transient. There are also other activities in the districts of Ouro Preto, and various shows in Tiradentes Square that happen as unexpectedly as the movie shooting I described before. Events have been mainly reported as occasions for socio-spatial distinction, as described by Teko, Ana, and Martins in the dynamics of 'finding your place'. Further, in addition to discomfort around tourists, jobs in the tourism industry are poorly paid, preventing those residents employed in these sectors from using local restaurants and shops.

The functionaries in the Secretariat of Tourism[16] explained that in tourism salaries are low, usually the minimum wage allowed by law (which in 2013 was R$678 per month, around £150). Many of the positions in restaurants are filled with temporary workers rather than employees with permanent contracts. This suggested that a lot of people working in the tourism sector earn a small share of what tourists leave in town. In addition, during many of the city events, the food, for example, is twice as expensive.[17] Consequently, residents, although depending on tourism, at times say bad things about the city to tourists. Many hospitality employees do not work to create a good impression of the city for outsiders. When a visitor compliments the city, the answer from a staff member is often that 'the city is a good stepmother but an awful mother'. This is an expression I heard throughout my stay in town, indicating that the city is good to those who are not her offspring but treats her own progeny badly. All this leads to it being hard to instil pride for the city's cultural heritage in residents, which makes it difficult to get them to participate in preservation efforts.

As they are paid directly by tourists, tour guides are among those who attempt to give a good impression of the city. They take the 'bunny from the hat', as phrased by an informant, to make sure tourists return home and say good things about Ouro Preto. Tourist guides created an association in the 1970s to regulate their work, as Nelson, the president of the Tourism Association, explained. 'But today it is difficult, there are no more tourists . . . so the money you make here is not enough to pay the bills', said Nelson, glancing at the horizon hopelessly as we talked in November, a quiet month in town. I contested, 'the city is full of people even now, you see tourists every day. How come there are no tourists?' He explained that the city is busy, but many tourists come for specific festivals, and though they pack hotels and restaurants, festivals often mean tourists will not visit the city's main attractions (churches, museums, mines). As a result, the profit is concentrated in the hands of the hotel and restaurant owners.

Both tourist guides and employees in hotels and restaurants seem to be affected negatively by cultural events. Even in rare cases when these residents attend festivities, they do not 'mix together' with other groups and instead stay close by, in Rua Direita. Additionally, events directly affect the work of tour guides who have fewer tours, as tourists may prefer to attend festivities. However, while all similarly affected, those working in the tourism industry offer a good example of what Angela referred to when she said that 'the people from Ouro Preto have a dispute, envy, and they want you to get nowhere too, instead of getting together and trying to do something together, they want you to go wrong. 'I cannot do it so you cannot do it either'. A relationship characterised by the dispute between workers in Ouro Preto was central in conversations when I lived for a month with a family that works as tour guides and owns two shops in town.

DISPUTES BETWEEN RESIDENTS

In Silva's family, the wife used to work in their shop next to Tiradentes Square. She described her days there as 'hell', because of the competition between tour guides and shop clerks to lead tourists:

> *The clients enter the shop and the others [other shop clerks] keep an eye on them, they do not want you to sell anything so that they can sell something. The guide is the 'owner' of the tourists; he wants to take them [the tourists] where he decides [usually tour guides earn commission from shop owners when they bring tourists to shop]. One day my husband got a tourist on Tiradentes Square that already had an 'owner'. After he finished the sale, the 'owner' almost beat him. They had to call the police and everything.*
>
> (Mrs. Silva, June 20, 2013)

Mrs. Silva seemed traumatised by the everyday disputes between traders and guides in Tiradentes Square and avoided visiting the place at all costs, having recently decided to work only from home. However, her husband had a different account, as his greatest life shift occurred in the Square.

The husband told me about his poor childhood as a tourist guide in Tiradentes Square with excitement. From a young age, he learned the value of precious stones and how to tell the city's story of gold and mines. He quickly became a tour guide, until the day he was standing in Tiradentes Square when a man in a luxurious car approached him, showed him a big gem, and asked where he could get more. He showed the man – and soon many other people – where to find gems. In a few years, he was travelling abroad selling gems. 'People would never think I had gems, look at me, do I look like somebody who has money?' He did not. Mr. Silva looked old beyond his years. His was a story of child labour that had marked his body, but he now owned two jewellery shops in the city centre. His house, like himself, showed signs of his economic flows, just like many others in town.[18] Large, with a big garden, two kitchens, a swimming pool, a billiard table, and memories of the many parties that took place there, the house was a sign of the development of a good life. On the other hand, parts of the house were in need of renovation or unfurnished, confirming narratives of difficult times. The wife mentioned owing to the supermarket, where they had a tab for their shopping. That bill was to be paid when things got better. 'Thank God we have a name, someone who has a "name" has everything', referring to the fact they are reliable in town and people know they would eventually pay their bills. The degree of informality for residents in the economy of Ouro Preto is noteworthy. Similar to other preserved and touristic cities in Brazil, like Olinda, many young people spend time in the main square and work as tour guides, hoping to find a better opportunity, as happened to some people like Silva. These young people promptly explain the city to anyone interested. Whether they have a training or are affiliated with Nelson's association is often questionable. Other residents rent out rooms in their houses or become artisans, musicians, photographers, storytellers, or other professions directly dependent on demand. This, however, does not mean residents who depend on tourists may defend the current focus on cultural stimuli for tourists. With the exception of those owning well-established hotels and restaurants, most residents working in tourism describe a situation typified by low and unstable salaries and continually live with a degree of informality in shopping, house construction, and employability. In addition, there is strong competition amongst residents, who depend on acquaintances to find work, and at the same time need to distinguish themselves from others through the services they offer. My interview partners often reported that 'men are envious of other men', and that 'successful businesses are immediately copied'. In a more metaphoric way, 'an ugly child does not have parents, but everybody wants to be the parents of the beautiful ones', which means that when a person has a good idea, many people in the city immediately claim it. This speaks to a relationship of coveting that typically results from the competition of offering similar services to a limited number of customers. The combination of unpredictable and low income makes their social network (friendship economy) essential (Rebhun 1999: 56). The pressure to cooperate is, at the same time, an expectation for reciprocity. When someone changes in socio-economic status, the life of others does not necessarily improve (even perhaps the opposite), and the investment made in every-day relationship is lost. Thus envy is a strong mark of such tight social network with strong economic dependency.

Stories and expressions of residents' disputes are abundant, as are stories of people who found valuable gems or opened successful short-term businesses. Sudden wealth and misfortune escalate feelings of envy, and such economic instability is not always easy to depict when looking at a central landscape that supposedly transmits permanence. Despite well-maintained façades, due to heritage policies, the insides of houses, especially in those outside central areas, are often unfurnished and unfinished. Houses, people's biographies, and stories of people's disputes reveal great social complexity. One aspect, however, predominates in conversations. This is that the city is viewed through conflict, especially the dispute between students and residents. The narratives during the June Protests in 2013 in Brazil,[19] when millions took up streets to protest against public transport prices and lack of public services while public money was spent to prepare the 2014 FIFA World Cup, will show that even when sharing a common agenda – lower bus fares – these two groups did not act together.

JUNE PROTESTS IN OURO PRETO

On June 26, 2013, some forty students blocked streets to press for lower bus fares, closing one of the access roads to Ouro Preto. They were drumming and holding posters, and every time a car or motorcycle tried to force its way through, the students would block them, sometimes lying on the asphalt and singing: 'if we do not disturb, it will not change'.

On the sidewalk nearby, while observing the students, three men wearing the uniforms of their respective companies (a driver, a fireman, and a third one that I could not identify) commented that students do not do anything, but

> *drink beer all day long, nobody there woke up at 6 am to protest. They are disturbing the workers! I spent the night working and stopped to buy food for my fish and now they will not let me through. Those vagabonds that spent the night drinking beer, partying in Repúblicas, only those who know the life in Repúblicas know how it is, consuming cocaine and smoking grass. If they do not have money to live here, they should go back home. Nobody in this protest is from here.*
>
> (Workers' conversation, July 2, 2013)

When I later talked to students about the lack of support from local residents, one rationalised, 'We protest for them [residents] too, when the tariff gets cheaper everybody will be happy; residents either have no political consciousness or are at work, but they will be happy if it gets cheaper'.

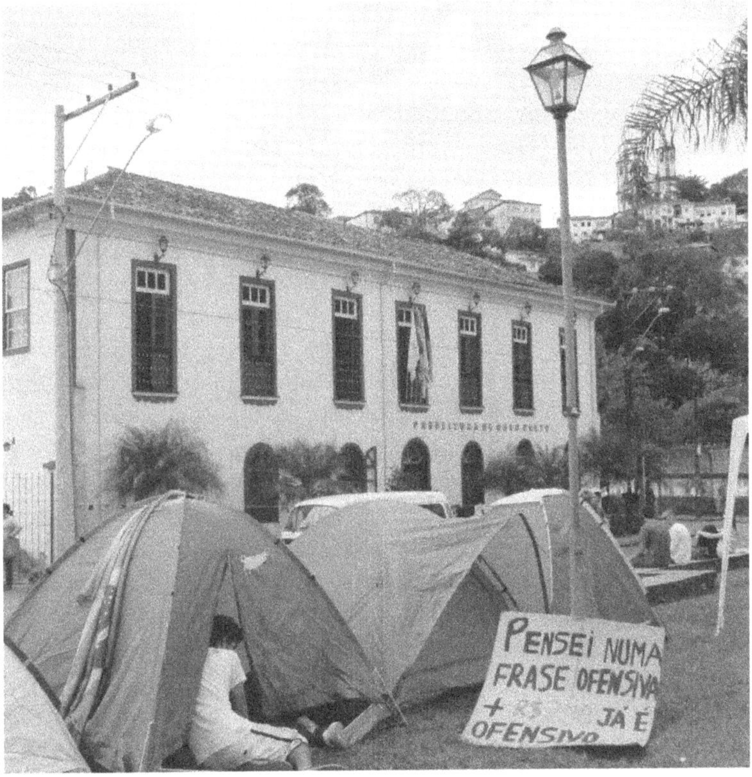

Image 2.4. Students protest in Ouro Preto, 2013. ***Source*****: Personal collection.**

Protests also included camping outside the prefecture and when the camp was set up, I heard an elderly lady talking to another after glancing at the protest against high bus fares: 'these rich students can afford to camp outside the prefecture to diminish bus fares, when I was their age and had no money for the bus, I walked' (Image 2.4).

The statements from the men in uniform as well as the woman surprised me. Ana had told me a few months before the protests that transportation fares rose and nobody did anything, because people in Ouro Preto usually do not fight those in power, such as the government authorities who raised the price of transportation. I thought that when people from elsewhere, in this case, students, demonstrated, residents would support them. However, residents did not sympathise with the actions taking place and, for them, the students were spoiled. Students, on the other hand, looked down on residents politically and justified their lack of support as a lack of social consciousness. The two groups kept a sense of otherness, drawing conclusions about each other. Further bolstering of the polarisation between the groups despite a shared agenda creates a relationship that reflects and perpetuates memories of previous oppositions in a contemporary scene of inequality.

There are complexities in relationships involving permanent residents and students in Ouro Preto. However, the idea of a standard relationship between 'us and others' or *Ouropretanos* and *forasteiros* remains. This aspect brings us back to the start of the chapter and the need to understand which values are associated with the preservation of the city. The normative experience of Ouro Preto relates to refined cultural activities and formal education, leading to a perception amongst residents that the city centre is often a place for tourists and the upper class. Even when directly profiting from students or tourists, most residents do not share a self-perception of association with those perceived as an upper class. Because 'those higher on the social scale make as many distinctions between themselves and the lower classes as possible – and the tendency of those lower on the scale [is] to resent upper class privileges' (Rebhun 1999: 39). For Ribeiro (2000: 32), one of the primary aspects that have prevailed in Brazil since its colonial period is its ruling class, which is 'exogenous and unfaithful to its people'. As Angela said, some people who migrated to Ouro Preto at the time of the change of capitals, when the city was vacant, even made money, but they arrived in town very humble and felt oppressed by the university that inherited the most important buildings. Thus the 'energy of the place', of power and powerlessness, ever since colonialism is further nourished in a present-day scene.

CONCLUSION

In Ouro Preto, one puzzling relationship is that of geographical proximity and social distance. Some residents live near students, but though they are geographically close, they live 'worlds apart', as expressed through conflicts mainly caused by noise and privilege. Teko, one of my informants, also explored this apparent entanglement of geographical proximity, but social distance. For him, sharing the same location did not mean mixing. The separation of the public is subtle – events that take place in Tiradentes Square are mainly for tourists and upper class residents, while just beside the Square, poorer residents gather in Rua Direita to socialise; and students gather in their own parties. The festivities do not necessarily aim to divide and select particular groups, but groups seem to find themselves already in 'their own places' (*cada um na sua*), in 'distinct cities'.

Everyday accounts unwrap the opposition not only between distinct groups but also within individual groups, which are crossed through with a spiralling sense of disputes. Students have organised themselves through representatives, but not all Repúblicas share the same values. Their students often rely on parties for house maintenance, which though successful in raising income, heightens the chasm between students from Repúblicas and those wary of those houses. On the other side, some residents report a degree of informality in the economy and often they rely on 'having a name', that is, having friends in town to postpone payments in a context of an unstable local economy and informal employment. However, those residents may often rely on acquaintances that offer similar services to a limited target group, the tourists, leading to internal competitions and envy.

Despite controversial descriptions of groups, disputes between city dwellers are at the centre of narratives. The system of quarrels in Ouro Preto is notorious in the city's history. Accumulated knowledge about the local history encourages an understanding of the place as composed of dualities (colonisers and the colonised) and a traditional focus on the rivalry between groups based on a violent history of conflicts (Moreira 2012: 215). When the antagonism of colonisers and the colonised was replaced in politics, the system of oppositions did not change, as a resident of Ouro Preto explained, 'but evolved, in the sense that the problems of today have contemporary narratives, but are similar to those from the past: a resentment about those who come from outside against those who are from here; and the main blame falls on students, who are the most visible [and audible] group of *forasteiros*' (Jorge, April 9, 2013).

The term *forasteiro*, often used in town, means outsider and derives from the conflict between those who first settled in Ouro Preto to extract gold, *paulistas* (also known as *bandeirantes*) and those who arrived later, *forasteiro/emboaba* (Portuguese). However, who were the oppressors in a mining economy that usurped lives and minerals? While the use of history today brings forth interpretations of the eighteenth century in a search for a national spirit, founded in sentiments against the *forasteiros*, oppressor colonisers, that rebellion challenges national heroism. The group of *forasteiros* included not only the Portuguese but also other Brazilian-born groups fighting to access mining areas *paulistas* controlled. *Paulistas*, on the other hand, if considered natives because they disputed (also) against colonisers, arrived in the area first because land expansion and enslaving indigenous groups also benefited the crown (Fausto 1999: 47–51). The conflict reveals not only disputes but also similarities among the different groups in their search for gold and regional control. This approach:

> allows us to break with the most common mistake in the traditional analysis about the War of the Emboabas: the anachronism expressed in the tendency to reduce the event to a rationality of our time. From there comes the strange feeling that everything seems to chain logically, as if paulistas and

> emboabas shared our view of the world and were driven by the same values and ambitions. There is no place for surprise, estrangement, or for history. The naturalisation of the past conducts inexorably to the suppressing of history as difference, replacing it with obviousness, where there are no questions or problems to be faced.
>
> (Romeiro 2008: 27, my translation)

Reducing events to express 'a rationality of our time' was part of the strategy when selecting places and monuments to include in the hall of national patrimony. The focus on Ouro Preto highlighted national martyrs such as Tiradentes but disregarded other interpretations of the Inconfidência as 'fundamentally a movement made by oligarchs in the interest of oligarchs, where the name of people would be evoked merely in justification' (Maxwell 1973: 139). Complexity in Minas' society, its insurgencies in the past, and the diverse interpretations of city dynamics today seem to give a way to a perception of groups in terms of otherness. As Brumann (2009) reminds us, the

> public recognition of things and practices as heritage produces pressure to fix those things and practices in time. Not only are they seen as unchanged survivals from an earlier day but they also may no longer evolve freely, being effectively placed under a glass case.
>
> (Brumann 2009: 277)

When cultural heritage focussed on the symbolism of national uprisings that took place in Ouro Preto, not only were locations enshrined under a glass case but so too was a perception that the struggles from the past were a dualism (colonisers and the colonised) that did not change. Instead, it evolved a constant sense of dispute between groups and the threat of betrayal within, as expressed through the use of previous terminology to name groups, or through narratives about 'the energy of the place'.

Negative perceptions of preserved areas and commemorative ceremonies convey ideas not of heroism but of uninterrupted inequality. Ouro Preto's cultural heritage is then not only a 'theatre of happenings of great historical relevance in the formation of our [Brazil's] nationality', as stated by President Vargas (Decree 22928, 1933), but also a stage for continuing spatial and social disputes. If all of the conflicts today are a continuation of the past, then preserving the past through heritage may preserve the conflicts as well. Thus, despite eventual (and controversial) profits associated with city maintenance, for most residents the city leads to an enduring socio-economic division, it is then not surprising that many permanent residents do not favour city maintenance. The authorities linked with cultural heritage think this apathy is a disinterest in culture and think they have to educate them (as I discuss in chapter 3). However, there is a deep-seated detachment from the town itself, because permanent residents perceive it as a place of conflict and unfairness and locate themselves as *Ouropretanos*, victimised by a (coloniser) upper class. Making the city attractive in its heritage is also de-mystifying the past as one of a dual conflict, or else how can residents see themselves, the city, and everyday life as part of a mutual and open-ended (and not maintained and polarised) conflict?

Chapter 3

Sightseeing the City

Departing from previous discussions that complex everyday interactions in the city are often communicated as a dual opposition, in this chapter I discuss how sightseeing could allow for diverse interpretations about the past that do not always find a representation in cultural heritage. This lack of representation about varied pasts matters as it leads to a perception amongst residents that their exclusion is both material and symbolic.

Tour guides seem to be caught between privilege and exclusion in regard to the preservation of Ouro Preto. Guides strive to offer sightseers a good impression of the city and directly profit from tourism, but as residents, they are often excluded from the city's cultural events and live outside the main touristic, commercial, and cultural zone. Looking at the interpretations guides have about the city, I discuss some stories and locations they favour in city tours. Do tour guides express the ambiguity of their lives in a city where residents have maintained a narrative about social and spatial divides since colonial times, or do they narrate a story that satisfies tourists' preconceptions about the place?

Guides' narratives are not the only ones to offer explanations about the city's heritage. For residents, there are government projects that create city interpretations. In the second part of the chapter, I look at programmes in Ouro Preto that hoped to familiarise residents with what the city offers for 'those coming from elsewhere' and thus alter perceptions of socio-economic unfairness and detachment from the city's sights. Directed at educating residents, especially those who articulate a perception of exclusion, programmes aim to create affective memories and joyful experiences in the city, mainly through cultural opportunities, such as pedagogic city tours and actions across museums and art galleries. When looking at those projects it is possible to locate theoretical debates discussing the opportunities and limits of cultural projects in the face of urban inequalities.

Mitchell (1991: 93–94) states that material (architectonic) control also has a non-material side, making 'the education of the individual suddenly imperative', because the power of city structures over individuals also aims to work from 'the "inside out" – by shaping the individual mind'. However, other authors such as Canclini (2012: 164) argue that the promotion of pedagogic tools to 'translate' the city often epitomises the lack of a shared perception of space and history. To insist in finding a common narrative for patrimony through education is also to ignore that learning in schools, museums, or art galleries is not an equal process for all individuals. Supporting his argumentation with the work of authors such as Bourdieu, in his studies about social distinction, Canclini (2012: 210) discusses the appropriation of cultural capital according to socio-economic inequalities.[1] In combining theories exposed by Mitchell (1991) and Canclini (2012) with my discussion about Ouro Preto, the material expression of the city does not on its own lead to a shared social meaning, thus pedagogic tools are important if cityscapes are to shape common city perceptions. However, not all individuals equally absorb cultural projects.

Finally, in the final part of this chapter, I offer a discussion about gold mines as a way to offer an alternative to polarised socio-spatial relationships (and normative pedagogic tools). Mines privilege more than a key focus on heroes and nationalism. Tours in mines offer non-official accounts of slavery as well as non-physical spaces, such as spiritual worlds. Could gold mines offer an alternative to geographies of exclusion with their metaphysical accounts and a history that challenges national contexts? This question guides the final section of the chapter.

SIGHTSEEING IN THE CITY CENTRE

Tour guides are generally residents who delve into the city's history for money or because of personal interest and do not have much in common with each other (as mentioned in chapter 2, they may compete with each other for clients and over access to shops and hotels). Guides often also have different ways of making money to live. For example, while Nelson is the president of the Tourism Association and dedicates his working hours to planning and leading tours and dealing with other guides belonging to his organisation, Silva is a guide for convenience. I had time to understand Silva's work and motivation when living in his house. The work of leading visitors through the city has been part of Silva's routine since his childhood and now, owning two shops in town, he continues to guide for pleasure and to attract customers to his shops. The different biographies and diverse commitments guides have when leading tours mean that talking about them as a group obscures the intricacies of their personal abilities and time budget context, amongst other particularities that impact their narrative of the city. As guides, however, they have in common an 'interpretative activity' (Reed 2002: 128); they offer more than the 'city's shell', as they say, but the essence of eighteenth-century stories. Despite emphasizing diverse corners of the city, street names, or local biographies, when explaining the city, guides view the city today through the same lenses most residents and tourists do: through the prism of the eighteenth century. The same lenses however will not mean they see the same picture – tourists look for a romantic city, residents often focus on conflicts – and I look at guides as ethnographic subjects to discuss how they communicate colonial memories:

> *To start, Ouro Preto was founded on June 24, 1698, but it is interesting to notice that it was founded twice. Antonio Dias who arrived through Itacolomi founded the city, this side here. But other people that came from down there also founded it. So we had people from Pilar and the people from Antonio Dias. People from the two groups met in this Square [Tiradentes Square] in 1711, Santa Quiteria hill at the time, and the meeting did not work out, because people from one side did not want to mix with people from the other side, and so they made an imaginary line in the middle of the Square dividing the two groups. So it was the people of Antonio Dias on that side and the people from Pilar in here. When the Crown had to create villages, instead of creating two, the Governor created only one and the village was growing and growing with this division between two groups; and so this is the only city that has two main cathedrals, we have the Cathedral Our Lady of Pilar on this side and Cathedral Our Lady of Conceição on that side. All the children that were born on either side would be baptized in the respective cathedral, and that continues up until now. During the Holy Week, as Easter is the biggest celebration of Catholicism, they agreed that each year one of them would promote the event, and so on even years it would be Pilar Cathedral and odd years it would be Our Lady of Conceição Cathedral . . . and so the city has always been divided.*
>
> (City tour with Nelson, November 25, 2013)

Nelson started explaining two important city landmarks – the two cathedrals – by portraying their association with the two distinct city groups that founded Vila Rica. Similar to Flávio (chapter 1), he described the first residential settlements to later explain divisions that took shape in Tiradentes Square (see Image 2.3 for a representation of the hills having the first housing settlements). The explanation finishes with the conclusion that 'the city has always been divided'. During another city walk, Silva again referred to Ouro Preto's cathedrals in terms of social separations, but this time, when mentioning Pilar Cathedral, he focussed on its interior artwork to describe the division between slaves and freemen:

> *Francisco Xavier de Brito made the pulpit on the right as the Portuguese Crown requested, but he died and the Crown then hired a slave and said they would grant him freedom (carta de alforria) if he made the second pulpit. But the slave already knew no freedom would follow so he moulded a similar piece on the left side but took the opportunity to expose the different ways of life in town for whites and blacks. If you notice, angels on the right (Image 3.1b) are better-dressed, stronger, paler; on the left side angels are poorly dressed, slimmer, darker* (Image 3.1a).
>
> (City tour with Silva, June 29, 2013)

Throughout the city's churches and chapels, guides such as Nelson or Silva usually explain how each church focussed on distinct city groups (e.g., mine owners, local traders, black slaves) that lived in the city in the eighteenth century. However, religious syncretism, music, dance, racial consciousness, are also described when temples are visited, sometimes clarifying city economic divisions, ostentation and racial exclusion and sometimes focussing on miscegenation and social complexity. Nelson, who started the tour by saying how the city was always divided, explains that when black slaves were excluded from main churches, they created their own temples. He then mocks São Francisco de Assis Church, named after a saint who preached poverty and humility, as a temple that was popular amongst mine owners and refused to allow blacks in its fraternity. On the other hand, Nelson talks with pride about churches like Lady of the Rosary of Blacks (Image 3.2), especially about its magnificent smooth-edged architecture, created by and for black people.

Bridging racial issues, architectural astuteness, history, and imagination, Aleijadinho, The Little Cripple, is a key individual in Silva's description:

> *Aleijadinho was the son of a black slave woman and a white Portuguese man, Manuel Francisco Lisboa, who was the greatest Portuguese architect and so the King sent him here to build city projects, churches, everything, but he made a slave pregnant. When they found out the mulatto boy was born, the father's punishment was to work for free for the crown the rest of his life and never see his son. Another architect, Francisco Xavier de Brito, baptised the boy and brought him up. The boy's first architectural work was at the age of nine years old . . . and he became the greatest Brazilian sculptor. . . . In all his images of Christ, he adds a hanging scar on the neck to pay a tribute to Tiradentes, and this is also a way to sign his work, because he had no fingers on his hands.*
>
> (City tour with Silva, June 29, 2013)

Image 3.1a. Angels in Pilar Cathedral, 2013. *Source*: Personal collection.

Image 3.1b. Angels in Pilar Cathedral, 2013. *Source*: Personal collection.

Image 3.2. Church of the Lady of the Rosary of Blacks, 2013. ***Source*****: Personal collection.**

Aleijadinho, the illegitimate son of a Portuguese man and a black slave woman, was more than the first well-known Brazilian artist; he was one of the greatest. Crippled and talented, he is hailed during tours as the product of a Brazilian miscegenation ideal:[2] creative, brown, overcoming through education and talent all the odds resulting from his deformed body and difficult family circumstances. In a short walk around São Francisco church, one can easily perceive how Aleijadinho sculpted more than the saints' images, encouraging and sparking ambition in generations to come. The city has a medal named after him, which is given annually to those who contribute in groundbreaking ways to the field of art.[3] However, besides miscegenation and upward mobility, imagination and inaccuracy are common in narratives about Aleijadinho's work. When pointing out Aleijadinho's sculptures, Silva emphasises a long list of his creative solutions in representing animals, saints, and historic moments in soapstone and wood:[4]

> *Aleijadinho did not know the animals, and when he portrayed Jonah's life, that one that was eaten by a whale, he could not make a whale because he had never left Minas Gerais to see the sea, so he imagined a duck and he made the whale with a beak and wings of a duck, can you see it there?*
>
> (City tour with Silva, June 29, 2013)

Narratives about Aleijadinho's creations give room for guides' and sightseers' imagination, who start to see resemblances of diverse animals when looking at the sculptures. Aleijadinho's intentionality in designing unconventional images has different narratives, starting from the need to make his work distinctive (since he could not sign his pieces), to his ignorance about certain animals, and his personal beliefs that would lead him to avoid certain forms.[5]

Less controversial than Aleijadinho, Athaide, the painter of the temple's interior, gains centrality in São Francisco de Assis Church. One cannot move beyond the church's atrium without being caught by Athaide's Virgin Mary. The ceiling, looking like the hull of a ship, makes Mary emerge from the clouds of the sky, as a ship does from the waves of the sea. Her presence, floating on clouds surrounded by musician angels is even more eye-catching as she has features of a mixed-race Brazilian. Black (or mixed-race) saints in churches are uncommon in Brazil, especially in a church built exclusively for white nobility, and that image was praised as a symbol of 'miscegenation and nationalism, already in colonial Brazil!', explained Silva with excitement (See Image 3.3).

Taking pictures at São Francisco Church is however to face a series of restrictions,[6] usually a contract needs to be signed previously, and one requires a private appointment. The church also charges admission fee, and because of its central location, São Francisco Church is an exclusive place. Even though locations such as the church offer entrance fee waiver for residents on specific dates or they offer a reduced price, permanent residents coming from poorer areas to visit the church feel self-conscious about clothing, and some might attend services from the door or seated at the back. On my visits to the Church I did not see people praying, priests, or candles, and there was no smell of incense left. Guides explain that learning the details of the church remains a privilege, and while black people could not enter São Francisco Church in the past, many local residents today do not visit the temple, nor can they access the diverse interpretations of its interior.

Embracing the interior and exterior of temples, interpretations of the city through tours with Nelson, Silva, and others referred to religious buildings to express both social exclusiveness and creative forms of inclusion and resistance (through saints or statues that denounce unequal ways of living and

Image 3.3. The ceiling in São Francisco Church. ***Source*****: Eduardo Tropia 1980.**

celebrate diversity). By exalting the creativity of artists tours did not only focus on a past of power and powerlessness. Nevertheless, tours depicted a city of privilege, when describing restricted visits to city sights (by residents) and limited interest on tours (by tourists). The work of tour guides, as they describe it, is often undervalued, and not all tourists are concerned with understanding the city as they detail it. Instead, usually tourists are concerned with consuming mainstream colonial images: 'the façade of the city'[7] and the city skyline suffices for them. This leads to a narrative of enduring separations. When guides interpret a city for few people, then they seem to agree with mainstream *Ouropretanos*' complaint: the city (and themselves) mainly caters for a few people 'coming from elsewhere'.

Nelson says that the exclusiveness of city attractions explains why many local residents do not praise tourists and the city, 'they do not feel they belong to it'. Residents have never entered some tourist attractions, and to them to work in the fields of city preservation or tourism means working for the satisfaction of 'others' only. Feeling apart, he maintained, changed their relationship to tourism and to the city. But guides such as Nelson, believe this situation could change:

> *One suggestion I gave in the 1980s was that we needed to go to schools to make a programme where everybody could get involved. At least everybody who depends on tourism should get involved, the prefecture, the House of Representatives, the university, the restaurants, the commerce in general; so that we could have a project at schools. So every week we would take one group of students from one school, and it would be a serious thing, take the kids from the school and make a tour as we do with people who come from elsewhere. We would take them to the churches, show them what the churches have, take them to the city sights and take them to have lunch in a restaurant where tourists also eat. They would have one day as a tourist that comes to see Ouro Preto. And hence we would show them tourists need respect. By doing so, they would learn, because that would be a wonderful day, it would be a great novelty, and they would learn to see Ouro Preto with other eyes. They would start helping with the preservation; they would respect the tourists, and would teach their parents to do the same.*
>
> (Nelson, November 8, 2013)

What seemed to have lacked in Nelson's account was a sense of the programmes that already exist and go in a similar direction to what he suggested. Those programmes, however, are not led by tour guides. The diversity of details in tours – evoking sightseers' imaginations – is often negatively articulated locally. The Vice-Mayor of Ouro Preto, in a conversation on November 21, 2013, explained that because guides each narrate different versions of city sights and often without historic accuracy, their work does not have a shared credibility. The Tourism Association, though trying to build guidelines, does not have many affiliates. Therefore, to solve the problem of local exclusion from touristic routes, regional and local governments are involved in pedagogic projects that encompass sightseeing, but the local art school directs those. However, there are several difficulties with explaining the city to excluded publics.

Firstly, learning about the past may not necessarily lead to preservation, when buildings express not only the continuation of material forms but also of privileges and discriminations. Secondly, learning about the city does not change the reality of the geographic and social distance between some residents' and the city's main attractions; in fact, it can make it more pronounced. In the following section I explore some methods used in Ouro Preto to allow poorer residential groups to develop a sense of the value of their city and how those methods compete with existing perceptions of the city.

ART FOR THE COMMUNITY

The steep Alvarenga Street leads to a neighbourhood called Cabeças ('Heads', a place where the severed heads of convicts were displayed in the 1800s). This location hosts one of the campuses of Ouro Preto's art school, with a gallery catering mainly for local residents. 'Art for the community' is how the curator explained the focus of the gallery and the reason why it stands outside the city centre. While accessing that gallery may be difficult if visitors are staying in the city centre, the location resonates with a focus on residents living far away from downtown cultural attractions.

The curator runs an educative programme at the local art school directed at children from state schools. Children are usually from the fifth or sixth class, and the age of the children (about twelve years old) is not selected by chance, as the fifth and sixth school years are associated with a large number of dropouts. The idea is to mediate their art appreciation without the social bias that conditions seeing art. The curator explained that children's impressions of art are impoverished, they do not visit central cultural locations (e.g., monuments, museums, art galleries), and do not feel a sense of belonging even in galleries closer to them, such as the one in which we stood. There is a 'distance', a social distance, and they walk past the door but do not enter. When they enter, they do not look at paintings, and are mainly relieved not to be attending school classes, she added. Mediating that distance with regular visits and engagement with artists and artwork faced the immediate disinterest of children as well as some lack of organisation from schools. The city, she concluded, 'is for the English to see' (for the tourists and *republicanos* – students who live in Repúblicas). The curator seemed to feel alone there, and on the desk at the entrance there was a computer, for she needed to do some work during times when no one was visiting the gallery.

The conversation at the art gallery illustrates what authors such as Souza (2011) discuss. To Souza (2011: 414), the pupils from a poor background that give up school at a young age, such as the pupils the above-mentioned art project invites for visits, do so because the school is a 'first experience that there is a world to which [they] simply [were] not invited' (my translation). In other words, schools or art galleries offer a world distinct from the one these poor pupils live in. Fine arts and formal schooling have little to do with the everyday life that often takes place in houses without books and paintings that are far away from fine cultural opportunities. Having access to visits to art galleries may increase, rather than correct, social distances. When individuals are offered educational and cultural opportunities but give up on them, what follows is often blame for their lack of interest, for example. Such blame on individuals harms a discussion about social circumstances that conditions seeing art, as the curator explained (see also Canclini 2012: 210). More importantly, local programmes like the one described focus on consequences (lack of attachment to cultural heritage), rather than on determinants, socio-economic conditions tainting cultural experiences.

Considering the conversation in the gallery and theoretical discussions, the lack of success of school visits to art galleries is not surprising. However programmes focussing on educating the population about the local cultural heritage – projects on patrimonial education – advance trying to smooth perceptions of inequality despite different forms of being in the city. One of the coordinators explained the controversies and limits of such programmes to me.[8]

'I AM FROM THE HILL, I AM ALSO PATRIMONY'

The programme 'I am from the hill, I am also patrimony' (*Sou do morro, eu também sou patrimônio*) caught my attention when I moved to town. When I first heard the name of the programme, I immediately thought of Ouro Preto's flag, the motto on which read since 1931: 'Precious although black' (*Precioso ainda que negro*). The gold found in the city was black because it was covered in other minerals and the idea of a saying 'precious although black' was racist according to FIROP (Forum for Racial Equality of Ouro Preto). In 2005, the motto on the flag changed to 'Precious black gold' (*Precioso ouro negro*).[9] Houses on the hill are immediately associated with a threat to Ouro Preto's cultural heritage entitlements (as discussed in chapter 1). The name of the programme suggests that these residents are part of patrimony, despite the fact that they are from the hill, recalling the segregation between centre and periphery even though the project hopes to bridge such separation.

To understand more about the programme, I visited one of its designers and executors in September 2013. Simone explained the aims and results of the programme to me in a long conversation. 'Ever since the city became a heritage site, the local population has not been valued'; therefore, the cultural reference for residents in their neighbourhoods is the church, a local landmark that resembles those in the city centre, and so is worth valuing, she explained. Simone also rationalised that, for different reasons, university students are detached from the monumental city. University students, she said, 'spend five years here and visit the city centre only to go to CAEM [the local student union where parties take place at night]'.

One project she coordinated was directed at university students called 'Urban senses: patrimony and citizenship' (*Sentidos urbanos: patrimônio e cidadania*). The programme offered a tour through the city to small groups of first-year students, so they could sense a different city from the one they would see every day. The idea was that by exploring city sounds, smell, textures, and uses, students would perceive and interact differently with the city. This interaction would lead to co-responsibility in city preservation.[10] But the programme also had to offer university credits to students to make it attractive. Students are mainly absorbed in their private realms, the life in Repúblicas, as discussed in chapter 2, hence the need to offer course credits. Despite a shortage in results with that community, Simone explained that in 2010, the programme expanded to encompass children from the periphery, and she mentioned the project named *I am from the hill, I am also patrimony*.

Schoolteachers in Morro Santana (a housing location mainly for poor residents) had the idea to design a project similar to that university students had in the city centre. The challenge was to create a route that would be attractive to pupils and hosted outside the city centre. Simone explained that teachers wanted to amplify ideas of patrimony to reach out to their location too, because children were often ashamed of living there. That, however, meant understanding cultural heritage beyond the colonial buildings in the centre. The idea was to encompass the memories and identities related to their location. One result was that they could find a brook where local women in the past washed clothes for their clients. Memories of the women's social gatherings led pupils to ask the local government for better maintenance of the brook, which was polluted but is clean today.

Simone explained that projects like these mean they were 'eating from the borders' (taking small steps) to bridge rooted experiences of detachment. When going to the *morros*, Simone explained, it was possible to sense the expectations created in the community, who would wonder if projects would offer infrastructure changes in that location. Thus, she added, their presence could only advance step by step. She concluded by saying that 'the programme is positively accepted, but is not magic, I would not say it transforms', but it addresses a historical dilemma of segregation between the centre and the rest of the city.

The programme *I am from the hill, I am also patrimony* is based on the idea that amplifying local patrimony to also include non-consecrated cultural goods can lead to affection, identification, social inclusion, and finally the preservation of those goods and the ones centrally located (Secretaria Municipal de Patrimônio e Desenvolvimento Urbano 2012: 6–7). Lynch (1960) presents a similar idea in his well-known study on city images. According to the author, it is possible to improve the image of the city

> by training the observer, by teaching him to *look* at his city, to observe its manifold forms and how they mesh with one another. Citizens could be taken into the

> street, classes could be held in the schools and the universities, the city could be made an animated museum of our society and its hopes.
>
> (Lynch 1960: 117)

Lynch (1960: 117), however, also states that pedagogical projects go hand in hand with physical reforms and need to be thought through continuously. The association of improving the image of the city and physically changing the environment, however, is not the focus in Ouro Preto.

In Ouro Preto, the methods used in *I am from the hill, I am also patrimony* focus on learning about cultural heritage through projects that allow for exploring the school and the neighbourhood, sparking interest in finding out more about students' family history, and learning about the school locality in relation to downtown Ouro Preto. The project may connect the pupil to the city centre (Secretaria Municipal de Patrimônio e Desenvolvimento Urbano 2012). However, some of the programme's complexity stems from the focus on the pupils' potential to perceive and preserve their immediate environment through memory, information, and affection. Many of the pupils, however, come from contexts where families are constantly improving the condition of the house and changing house location, because most houses are illegal and many have been built in a hurry. Improvised and temporary, houses may not evoke a relationship of identity, affection, memory, and preservation. Finally, focussing on the individual to insert values of city preservation sets individuals in an 'existential dilemma of autonomy and dependency . . . having to act while being powerless' (Dalsgaard 2004: 25–26), in other words, pupils are encouraged to look for their own monuments – the locations, memories, and objects that they value as a way to challenge the dualism centre and periphery. But socially, those pupils are part of a system that excludes them from the main patrimonial reference, the city centre. These individuals are also perceived by residents in downtown neighbourhoods as sources of endangerment, for the mere existence of a periphery on hill slopes threatens the city's preservation status. If individuals can learn to value and preserve their vicinity, it does not mean their houses will become legal, or that the city in general will share ideas of value and preservation to encompass those locations. It is then not surprising that the programme has developed sophisticated methods (such as building maps, photography, collecting favourite family objects) to encourage participants to sense and reflect about Ouro Preto but has still achieved little results.[11]

Executors of programmes that focus on offering a new perception of the city, when everything else remains the same, explain that projects do not achieve much but address rooted perceptions of segregation. However, programmes that address segregation by focussing on individuals and not on socio-economic circumstances run the risk of both maintaining the status quo and denying the production of inequality (Souza 2011: 20), as such projects miss 'key structural question of why people live where they do in cities' (Slater 2013: 367).

Nevertheless, the discussion on sightseeing (the formal and informal) city would not be complete without going underneath, into former gold mines. Visits to gold mines do not change the paradigm of working towards city inclusion through cultural and touristic activities. Former gold mines are a touristic attraction in town. However, mines are located outside the city centre, and they convey the idea that central buildings existed only because of the gold extracted in those areas. Mines then could be seen to break with the dichotomy of the centre and the *morros*. Moreover, mines tell stories not officially accounted for, such as the biographies of black slaves, hence offering the possibility for permanent residents (often black or mixed-race, *pardo*) to be included not only in city tours but also in city history. In Ouro Preto, Cuzco, or in other preserved cities in Latin America, residents 'have multifaceted and contradictory relationships to ancient remains. . . most obviously because the descendants of those who created the admired ancient civilization have been socially denigrated' (Silverman 2002: 883).[12] Finally, socio-economic hierarchies are metaphysically challenged in those spaces, when black slave spirits control the location.

GOLD MINES

Touring gold mines in Ouro Preto offer an opportunity to learn about slavery through the recreation of the working conditions in mines and through the accounts of slaves' spirits that act upon visitors' bodies. In tours, the history of slavery gains a 'memory' in the form of spiritually (and bodily) experienced past. Before exemplifying how mine visits work, I briefly discuss slavery and spirits, relating my analysis of Ouro Preto to other ethnographies.

In his ethnography about rituals of spiritual possession in Cuba, Routon (2008: 633) shares the explanation offered by a local medium that 'the spirits of runaway slaves are always out of breath . . . they always come running in order to escape from the overseer and his dogs'. Cuban slavery in that case 'becomes real for present generations through ritually stylised forms of social mimesis' (Routon 2008: 633). In the case of Ouro Preto's mine tours, it is unlikely that visitors witness moments of spiritual possession; at least, I did not come across any such descriptions. The history of slavery is represented there through the recreation of earlier working conditions – including sounds, sights, and sensations – while slaves' spirits are narrated, expressed in detailed accounts rather than in rituals of spiritual possession. However, although taking narrative form, this does not mean spiritual practices are not physically manifested; indeed they are. When visitors describe physical pain or have an accident in the mines, they are said to be victims of slave spirits. Spirits then act directly upon visitors' bodies through negative experiences.

The association between colonial slavery and spirits is not uncommon (Routon 2008; Hale 1997; Stoller 1994). This is because a violent past is often retold through narratives involving spirits and ghosts. Ulturgasheva (2017), looking at the legacy of Gulag, in Siberia, describes how memories of a violent past are reproduced through ghosts that inhabit buildings, thus blurring past and present of Gulag experiences. In this chapter, the analysis of the 'phantom of slavery' is twofold. Firstly, ghostlike memories of slavery illustrate that slaves are found in narratives about Ouro Preto through mystical oral tales rather than local statues, statistics, or biographies.[13] Off-the-record spiritual or imagined remembrances by residents enact a history overlooked by official accounts. Hale (1997: 396) observes that slavery in Brazil is usually portrayed in museums, with great emphasis on its violent occurrence – in exhibitions of torture objects, for example– rather than focussing on its cultural or biographic legacies. This is the case in Ouro Preto. Goldman (2013: 114), drawing on his own and others' research in the region of Ilhéus, Bahia, narrates that there is a 'dominant version [that] cacao-based economy was founded in the small estates and work of the landowners, almost without any intervention from the slave labourers'. This 'dominant version', he clarifies, is far from what documents say about the participation of slaves in the local economy. In sum, in mine tours one can move beyond the typical torture tools recollection or the non-existence and denial of black memory.

Secondly, the 'spiritualisation' of slavery allows previous occurrences to have a phenomenological manifestation. Visitors learn about slavery in mines both by revisiting the working conditions and when sensing the spirits that are said to reside in the mines. Stoller (1994: 637), writing about spirits, the body, and colonialism in Niger, explains that spiritual possession is a bodily practice and that it allows for colonial memories to have a phenomenological arena. A phenomenological arena, as other authors such as Harris (2007: 2) support, offers the possibility of knowing 'the world as it is lived and experienced'. Spiritual manifestation in Ouro Preto (though not occurring in the form of spiritual possession rituals) fosters a 'living past'. In short, in gold mines, previous events are physically experienced in the present, mining settings provoke bodily sensations, and the 'energy' of mine spirits, as tour guides narrate, equally affects the body.

In the following text, I share a brief account of a tour through gold mines in Ouro Preto before engaging further in the analysis of spirits, past and present in town:

> *November 25, 2013, a drizzly rain persisted all morning before we arrived at the first gold mine. Big J. guided me through the dark, cold and wet mine. While leading me to crouch in narrow and low corridors he would say: 'Imagine if time went back by 200 years and you were a twenty-year-old man, a black man working in mines, poor', Big J. insisted I should imagine that to release my fears.*
>
> *As we walked through the mine, Big J. and my city guide stopped walking and I had to set the pace on my own, for I was the one who was there to 'learn the past through sensations'. I kept on walking; it was very dark, and I could still hear the voices of the two men, though the voices became more distant, 'You need this to understand what the slaves went through back in those days', they said, while I moved through the unknown in a narrow corridor. The ceiling would get lower and lower as I walked. I had to squat in a very uncomfortable and claustrophobic position, and I wondered if I could still move forward or how I would move backwards to leave the place, at which point Big J. yelled: 'Can you imagine if we both would go away and you would have to stay for two or three days here?' No, I could not imagine that and wanted to return, but Big J. started to hammer against the wall, producing a sharp and repetitive sound. 'Men died from the noise; while digging stones some particles would reach their eyes making some men blind, while others would have their lungs turned into stone when breathing the powder day after day'. The noise continued for a short while until it became irritating, at which moment I tried to make my way back to the exit, but I fell down while moving backwards. It was very slippery.*
>
> (Field notes, November 25, 2013)

Experiencing humidity, darkness, noise, and the claustrophobic feeling in the low and narrow corridor in the mine illustrated how Ouro Preto's slaves lived back in the eighteenth century.

In addition to bodily sensations included in the tour, Big J. offered me a glossary of expressions and facts connecting slavery and suffering in the gold mines. One example is the explanation given about how the low, narrow corridors of the mines led slaves to be short. To stop male growth, many mine owners would castrate young slaves before they reached puberty and select short slaves for reproduction. Additionally, death in the low corridors of the mine as a result of a lack of oxygen or an inability to navigate the labyrinths quickly led to the development of some habits that are still in use today in town. As another guide explained, slave miners would bring a bird to work with them in the mine. When the bird stopped singing, they would take it as a sign that the oxygen had almost completely been consumed by the torches and the men, and when the bird died, that they had only a few minutes to get out of the mine. The guide explained how local families believe that having a bird at home is a lifesaver and keeping it at home remains customary in Ouro Preto (and in other places that faced a similar context).

While stories of violence against slaves are told in mines, Routon (2008: 638) points out that there are 'paradoxical colonial attributions of power'; and the same people who were enslaved, whipped, and chained were also believed to have the power of sorcery. In Ouro Preto, the power of slaves as sorcerers is indeed common in local stories. But this power did not cease with acts of sorcery in the past, for nowadays the spirits of slaves, rather than those of mine owners, dominate mining territories. Spirits may not allow entrance to mines, explains the guide of another mine:

> *You need to be approved by the spirit from the people there; otherwise you do not enter the mine. There are people who arrive here and ask me to enter, but I arrive at the entrance and I fall down, they beat me up, throw me on the floor, 'with that person you do not enter'. But when the person has a clean soul, a person with the mysticism (mediunidade) and the sensibility that matches theirs and mine, we can enter the mine.*
>
> (Guide in a gold mine, November 25, 2013)

The 'people there', the guide explained, are the people who worked as slaves in the mine in the past. When they do not want a sightseer to enter the mine, they beat the person up by making him or her or the guide fall down, or hit their heads against the ceiling or the walls, or by inflicting headaches after visits. Those are seen as the typical signs that the spirits had not granted permission to enter. Local stories involving the spiritual infliction of pain in mines are so common that guides report offering tours for people across the world and Brazil, while the local population is usually afraid of the mines and do not visit them.

In my case, when I arrived home and told my *Ouropretana* landlady of my tour through local mines, she not only thought I was brave in my expedition, but when I reported feeling a headache and sore throat, she also immediately attributed the symptoms to the 'negative energy of mines'. While I thought my headache and tonsillitis were a product of the humidity and a long day crouching in dark spaces with limited oxygen, my host disagreed and said that my illness was the result of 'the energy of the place'. Instead of taking medicine, I was told to light a candle for the oppressed spirits of the enslaved, as many residents in Ouro Preto do. Candles are a visual expression of reports about physical pain caused by spirits. Spirits bother residents who report hearing noises, seeing images, or having revealing nightmares.[14]

During my tour, Big J. told me a dream he had had the previous night. In his report, the dream, like his stories while awake, explained relationships of power and violence during the days of slavery:

I went to bed and I had a nightmare as never before. It felt as if my spirit was imprisoned there [in the mine] and there were people there beating me, and I tried to leave but I could not. I felt that affliction that you felt there [when I was left alone in the dark in the mine] and I felt I was going to die of that affliction. Suddenly when I least expected a Preto Velho [black old slave] appears saying 'you will leave this place and I will help you'. And he helped me to leave, but he was cursing me all the way out. When we got out I saw a lot of people working inside the mine and my spirit leaving it. . . . Do you know why I had this dream? Enemy groups from the 18th century, enemies there and enemies here, and the blacks did not get along, that is why there was never a rebellion. The majority of the afro-descendent here [of Ouro Preto], they do not like entering the mines. A lot of the time the problem is not you, you are white, it is with another black like me.

(Big J., November 25, 2013)

Society in Minas, as I described elsewhere, has demonstrated great social complexity since the eighteenth century. More than a society of slaves and masters, 'numerous skilled musicians, painters, sculptors (many of them of [mixed race] *pardos*) formed an urban artisan class which stood between the slaves and the white minority' (Maxwell 1973: 94–95). Likewise, within groups of slaves, as Big J. reported, complexities meant there was often no common ground for relationships. While some slaves would look for their own personal fortune smuggling gold, others would try to escape slavery violence in small groups, leaving no space for rebellion.[15]

Ghostly mine tours fill gaps in the official history when they show where slaves worked, address the lack of a revolution led by slaves, and connect the wealth one sees in churches and central constructions with the gold that cost human lives. Mine tours also present the biography of notable black residents, such as Chico Rei. The story of Chico Rei summarises the limits of power relationship inversion in town as a result of mining.

While crouching in the mine where Chico Rei worked, Nelson explained the story of a black slave who used to be a king in Africa until he was forced to work as a slave in Brazil. In my own words, I summarise the explanation offered that afternoon:

Chico arrived in Ouro Preto and worked in an unproductive gold mine, until his master became ill and offered the mine to him. Chico knew about mining and knew that one had given no gold yet, and he would not be able to pay for the mine if there was no gold inside it. Nevertheless the slave accepted the offer. When he started exploring the mine, mysteriously, he finally found gold there. Chico paid for the mine, bought his freedom and that of those who were part of his former tribe. He started a new tribe in Vila Rica and was king once again. He became very rich and the Crown said 'look at it, in Vila Rica there is a slave that owns a mine, freed his people, and is today the king of the slaves'. Portugal, afraid of a rebellion, offered Chico Rei all he needed to return to Africa and he could take with him all the wealth he had accumulated. Chico accepted the offer because there he would be free; while in Ouro Preto, though he was king, he was a 'nobody'. Nobody respected him, he was black in the eyes of the whites and so he never had freedom; he was no longer a slave, but he was always seen as inferior and so he left.

(Nelson, November 25, 2013)

Concluding the tour with the story of Chico Rei, who became free and rich, yet remained chained to the social organisation of the colonial society, seems to suggest that the city, material or immaterial, official or non-registered cultural heritage, excludes, rather than brings, groups closer. In mines, the dualism of oppressed and oppressors gains a new contour, when stories of black slaves' spirits express the power of the oppressed. The power of the excluded, however, does not go beyond mining territories. In the city, there is no statue for black slaves, and the one museum that dedicates a room to slavery exhibits only instruments of torture. Additionally, only a few residents visit mines, partly to avoid encounters with the spirits and partly because mines, like other tourist attractions, cater mainly to tourists. In addition, there is no space for a narrative about geological knowledge amongst mining slaves, and one is invited only to imagine how mining tunnels were carved and still resist over time. Similar to city tours, mine tours finish with narratives of enduring separations and privileges:

We are sad because I think the prefecture or the regional government should grant residents the right to visit mines, so they would know their history. The majority of the children do not know it; they do not know about the mines. If I were a millionaire, you know what I would like to do? I would like to get some thirty kids, some five or ten from Morro Santana, five from Morro São Sebastião, those black and poor kids and would take them to São Geronimo Museum in Portugal, so they could see what was taken from here. They do not know. We do not know. Have you been to Europe, Nelson? Nelson shook his head.

(Conversation between a mine guide and Nelson, November 25, 2013)

CONCLUSION

When Ouro Preto was nominated 'a theatre of happenings of great historical relevance' (Decree 22928 passed on 1933), the preservation of its colonial constructions followed. However, as the number of inhabitants in the city grew, only the façades of some colonial houses were maintained, as the interiors of many of those structures were changed to support the needs of contemporary families. Similarly, the use of hills changed to house the growing population. The local saying that Ouro Preto is a city of façades is then justified by the split between the outside and inside of the houses, between the preserved centre and improvised periphery, and between the national symbolism of heroism and revolution and a local narrative that speaks the maintenance of privileges and prejudices. Not surprisingly, city accounts focus on a 'negative energy of the place'.

Tour guides are often amongst the residents who are spatially excluded from the cultural opportunities of the centre yet profit from the existence of a preserved city centre that attracts tourists. Nevertheless, because mainly a few tourists hire guides, they speak of a city that has never changed and benefits a small elite. According to those guides, however, offering tours to local residents could be used to change their historically negative perceptions of the city. They maintain that if residents could experience the city centre, they would feel part of it. Such offering of cultural experiences exists through pedagogic projects that invite pupils from poor areas and university students to experience the city. Pedagogic programmes are however limited. The programme *Urban senses patrimony and citizenship* offers university students the opportunity to sense the city but dialogues little with students' domestic sphere, which seems to dominate their university life, as described in chapter 2. Other projects such as *I am from the hill, I am also patrimony*, must be applied in a context of unequal socio-economic situations. Poorer residents maintain the opinion that they will always cater for tourists and students and hence be poorly paid and materially excluded from the city. To those residents, programmes on patrimonial education offer cultural moments in their immediate location and in central ones. But this inclusion in the city is unpromising when it disregards the social and material separations between poorer residents and the other residents of the city. Consequently, local inequalities have not been altered, nor centrally attended through such programmes. The importance of such pedagogic tools, that address how one can think differently about a location when the location and the position of the individual in the city (socially and economically) remains the same, will be also discussed in chapter 6.

Yet, when visiting the touristic gold mines, a change of perspective gains traction. In mines, colonial memories are 'stored . . . in flesh' (Stoller 1994: 641); visitors can physically experience the eighteenth century from the perspective of mining slaves. Moreover, in mines one can hear about some slaves' biographies and perceive the centre as a result of the work of the periphery (the slaves in the past, the poor habitants today) and begin to break down the juxtaposition that predominates in town between the centre and 'the rest'. However, the use of mines as historic and cultural centres remains mainly connected to tourists (especially foreign tourists), and the stories of black slaves linger in folklore and remain undocumented. Hence, prevailing ideas of racial consciousness in town privilege miscegenation and characters such as Aleijadinho, who shows the ascension of the Brazilian mulatto through education. The problem with a predominant narrative of artists such as Aleijadinho, focussing on artistic creativity rooted in miscegenation, is that it taints the discussion of racism in Brazil. Sheriff (2001: 220) discusses Freyre's work – suggesting a hybrid making of the Brazilian urban culture – and as opposed to Freyre, the author identifies racial democracy as a myth yet a dream. Aleijadinho's work, however, shows more – black inclusion in discriminatory temples, tribute to rebellion against colonial injustice. But the many stories around him that tour guides narrate are attended only by few people and often have their credibility diminished by the lack of factual information given by guides.

In sum, sightseeing the city offers a 'baby step' towards making local cultural patrimony of equal significance for the city's diverse residents. While most residents would not seriously contest the importance of maintaining the Tiradentes statue, São Francisco Church, or the many other local sights, relationships with those monuments and commemorative celebrations are diverse. To mediate disputes over the meaning of city spaces, there is participation, as a way to diminish exclusion after patrimonial education failed. In that context, the Municipal Council for the Preservation of Cultural and Natural Patrimony – a policy group that brings together technicians, politicians, and civil society – gains importance as a platform that offers a new sort of heritage inclusion: participatory politics.

In the following chapter I will discuss how this group struggles with a shared local perception of patrimony as prohibitive and excluding and disputes over the scope of its influence. When at a crossroads, those working in the Council are both involved in directing preservation efforts and directly affected by it; they are residents and professionals related to that area. To examine the Council is therefore to examine the politics of patrimonial preservation under various prisms: how the process of hailing mundane objects as monuments takes place, with what purposes and results, and how cultural heritage affects residents and policy makers, or policy makers that are also residents. The Council, better than any other group in town, scrutinises questions pertaining to a sociological and anthropological discussion on cities and citizenship (Holston and Appadurai 1996). Looking at the Council, my discussion in the second half of this book addresses the following questions: Is the participation of civil society in the work of cultural heritage an opportunity to reduce perceptions of exclusion by offering a platform for change? Could participation allow for varied and fluid interpretations and uses of the city's past and present? Or does participation feature as a process to give credibility to a preset national narrative of the aesthetic and historic symbolism of Ouro Preto's monuments? If so, what are the structural conditions behind (in)effective participation?

I will address some of the challenges for the Council, especially in attracting contributors in the face of the local association of cultural heritage with socio-economic inequalities, and of local misgivings in disputing with people in privileged positions. In doing so, my challenge is to invite the reader to consider democratic innovations in the governance of urban spaces in Brazil, while demonstrating ethnographically the limits of political participation locally.

Chapter 4

Opportunities for Participation in the Governance of Cultural Heritage

The bus station in Ouro Preto, a hub for local and regional buses, greets passengers with a poster that says: *Bem-Vindo a Ouro Preto – Patrimônio Cidadão* (Welcome to Ouro Preto – Citizen Patrimony). While it is common to see a welcoming slogan when arriving in a city, the lower part of the poster combines the words 'patrimony' and 'citizen' in a way that does not make sense in Portuguese. But in Ouro Preto, during the period of my fieldwork in 2013, the words 'citizen' or 'citizenship' and 'patrimony' often came together in city slogans (see Image 4.1).

The intention behind this combination of words is twofold: it reflects the government's attempt to view all citizens as part of the patrimony, fostered through projects related to pedagogic and cultural inclusion (chapter 3), and allows non-state actors to participate in heritage policies and urban governance. In this chapter, I will discuss participation: how politicians, technical experts (urban planners, environmentalists, engineers), and community representatives come together, especially in municipal policy councils, to direct cultural heritage. I further explore the search for the meaning of, and the limits to, urban cultural heritage in these forums.

Initially, I focus on bottom-up approaches in urban administration and how Brazilian laws have made local participation central to these processes. The 1988 Constitution[1] established new norms in the administration of urban development, granting key functions to local administrations. More specifically, the community was included in promoting and managing the protection of cultural patrimony.[2] In 2001, Law 10257, known as the City Statute, structured ideas of local governance and community duties, 'imagin[ing] a society of citizens who are active, organized, and well informed' (Caldeira and Holston 2005: 406). Different from modernist planning, 'the social is not imagined as something for the plan to produce but is, rather, something

Image 4.1. Welcome to Ouro Preto Citizen Patrimony, 2013. ***Source*****: Personal collection.**

that already exists' (ibid.: 407). Presumptions about 'the social' are slowly being replaced by studies, usually made on a case-by-case basis, that look at the dynamics of new spheres of participation – how communities organise to address common problems and how they may cooperate with the state. What requires investigation is who the involved actors are, how they may cooperate in communicating problems and solutions, and if their ideas are taken into account by the government. In the protection of cultural heritage, participatory instruments can include collegiate groups, debates and public audiences, conferences, and popular initiatives for legislation. The investigation I offer examines how one of these instruments, collegiate groups – the Council – resonates with existing ways of being in the city and governing the city in the case of Ouro Preto.

My analysis takes into account several arguments I presented in previous chapters (especially chapter 2). It investigates civil input in urban governance in a context where residents perceive themselves as victimised by – but are invited to take responsibility for – cultural patrimony. The patrimonial legacy, representing both pride in history and aesthetics as well as exclusion and inequality, makes the Municipal Council for the Preservation of Cultural and Natural Patrimony (known in town by the acronym COMPATRI and in this book simply as 'the Council') an extraordinary place to ground a discussion on the process and results of the politics of cultural heritage. Considering stories about the enduring 'energy of the place' of injustice and oppression, when looking at civilian participation in a topic as controversial as cultural heritage, I explore aspects of everyday and unavoidable economic interdependency and social conflicts to discuss the likelihood that residents will voice demands and take part in heritage decisions. Lastly, this chapter introduces the Council, its work, and the controversies surrounding it, which will be central to chapters 5 and 6.

THE BOTTOM LINE IN BOTTOM-UP GOVERNANCE

Community associations, policy councils, city conferences, public audiences, and other spheres where non-state members participate in public administration have grown in number in Brazil. The strong decline in modernist central planning combined with the strong base encouraging civilian participation arose with the 1988 Constitution. The modernist state-centred design and execution that dominated in Brazil in the 1950s and 1960s could not foster the social transformations envisioned in the modernist city-planning blueprints, subsequently weakening this model for top-down urban planning (Caldeira and Holston 2005). New norms helped develop new ways in which non-state actors could participate in city governance. On the other hand, the growth of democratic participation increased in the face of escalating urban problems. In the 1980s and 1990s, Brazil faced 'on the one hand democratic citizenship; and, on the other, economic crisis, privatisation, and violence' (ibid.: 404).

What we can see in the case of Brazil and other Latin American countries is that neoliberal policies in the 1990s were implemented to overcome what was known in Latin America as the 'lost decade'. The debt crisis that afflicted the region led to state scepticism and a stronger belief in the private sector as an actor to promote economic growth (Rodrik 2006). The regulation of the market would then be done, not by the state but by civil society (ibid.: 985). The role of participatory governance thus grew in the region at the same time as inequality and unemployment spiked (Hellman 1997). Not surprisingly, the results and processes of these new city planning practices, especially those focussing on popular participation, are still indeterminate and contested.

When citizenship, here understood as 'the capacity of citizens to use their basic rights' (Bertorelli et al. 2017: 48), is investigated in relation to class (ibid.: 47), political culture (Cornwall and Shankland 2013), and inequality (Lombard 2013: 137), we see a mesh of old political practices and economic systems amidst new democratic tools. In this situation, it is hard to generalise the importance of specific outcomes.

The view of participation as good governance often ignores a literature on political economy demonstrating that participation is 'decorative' (Lombard 2013: 141) in contexts of deep-seated inequality. How can we respond to this literature that epitomises reinforced economic inequality in participatory decisions and yet consider that 'if the poor did not participate in political and civic life, they would receive less from the State' (Bertorelli et al. 2017: 48)? The answer to this question lies in understanding the historical conditions that could make participatory platforms effective. What is still sorely lacking in Brazil for such understanding is the investigation of participatory platforms in medium and small towns, as much of the scholarship has focussed on larger cities such as São Paulo, Porto Alegre, Recife, and Rio de Janeiro (Avritzer, 2006, 2010, 2012b; Holston 2008).

Locating new practices in city planning in Ouro Preto is not only timely but also highlights several paradoxes. As discussed in chapter 1, modernist city planning (leading to cities such as Brasília) and city preservation are interrelated projects. However, modernist cities have recently looked at historic and small cities as the remedy for violence and chaos (Ellin 1996: 124), and historic cities such as Ouro Preto serve as model. Ouro Preto, however, not only looks for modern amenities to avoid social and economic isolation, but also deals with an official narrative of past that, likewise modernist architecture, was prescribed top-down. The conflict of being a window into the (contested) past yet yearning for modern conveniences is to be solved through participation. Participation thus exists in a context where not only the process of participating but also the end goal – preservation – is questionable.

The appeal and uncertainty of process and outcome towards broader public engagement and participation in public administration can be seen in other parts of the world and in other spheres than urban planning. For example, Marks and Bonnin (2010: 56) investigated community safety groups and policing in South Africa and concluded that 'policing functions are being carried out by agents other than the police . . . and instead of trying to be all things to all people . . . the state police should hone in on their core functions and intervene when communities request interventions'. To Altbeker (2007: 27), participative theories draw from convictions that 'the "professional model of policing" resulted in policing that was too remote, too isolated from the community to deal with the social problems that gave rise to crime'. However, there has been on one hand more democratic participation, while on the other more incidences of criminality, thus raising questions about process and outcome (ibid.: 31). Moreover, it remains unclear how ‘community and belonging’ (Hughes 1998: 7), as a replacement to an inefficient state, may still look to the state to guarantee interconnection among citizens, and how those citizens will engage in spaces organised by the state (Albert 2016: 13).

In post-dictatorship Brazil, as in post-apartheid South Africa, urban centres have encountered both more access to participation in city governance and a context of more urban violence. The question that follows is whether people could transfer blame for failure from the state to the individuals who direct communitarian discussions. The difference between blaming ‘the state’ and blaming civilian associations is strong. A bureaucratic culture (Cornwall and Shankland 2013), technical language (Abram 2017), and broad access to information are not common amongst all participants in policy councils, and decisions may still be a guessing game. On a socio-economic level, intimidation and co-optation need to be considered in locations with a high social cohesion and levels of economic dependency (De Souza Santos 2018). In such places, individuals tend to vote consensually to avoid being easily identifiable (ibid.: 437). Finally, participants may not share the same goal; ‘who “really” speaks for the community’ (Sennett 1976: 310) is an enquiry that speaks both about issues of representation and fragmentation. Seeing it from the frame of community policing, Marks and Bonnin (2010: 59) state that ‘while non-state actors are encouraged to participate . . . they are not always adequately supported in their attempts. Nodal actors may even compete with one another’. When the state shares with ‘citizens’ the responsibility to decide on infrastructure investments (chapter 5), environmental licenses (chapter 6), budget spending (Avritzer 2006, 2012a), health priorities (Cornwall 2008; Cornwall and Shankland 2013; Guareschi and Jovchelovitch 2004), or security control (Marks and Bonnin 2010), it should not be assumed that instruments for informed and autonomous decision have equally been shared or already existed.

PARTICIPATION AS STATUS QUO

Everyday experiences in Ouro Preto, described throughout this book, demonstrate that preserved areas do not enjoy shared local engagement. Places and stories did not live up to their reputation as celebrated heroic spaces, but rather were often viewed as echoing colonial injustices. On a practical level, the lack of local acceptance discourages local politicians from maintaining the preservation of contested locations. Local residents, who might be negatively affected by preservation, are invited to participate in making decisions relating to it. Contrary to the desires of the residents, however, this process of participation may solidify preservation and prevent change.

Abram and Weszkalnys (2013) discuss credibility in the work of urban planning. The authors suggest that planning can be an 'expectation, an instruction, a policy, a project, an exercise of democracy, a blueprint, a law', but all plans need to produce conviction (Abram and Weszkalnys 2013: 12). Focussing on ideas of conviction, the authors refer to self-representation – 'when the plan may be presented as a personalised product' – or when planning is non-representational, such as when it is turned into law and the focus on the personality of the planner is removed (ibid.: 13). In Ouro Preto, residents do not equally engage with their surroundings and have different reasons to maintain or change the cityscape. This gap between 'flesh and stone' (Sennett 1996), when individuals feel detached from their surroundings and one another, means that the historic and aesthetic appeal for the development of a national bond, established by law, is de-contextualised along local fault lines (as discussed in chapter 2). Self-representation might be a promising way to encourage residents' belief in the value of preserving the city, rather than being an opportunity to contest preservation.

However, there is little evidence that residents are willing to take part in the work of preservation. They often shy away from 'patrimony people', afraid of embargoes on and fines levied for house construction. Those who participate may perceive the city differently from each other, according to personal, economic, and professional ties, and may be in favour or against preservation. Thus, participation could produce belief in the value of preserving the city, if participation is a shared value. However, participation is not a clear resolution in a city where people have strong economic reasons to avoid confrontations.

AVOIDING CONFRONTATIONS

> *In the afternoon of October 15, 2013, I arrived at a public building and waited for my appointment. In the same waiting hall and sitting opposite of me, there was a woman smoking quietly. After a long waiting time, and annoyed by the smoke clouding in the hall, I asked the receptionist if it was permitted to smoke inside public buildings and he replied, to my surprise, 'no problem'. The smoker heard my question, but continued smoking, however, now looking intensely at me. The staring was threatening and I read on my phone to avoid eye contact. I looked up smoking laws to find out smoking was forbidden where we were. A few minutes later the receptionist went outside to smoke. I asked him 'if you allowed that person to smoke inside, why did you come outside?' His answer was short, 'of course it is not legal to smoke inside, except if you are the prosecutor'.*
>
> (Field notes, October 15, 2013)

Here the receptionist followed the law, while the smoking prosecutor broke it shamelessly, with facial and bodily expressions of someone who is unmoved by my outrage. More interestingly, she broke the law while being a professional in charge of enforcing it.[3] For the receptionist the choice to retreat, rather than dispute with the prosecutor was obvious, as she was his boss. In that social encounter, the result of waiting for long hours in public buildings, the well-dressed woman did not control me. However, I was silent against that inequality and law breaking.

At this point, as I write, I put myself as an ethnographic subject rather than the ethnographer and reflect on my own experience as a resident in Ouro Preto. In a city with about 70,000 inhabitants and only a small number working in public administration, I would probably see that woman again. My work in town relied largely on my social relationships, and I wondered how a dispute would affect my social interactions in the short run, when meeting upstairs with another prosecutor, or in the long run, living and working in a place where everybody knows everyone else. Moreover, after learning she was a prosecutor, to whom would I complain when the episode happened in the place one goes to seek justice? I was discouraged by the potential social consequences and a lack of any result, a hopeless and hostile situation. I understood the saying my informants had shared with me a few times, 'those who command do so because they can; those who obey do so because they are sensible'. That saying, to my personal frustration, made sense to me.[4]

Many of my informants depended on friends and kinship ties for employment and housing; to some extent, everyone does in Ouro Preto, and if a conflict does not affect one directly, it may affect in-laws or friends. Everyday bureaucratic interactions in Brazil reveal privilege for the rich and humiliation for the poor (Holston 2008: 16). How people will contest or concede to unequal treatments is a result of cost-benefit calculations. Encounters between 'anonymous others' and people who 'know each other in a variety of employment and servant relations' (Holston 2008: 276) can generate only different compromises. Where people have hierarchical bonds, disputes about rights then may not happen through a 'direct verbal confrontation' (ibid.: 277), because 'most subordinate classes throughout most of history have rarely been afforded the luxury of open, organized political activity' (Scott 1985: XV). When silence suddenly becomes an important variable, it brings complexity into anthropological research: Is it an act of insubordination, acceptance, or oppression? By breaking this silence with ethnographic research, one can find the answers. As much as I look at Council members' participation, I also noted moments when members avoided making decisions and had conversations before and after meetings to understand what remained unsaid in public. Finally, as much as it is important to know who Council members are, it is equally important to consider why many other residents may not be willing to take up such positions (or those participating might leave after some time). One's view about city change or preservation – a hot topic – may not always be unswervingly broadcasted. A significant number of Council participants are not *Ouropretanos*, and the Council has more seats available than participants discussing (De Souza Santos 2019).

MUNICIPAL COUNCILS IN OURO PRETO

Municipal policy councils are collegiate groups that exist to advice or direct public administration in diverse areas, such as social assistance, health, or transportation. In Ouro Preto, there are twenty-four listed councils, but only fifteen of them were in operation in 2013. However, the number of councils in 2013 was still large compared to the five in operation in 2005. The first municipal council to exist in town was on health, created in 1991, to respond to a nationwide demand to supervise the transfer of national funds to municipalities. Likewise, most of the councils created at the time in Ouro Preto, or elsewhere in Brazil, were related to the local duty to control public spending. However, a few are more recent, and Silvana, the coordinator of Ouro Preto's councils from 2005 until 2012, explained some of the problems in the process of forming and sustaining councils in town during an interview with me:[5]

> *People don't find out about ways they could participate in public governance . . . and one way to do so is through municipal councils. . . . Many councils will need popular movement to be formed, because if society is not mobilised then the council does not need to exist, does it? Why would we have a council if society is not articulated? . . . So in 2005 . . . five councils worked, of course other ones were created by law, because the law says we need to create municipal councils, but they did not work. So I started them . . . and those councils started to work again and I began other ones and many others I tried to start but these attempts were frustrating because society was not ready to mobilise.*
>
> (Silvana, July 11, 2013)

Silvana explained the importance of civil society's mobilisation to have municipal councils. In the case of cultural heritage elsewhere in Brazil, some protection petitions approved by the municipality of Porto Alegre were initiated by residents who were neither owners nor professionals associated with planning and architecture, suggesting social mobilization preceded preservation (Meira 2004, as cited in Collins 2009: 293). However, in other locations it is possible to have a municipal council on preservation regardless of local eagerness. In Minas Gerais, a regional law[6] establishes conditions for municipalities to access state funds to finance cultural projects, such as having patrimonial education projects (some were discussed in chapter 3) and a municipal heritage council. Therefore, about 70 per cent of the 853 municipalities in Minas Gerais possess a municipal council for patrimonial preservation (IBGE 2012: 83). In comparison, in the southern region of Brazil, where Porto Alegre is located, approximately only 8 per cent of municipalities have such a forum (ibid.). Regardless of laws that prompt to the creation of councils on preservation, most decisions discussed in the Council are binding and not merely suggestive; that is to say, the Council directs most policies concerning preservation regardless whether civil society is well organised on the topic. However, what defines preservation or alteration, or which areas are to be preserved, are questions that have to be answered first.

THE COUNCIL IN OURO PRETO

When Decree 25 from November 30, 1937 organised the historic and artistic national patrimony, the idea of a national council was already established. That law prescribed a consultation group to decide in cases of dispute. For example, when houseowners disagreed with a protection status, they could appeal to the consultation council. The consulting group, however, was not diverse in membership. IPHAN (Institute for Historic and Artistic Patrimony, the national organisation for the preservation of heritage) selected locations of aesthetic or historic value, and the President of Brazil selected council members. Nominees were mainly those working in national museums and were well known for their political and intellectual activities (Chuva 2009). These nominees worked to establish the legitimacy of the state in its preservation actions, rather than casting votes on the populaces' disputes (Chuva 2009: 224). In addition, council meetings were rare: from 1938 until 1946 (a period of great preservation efforts and numerous controversies), there were only thirteen meetings (ibid.: 227).

Ouro Preto's municipal archive reveals two periods when the municipality featured consulting councils in its contemporary history. First, from 1931 to 1936, here members of the councils were the greatest tax contributors in the municipality, while others were chosen directly by the administrator. The consulting group in Ouro Preto offered advice about construction, demolition, street repair, public lighting, and local budget. In a second period, minutes reveal a consulting council in 1971, during the military dictatorship in Brazil. Members were selected regardless of economic status, which did not mean the group was not exclusive. The mayor was the president of the council, the vice-mayor the vice-president, and some of the individuals composing the group in the 1970s were from the same families as in the council in the 1930s.[7] Consulting councils thus did not always lead to increased public participation and were not always related to democratic governance. In the national council concerning patrimonial issues, or in local ones supporting an embracing agenda on public administration, the selection of members epitomised exclusivity.

Currently, municipal councils in Ouro Preto work in parallel to other spheres of public administration, such as the prefecture and the House of Representatives (*Câmara de Vereadores*). They have greater autonomy than in the past in relation to the mayor, who does not directly select members. However, members in the Council are usually technical experts, and as such work in the municipal administration in one of the thematic secretariats. In addition, some of the council members are *vereadores* (local representatives). Therefore, in the municipal council on patrimonial preservation, membership remains exclusive. Lastly, though the Council was already mentioned in the local law that organises the municipal administration in 1990 and was planned in 2002, it started functioning in its current format only in 2003.[8]

In its 2013 format, the Council was composed of eight volunteer members from public administration, including representatives from the following areas: cultural patrimony, urban development, tourism, environment – two representatives from the national and regional level of IPHAN, one representative from the university, and one representative from the local art school. The Council also has another eight volunteer representatives from civil society, including two representatives from preservation associations, two representatives from the federation of residents associations, two representatives from cultural associations, a tourist guide representative, and one representative from a commercial association.[9] However, there are usually more places available than people involved, especially amongst the representatives of civil society, who in 2013 were mainly those from residents' associations. Reasons for low participation were various, including meetings taking place during working hours and many residents preferring to avoid public confrontations. In this chapter, I discuss some of the limits of direct participation for members of the Council. One clear limitation is the Council's agenda. The work of the Council usually starts because another sector of public administration did not want to take decisions, passing on the burden of history to the Council.

THE BURDEN OF HISTORY

The main actions of the Council relate to laying out the basis of preservation policies. It disseminates advice in cases of protection or cancellation of a previous protection status, oversees the process of maintenance and restoration of preserved goods, issues licenses for works in protected areas or their surroundings (or areas examined for protection), and approves or revokes urban projects if they interfere in the aesthetic 'integrity' of protected goods or their surrounds.[10] Therefore, house owners, the local government, or companies may eventually need the approval of the Council to carry out construction, demolition, or renovation. However, such activities are complex because the Council has to decide on 'notable features' or on a reference for memory and identity, and those items are not legally defined.[11] Moreover, which changes constitute an act of restoration or end up being an act of destruction? It follows that deciding on the aesthetic, historical, or landscaping value of a certain building or area to justify preservation is a subjective matter.

Architects working for the prefecture commonly apply for the Council's advice to avoid deciding alone if new constructions, renovations, or demolitions will affect the existing heritage. Their strategy is not only to seek for a democratic decision but mainly to diffuse responsibility. Considering that heritage can affect the construction or expansion of private houses or large business entrepreneurships, there are great economic interests at play in a town where individuals need to avoid being directly associated with controversial decisions. Members of the Council, however, often return the decision powers to the prefecture, in an exercise of kicking decisions into the long grass, *jogo de empurra-empurra*. The Council itself can also suggest other topics for discussion. Once the agenda is set, meetings start with a technical appraisal of the issue (*parecer técnico* – often stating technical limits) and discussions follow. I summarise meetings in four stages: presentation of problems, discussion, negotiation, and decision.

The discussion is participatory, meaning that any member can tackle the problem from his or her own perspective and numerous times, as long as there is still time. Non-council members can also participate in the discussion, but they cannot vote. One limiting issue for the participation of short-term participants in the Council is the language used in meetings. Often, to refer to locations, policies, or institutions, members use acronyms or technical terms common to areas such as urbanism or architecture. Another limit to participation is time. The Council meets every first Tuesday of the month, and usually meetings take three to four hours, generally from 9:30 am to 1:00 pm. This choice of day and time means that technicians working for the prefecture have a greater possibility of participating, as they can be excused from work, which is different in the case of community leaders who may have jobs unrelated to public administration.

Extraordinary meetings are common, and in 2013 there were fifteen meetings, including ordinary and extraordinary meetings, and joint meetings with the Council for Environment. There was also one technical visit to a district. There were two cancelled meetings – one due to the low number of members attending and another cancelled for internal reasons. The Secretariat of Culture and Patrimony provides administrative support for the meetings. Decisions are made through open vote and simple majority.

Although the details provided here regarding the composition and function of the Council hint at its power, one realises how powerful the Council really is only when following its agenda. Almost any building in town could be within the Council's purview. However, the Council is constantly discussing its own competence. Assuming that constructions will not interfere with the ambience of an area or may not be within the protected perimeter or a surrounding area is to declare that the Council cannot decide the matter. In 2013, the mayor introduced a project limiting cultural heritage to the city's preserved perimeter, thus assuming the position to decide on the limits of urban cultural heritage. Such a project showed how city preservation is politically and socially disputed.

SETTING PRESERVATION BORDERS

In early 2013, the Mayor Zé Leandro proposed to change the Secretariat of Patrimony and Urban Development and created two organisations instead: the Secretariat of Culture and Patrimony and the Secretariat of Urban Development and Constructions. By doing so, the mayor clearly stated his position in the local political polarisation. As Flávio explained in chapter 1, municipal mayors have polarised local perceptions about city preservation politically, the candidate for modernisation against the one for preservation. Zé Leandro was a mayor for city modernisation. While he upheld the importance of the city's preservation, this was not to be conflated with urban development. Areas for preservation were to be limited to the city centre, and the town could grow outside its preserved setting through the Secretariat of Constructions, a popular proposition.

By observing the work of the Council in that moment of change in municipal administration in early 2013, it was clear to me that they were the 'architects of memory' (Chuva 2009) in Ouro Preto, while some residents and politicians tried to limit the scope of cultural heritage. However, different from the 'architects of memory' who defined and promoted Ouro Preto as a place to be preserved in Brazil in the early 1930s, the 'architects' of today not only defend preservation but also reflect on the economic impact of housing and industrialisation while being at the same time residents in the city. The members of the Council each faced the conflicts of a fragmented city and residents' scepticism about cultural heritage. Moreover, the mayor's proposition set the Council at the forefront for preservation and the prefecture on the side of loosening stiff regulations, making the Council unpopular locally.

When the new mayor announced the structural change[12] as soon as he took power in January 2013, he sent a letter to the House of Representatives to explain his intentions. What he clarified was that the structure at place was time-consuming, when constructions inside or outside the preserved perimeter were viewed through the same lens of patrimonial preservation.[13]

The Council also expressed its view in a letter. On March 8, 2013,[14] the Council met, and the administrative change was on the top of the agenda. Most members of the Council expressed disagreement and showed scepticism about such a change. Reservations about the project included possible confusion for residents, who would need to know if their house was within the preserved perimeter before they could seek approval for construction. The Council reinforced its position against a fragmentation of city areas.[15] In addition, to the Council, patrimony extends beyond a preserved area, so that heritage policies should also include housing, urban mobility, and the quality of life throughout the city because, as an architect and Council member said, 'Patrimonial preservation happens within everyday life'. Despite opposing the project, the Council did not hold much hope, as they were certain the project would be approved later in the evening in the House of Representatives. Their goal at the meeting was simply to voice opposition. Council members then wrote down such views in their letter, also addressed to the House of Representatives.

The decision was made in the evening of March 12, 2013. The plenary in the House of Representatives was full of residents interested in the decision. Before the discussion of the project began, one of the political speeches that night was about *forasteiros*, the people from outside Ouro Preto, who come to the city and take the jobs and houses that should belong to residents, as the discussant explained. Such speeches only strengthened the mayor's project and the need to limit the impact of cultural heritage across the city. Local politicians said that approving the project would be an improvement for residents. They argued that 'the patrimony' was 'that thing that does not allow us to do anything', and highlighted the fact that residents of Ouro Preto do not feel part of cultural heritage and do not feel included in the city's legacy. As a result, restricting the scope of the Secretariat of Patrimony to the preserved perimeter was seen as a way to speed up the analysis of projects and to avoid the many embargoes applied to people's houses. There were also those who argued against the project, but the reason for this opposition was mainly connected to the impact that the creation of new posts would have on the local budget. Defending cultural heritage was undoubtedly politically unpopular.[16] The letter from the Council was read in plenary but voted against, and the division of functions took place.

The idea of establishing preservation borders that sparked political discussion in 2013 moved forward with two projects – one to asphalt cobblestoned streets just outside the preserved perimeter and one addressing mining on the edges of one of Ouro Preto's district (topics addressed in the following chapters). Clearly, setting a border for preservation was important for the government in that it allowed for the development of infrastructure and new businesses in the outskirts. The administrative change that took place that early March increasingly politicised cultural heritage. What became central in my investigation was to see how the Council would deal with the pressure to dispute heritage borders.

Finally, in the case of the mayor's project, the opposition of the Council was to be expected. Members were mainly associated with architecture, tourism, culture, and education (as I will detail in the following), and the project was administratively reducing the importance of those areas. Thus, a clear defence of cultural heritage could be associated with self-defence, when some professionals may directly benefit from city maintenance. For example, architects would be one of the groups to benefit from stiff regulations, being necessary for those who need construction projects. This aspect explains why the position of the Council may be disliked in town. More importantly, whether based on technical, personal, or economic interests, some members of the Council work for the municipal administration, and though they may have their (private, professional, community) interests, they cannot always voice those when directly opposed to the prefecture. In the next section, I look at Council members as residents and technical experts for the municipal administration (when that is the case), to discuss how political, economic, and social ties may blur city visions.

COUNCIL MEMBERS

By following a group of people throughout the year, I got to know them as friends, but it took some time to gain their trust (see Table 4.1 for a view of the Council's composition). Especially towards the end of the year, after various complex decisions made by the Council, interviews revealed the dilemma faced by Council members, whose personal and professional roles intertwined when making decisions. Most of them invited me to their homes, to local cafés or offices, where we could talk privately. When we set meetings in local cafés, before our conversation, they would first check who was seated nearby or if a less visible table was available, for example. It was also usual that they would lower their tone of voice every time they engaged in a controversial topic, regardless of whether we were talking in a place packed with tourists, or in a house where there were only the two of us. I offered to switch off my voice recorder and stopped taking notes a number of times to avoid the feeling of apprehension that I sensed. However, it was not my presence that threatened them but a constant feeling of being watched in a city where people recognise their positions in embargoing or allowing local constructions. As a Council member told me, I was the least of their concerns, and they were willing to contribute to my research and were aware their positions were not anonymous because meetings are public, publicised, and of interest for most residents and businesses. Nonetheless, it seemed difficult for them to get used to being constantly exposed, and despite a sense that their actions were public, they continued to look over my shoulders before responding to questions. Such a concern proved correct when one member was fired from her job and another changed jobs to avoid the same fate. In both cases, according to them, their roles in the Council motivated professional changes. Before sharing information about their biographies, I offer an outline of members and affiliation. Mainly because of a blurring of private, professional, and participative roles, I decided to introduce the members of the Council as they introduced themselves to me in the interviews, but when I address their arguments in the meetings (chapters 5 and 6), I do not disclose their names. I understand most Council meetings have minutes, and the data I present is not confidential. However, as my notes may be more detailed than the minutes available, I am careful when using them to discuss controversial decisions that took place in 2013 to protect my informants.

Throughout the year 2013, there were various controversial Council meetings, some of which will be addressed in coming chapters. Deolinda and Marcelo pointed out that decisions are controversial because some will have great economic impact. Deolinda mentioned that because of the many changes the city faced, being first a mining town, later a political capital, and afterwards a 'city of alcoholics and widows', the city's ups and downs made

Table 4.1: Council members

Member	*Main Occupation*	*Represent in the Council*
Deolinda	Folklorist	Folklore Commission
Flávio	Politician	Residents Association
João Paulo	Historian	Secretariat of Culture and Patrimony
Gabriela	Art teacher	Art Foundation of Ouro Preto
João Carlos	Architect	IPHAN
Marcelo	Pensioner	Residents Association
Roninho	Environmentalist	Environmental NGO
Marilia	Architect	IEPHA – Minas Institute of Historic and Artistic Patrimony
Guilherme	Forest Engineer	Secretariat of Environment
Gabriela	Museology Professor	Federal University of Ouro Preto
Debora	Architect	Secretariat of Culture and Patrimony

economic interests more pronounced. To her, the Council also exists because of economic interests: 'The external funds can only enter the municipality if there is a council', and one of the main challenges of the Council relates to the pressure to decide on issues that may compromise lucrative businesses. Like Deolinda, Marcelo saw the pressure money puts on the decision-making processes.

Council members also felt pressured by the fact that residents share a perception of patrimony as something prohibitive and forced upon them from the outside, and Marilia mentioned feelings of frustration amongst residents who perceived tourists in a position of advantage and for that resisted preservation. Flávio mentioned that people felt excluded from heritage concerns by explaining that residents approached him to say, 'You do not like people like us because we are not historic'. According to João Paulo the city was plagued by the problem of channelling 'everything to the centre; they invest more in the roof of a church than on sewage system'. In another example, he said, 'I thought people would not know what patrimony is, but everybody had an idea: "patrimony arrives and does not let us do anything"'. This means members make decisions that might be unpopular with most residents, and this helps to explain why residents are not willing to participate in meetings and four out of eleven council members are from outside Ouro Preto. Those members who mainly come from large cities such as Rio de Janeiro and Belo Horizonte have to fight against the perception of being an outsider. At the same time, they are part of the Council because they moved to the city as *concursados* (permanent civil servant positions), and their job stability is attached to political capital (Cornwall and Shankland 2013: 319). For Flávio, who is from Ouro Preto and whose father was director of patrimony in the city in the past, the difficulty since the 1950s was to get people to understand that whether in the centre or in the outskirts houses needed an architectural plan. However, the idea of separation is so strong, Flávio explained, that a man who lives outside the city centre says that he goes to Ouro Preto when he heads downtown and does not understand why his faraway house could be embargoed.

For reasons of segregation and unpopularity, as Debora explained, technical experts prefer to have the Council's assessment, rather than making decisions alone. However, businesses and other interested parties are not always willing to spend time discussing projects with people directly affected or with the Council, explained João Carlos from IPHAN. Guilherme added that meetings are not only unpopular with businesses but also within the community in general. Also in meetings, Council members decide on contentious topics that fall outside legal and technical limits. Guilherme saw the lack of legal certainty as positive, because often the Council needed to avoid damage and minimise negative effects and, the law cannot always regulate this in each different case. He praised the opportunity to have 'subjective criteria' that are also rooted in technical knowledge.[17] What this approach does not consider is how decision-makers are affected in the absence of clear laws.

Roninho identified local pressure in small communities, and members such as João Paulo, João Carlos, and Professor Gabriela said that such local pressure affected personal and professional relationships. For João Carlos there is a personification of public positions, and 'you cannot go to the bakery, have a pizza, a beer, your private life is always mixed with your public one, I find this a great mistake'. For that reason, João Carlos opted to live in a different city and commute to Ouro Preto. For Roninho, residents in general do not want to get involved in any common discussion for fear it would spark conflicts with neighbours. He described the situation by saying that 'here the bank manager knows all your life, in a larger city you are one more client . . . this exposes us, we endure more pressure'. Gabriela also spelled out the pressure Council members endure, and for her, members 'cannot decide on something as technical experts without impacting their future'. As technical experts, members often work in institutions addressed in meetings; hence, participants may be judging a project that was previously agreed upon by their bosses. João Paulo reflected exactly on that point and mentioned that working as a technical expert, a public servant of the prefecture, he represents conflicting positions and often his technical account can go against political decisions.

Council decisions were subjective and members were identifiable subjects. While many residents may not attend meetings, they know the work of Council members and their association with the preservation of patrimony, as Flávio explained. Even when members vote consensually, hence removing culpability from the individual, the group is small enough to make participants distinctive. Moreover, a consensual decision is not always the outcome of discussion. When singled out as stakeholders of specific decisions or discussions, a member may not be detached from her professional role and may suffer consequences at work. To avoid confusion, however, members often announce in what capacity they are voicing an opinion: the technical expert, the resident, or the Council member in a volunteer political role. Professor Gabriela, for instance, noticed this in some members' participation, who would start a speech by introducing themselves as a technical expert to then shift to being a Council representative. By positioning themselves as different entities, members do not only voice multiple roles in the city but also hope to avoid being seen as an employee when they speak as a resident. The few sentences in the following shall give the reader an idea of how participants introduce themselves before engaging in Council discussions. In the same meeting, the same person may make different remarks on who is talking; some of them are controversial, sometimes the identification may be narrowed down, such as speaking as a professional of an area, or as embracing as talking in the name of society:

- 'I am talking as a member of the Council and not as a technical expert' (July 2, 2013).
- 'We, the prefecture . . . as a member of the council . . . as a technical expert . . . as the civil society . . . I talk as a professional' (July 2, 2013).
- 'As part of the Secretariat of Patrimony, . . . as part of the prefecture' (July 12, 2013).
- 'As part of the Council . . . I speak as a citizen, I am nothing else' (July 12, 2013).
- 'My role as a technical expert . . . my role in the prefecture' (September 24, 2013).

The Council could potentially offer 'a more comprehensive understanding of the social life of cultural heritage', that is, to listen what different people 'have to say about their heritage and their own motives for keeping it up' (Brumann 2009: 295). However, that opportunity will need to encompass the perspectives of different citizens, but these different perspectives on the city have not yet been incorporated through widening participation. Not only there are few members and those are mainly connected to cultural, educational, and touristic areas, but Council members can not always express multiple views on the city without being perceived, addressed, and affected as if holding a single role. As McGranahan (2010: 768) asserts talking about narrative dispossession, 'Possessing one's own life story, however is not a given . . . it involves social processes and conventions operative well beyond individual processes of reflection and experience'. Regardless of the announcement of who is voicing the opinion, Council members cannot control how their representation is perceived. Nevertheless, this group is the one that has the burden to preserve the architectural legacy of (continuous) social injustice. As challenging as it might be, the Council plays a key local role in re-thinking the process, the results, and the participative possibilities within the cultural heritage of Ouro Preto.

CONCLUSION

Cultural heritage preservation in Ouro Preto more recently started to include ideas of participation. The combination of patrimony and citizenship is twofold. It means residents are the patrimony, and it means patrimony should be directed by residents. The idea that residents are patrimony was discussed in previous chapters and refers to the projects that hope to alter the notion of socio-spatial exclusion from city's main sights by focussing on cultural and pedagogic inclusion, as well as by expanding ideas of historic and artistic to locations beyond the city centre. In this chapter, the focus has been on the idea that patrimony is participative, and I looked at the municipal council that deals with cultural heritage.

Locally, patrimonial preservation has been controversial, and not all politicians endorse city preservation. Many residents view the investment in cultural heritage with scepticism, as the outskirts of the city lack infrastructure but resources are directed to the centre. In addition, an embracing concept of preserved areas or surrounding areas of preserved sites may lead to concerns regarding restrictions in house construction, which affect many households. The mayor used these aspects in 2013 to justify restricting preservation efforts to the city centre, as opposed to the previous mayor who tried to combine urban development with patrimonial preservation in Ouro Preto. However, the mayor does not govern alone, and the House of Representatives voted after listening to both sides: to the Council stating that the project would increase existing perceptions of polarisation between centre and periphery, and to the mayor who argued the idea would allow the outskirts of the city to grow in housing and business opportunities. The mayor's project was approved.

The mayor's project was intended to limit the scope of patrimonial preservation to preserved areas. However, this does not mean the Council discuss only the city centre. There are intricacies in the governance of cultural heritage that relate to the surrounding areas of a preserved site, making the boundaries and terminology associated with preservation constantly disputed. As a result, the mayor's project did not diminish the importance of this group. The Council remained the main forum in which to discuss aspects of preservation. However, I sensed amongst Council members that it was up to them to 'save' the patrimony, a word often used in meetings, while the prefecture would restrict cultural heritage (at least administratively).

However, when a sensitive topic like housing is discussed through the lens of aesthetics and historic importance, patrimony generates local indignation. It concentrates resources in the hands of hotel and restaurant owners, it excludes residents spatially, and it may even privilege a future generation for whom the city is to be maintained at the cost of the present one. The Council exists in a context of social inequality wrapped in social responsibility, aspects that limit broad participation and generate unpopularity, as I will address in chapters 5 and 6.

Nevertheless, local controversies call for strategies, and Council participants have multiple voices in their capacities as residents, technical experts, or members of the government. However, there is no guarantee that it is possible to distinguish between those multiple roles in town, and Council members highlighted a blurring between their personal, professional, and political relationships in town. In council meetings, there seemed to be a chasm between a national call for local representatives and a local possibility to represent different everyday roles.

In sum, the local encumbrance of preservation, which the municipality often passed on to national organisations such as IPHAN, is now in the hands of local residents who make up the Council. Far from representing all sectors of a fragmented city, the composition mainly unites sectors that support patrimony. However, Council members have personal and professional roles, which intertwine with their decision-making. Members' participation vary according to whether they represent 'an expert, a citizen, a resident, a council member'. By engaging in Council discussions in specific cases, I demonstrate in the coming chapters that granting the right to participate in city governance does not mean participants will necessarily voice different perspectives, nor that local participation is necessarily to a participant's gain. Silence in participatory meetings will also be considered, because the costs of publicly voicing concerns, often against established powers in town, needs to be observed considering the size of the city and the economic dependency of participants. Sub-optimal decisions or non-participation may be less costly for participants than direct confrontation. Whereas grassroots politics has been recognised, especially in Brazil, as an important resource to press for urban amenities, it is important to consider which spaces are adequate for effective participation to avoid romantic and seductive rhetoric of a 'fix-all' model (Cornwall and Shankland 2013: 310).

Chapter 5

Infrastructure in Heritage Sites

Did you hear how noisy the street was last night?
No, I did not. When I arrived things were calm.
We called the police; there was loud music all night. It was all about songs that tell you to shake your ass and the like. It was only the 'muddy feet' here, from Morro Santana and beyond.

(Conversation with a neighbour, October 27, 2013)

In Ouro Preto, some wealthier residents and students refer to the poor, who live in unauthorised settlements with unsealed roads, as *pés vermelhos*, 'red feet', or *pés de barro*, 'muddy feet'. The term 'red feet' is used often during the dry season, when walking on unpaved roads results in shoes covered in red dust, while 'muddy feet' conveys the same sentiment during the rainy season. When one's appearance announces place of residence through shoes, it also serves to identify and distinguish class. In such dusty/muddy locations, asphalt is highly valued as it diminishes commuting time, signals public service delivery (such as postal-delivery and garbage collection) and potential housing regulation. Above all, asphalt makes poverty less obvious, as it is no longer displayed on people's shoes.

However, in Ouro Preto, not only does asphalt contrast with dust and mud but also with historic cobblestoned streets. In this chapter, I explore the various roads made of dust, asphalt, and stones as lenses that demonstrate class perception and ideas about cleanness, aesthetics, and historicity, carrying with them promises of social inclusion or exclusion. I discuss the moment when the municipal government decided to improve urban mobility by paving over cobblestone streets with asphalt in 2013. This process laid bare the clash between contrasting sets of values that different groups of people place on cultural heritage and urban infrastructure. When the idea of city preservation is related to the appearance of the city, where are the boundaries of the preserved site drawn? Should everyday roads that also lead to a historic monument lead a visitor into another time? More importantly, when do such questions arise, and who has the privilege of answering these questions? Honing in on these questions, I analyse disparate and competing realities of urban life in Brazil's most iconic heritage site and illustrate who mediates such contrasting priorities over city infrastructure. Terms usually used to govern cultural heritage in Brazil and elsewhere, such as historicity, aesthetics, authenticity, are however often 'erratic' and 'inconsistent' (Canclini 2012: 97). In Ouro Preto, such terms were not helpful to inform decisions on the use of asphalt. The Council may have the potential to correct the ambiguity of these imprecise terms, by focussing on policy process in the absence of clear rules and terminologies. However, as illustrated by the following newspaper headline, the prefecture paved roads with asphalt but did not consult the Council in advance:

> One of the most polemic points of PROMOVA Ouro Preto,[1] with a total cost of 25 million [Brazilian Reais], is the use of asphalt in the street Engenheiro Correa, access to the Museum Casa dos Inconfidentes, in Vila Aparecida, where asphalt pavers covered cobbles without consulting the Municipal Council for the Preservation of Cultural and Natural Patrimony.
>
> (Do Vale 2013a, my translation)

When 'the city of stones', as Ouro Preto is known, was paved with asphalt, the details of such radical transformation affected residents throughout the city.

OURO PRETO, THE CITY OF STONES

Ouro Preto is known amongst tourists as *cidade de pedras* ('city of stones'), a term of endearment paying tribute to the cobblestone streets, the gemstone trade, soapstone art popular with tourists, and the gold from which the name and fortune of the city were drawn. Stones thus work not only as a powerful reminder of Ouro Preto's history and economy but are also useful to many professions directly involved with the material preservation of the city. For artisans, architects, historians, storytellers, archaeologists, and those working in the tourism industry, the maintenance of the city's design is economically essential. Thus in Ouro Preto, everything from the colour of the houses, the features of the colonial roofs, the choice of the window material, and the colonial façades of buildings, among other elements, are carefully maintained and are points of much discussion in cases of intervention. However, as happens in historic cities around the world, maintaining buildings of historical relevance will also include pairing together ancient buildings with equally old-fashioned modes of transportation, public illumination, and road layout to increase the experience of historicity. Examples of this are the gondolas in Venice or the *fiakers* in Vienna. Even though there are no carriages in Ouro Preto, central streets and smaller connecting roads are paved with cobblestones. While this feature makes these streets unique, it simultaneously makes them unpractical for the residents of the city who usually commute from the outskirts of the city to the centre.

Roads in Ouro Preto can thus contrast with the fundamental aim of transportation and become destinations themselves, attracting tourists who appreciate the cobblestones. In addition, instead of connecting individuals and places, roads in Ouro Preto segregate and alienate. Roads made tangible existing class divisions that fall across historic (cobbles) and non-historic areas (dirt and asphalt).

Such nuances in the perception associated with asphalt, cobbles, and dirt explain why street material abounds in residents' conversations in Ouro Preto. While some people complain about the width of the streets, it is the paving material that is most central in local conversation. The unmistakable smell of burned tyres coupled with the sound of cars screeching as vehicles force their way up a cobblestoned street are typical for Ouro Preto, disrupting the historical experience of visitors and upsetting residents. Together, vehicles lacking road traction, pedestrians falling in the street on rainy days, and the smell and sounds of the street fuel negative narratives about the cobblestoned pavements in downtown.[2] Modifying the layout of roads could potentially 'increase the speed of travel, cutting journey times' (Knox and Harvey 2011: 144), and paved roads could arguably be seen as bringing people together.

In Ouro Preto, as the population grows, people are forced to move further away from the city centre, where most working opportunities are located, and narratives about distances within the city abound in everyday conversations. Transportation is locally important and is expensive (as demonstrated by the case of the protests about bus fares in chapter 2). To commute from the periphery to the city centre is not always easy, due to the hilly landscape of the city and the lack of grip in streets paved with cobbles. Asphalt, on the other hand, allows vehicles to drive faster and reach remote locations that were otherwise unreachable by bus. Asphalt is popular in this context. Due to these reasons, on top of the aforementioned association between dusty/muddy feet with lower social class, asphalt became a popular solution to address separations. As a result, the mayor wasted no time paving over some roads with the new material.

THE MAKING, UNMAKING, AND REMAKING OF STREETS

PROMOVA Ouro Preto is a local policy initiated by Ouro Preto's prefecture in 2013. Though the project encompassed various areas, in this chapter I focus on one aspect, that of urban mobility through the paving of Ouro Preto's streets with asphalt.[3] The project generated great local controversy. Evidence of some of these disagreements can be found in the prefecture's promotional material, a twelve-page government bulletin freely distributed in town, which connected the ideas of 'seeing and living in a new Ouro Preto' (Assessoria de Comunicação Social 2013: 5, my translation). Road improvements were controversial interventions because they were visible modifications to an aesthetically preserved city. According to material about the project, some roads connecting remote areas to the city centre were paved with asphalt and some cobblestoned streets in locations closer to the centre had been altered or considered for modification. Defining which streets could change and which others had to be kept unaltered was controversial. There are different preserved perimeters defined by national institutions such as IPHAN (Institute for Historic and Artistic Patrimony) and local ones such as the Prefecture, and there are areas of historic interest outside such perimeters. Thus borders for intervention or maintenance are disputed (as discussed in chapter 4). Although a participative process involving the Council provides a possible solution in cases where the rules are unclear, this lack of clarity can also mean the Council may not be included in discussions at all. This was precisely what took place in Ouro Preto when discussion followed the introduction of asphalt in areas that lie just in the intersection of different preservation perimeters.

Even though asphalt heightened local disputes about aesthetic and historic areas, the programme to modify streets was aimed exactly at bridging perceptions of social disconnection. The prefecture of Ouro Preto invested in urban mobility – mainly through the use of asphalt – to overcome socio-spatial divides, as indicated by the mayor's letter informing local politicians about the modification of street material. The letter, sent to the House of Representatives on September 10, 2013, justified the importance of PROMOVA by emphasising the need to bridge the perceived divide between local residents and visitors. In the official communication, the mayor explained how the programme was considered important as it was to

> maintain the city as Cultural Patrimony of Humanity and at the same time be the city dreamed about and expected by *Ouropretanos* . . . the project now submitted for consideration . . . will prompt the revitalization of public spaces and as consequence, greater integration with the population and visitors.
>
> (Oficio Mensagem 61, 2013, my translation)[4]

What I saw in Ouro Preto during my fieldwork, however, was that modifying existing lanes did not ultimately change the perception of a disconnect between residents and visitors. If anything, the polarisation that resulted from the positive and negative perceptions of road interventions exacerbated the already existent social distances. This was mainly because streets were not only viewed as avenues of access to a historic site but also perceived as a historic destination in themselves, an element of another time, which made being in Ouro Preto a unique experience. On the other hand, the same lanes that lead people into another time also lead residents to their everyday home and work. 'Plain' (asphalt) or 'fancy' (stones) streets sharpened an existing disagreement about cultural heritage and everyday activities and became a particularly central feature in the discussion about the boundaries of preservation.

The boundaries of preservation had already been controversial in other local urban projects. As discussed in chapter 1, the preservation of the city was justified and regulated through its appearance.[5] Nevertheless, ideas of national development also underpinned the declaration of Ouro Preto as cultural heritage. As a result, the preserved perimeter has not been entirely static. For example, the construction of the Grande Hotel in the centre of the town by Oscar Niemeyer in the 1940s was a controversial architectural intervention, but one also related to tourism and thus to economic aspects related to the preservation of the city. When describing asphalt interventions to me, the vice-mayor explained that his rationale for this shift was to find an urban change that could fit within wider concerns for maintaining the city's architectural importance. In the conversation we had, I asked the vice-mayor about asphalt, and Chiquinho explained that

> *already in our government, the problem of urban mobility is very pertinent and in the long term, it will be even more pertinent. Ouro Preto, because of its colonial history, has very narrow streets, very unstable terrain, the geological formation is very bad, and that already concerns us. So we are investing so as to have a higher quality of life in the long term. It will be a nuisance now because we . . . want to improve the mobility of the people. . . . Abroad it is a bit different because you go for example to Paris, the historic centre has asphalt, with the concept that trembling, the movement of cars on irregular pavement, harms the buildings. In Ouro Preto it is exactly the contrary, here we preserve the patrimony and the pavement. So we want to have fewer factors that could spoil the patrimony we are trying to preserve. . . . Ouro Preto is very unique . . . the public transport in other cities is very different than that in Ouro Preto. If you ask a public transport company they will tell you that the costs are much higher here, and they are. Because the pavement is not good, the topography is not good, you see. This is also a university city, which generates a different kind of transportation. . . . So this is my concern . . . in*

twenty or thirty years the population that comes to live in Ouro Preto will have a good quality of life.

(Chiquinho, Vice-Mayor, November 21, 2013)

The argument made by the vice-mayor suggests that patrimony and pavement are related but distinct. These concepts are intertwined as the choice of pavement can affect the preservation of buildings, and his statement implies that these should be maintained and for that the pavement itself does not have to. The choice of pavement can also influence how visitors and residents can move around in the city and how transport can be made more efficient, especially given the hilly nature of Ouro Preto.

While the introduction of asphalt can be seen as an asset to preservation – based on the explanation that it can help maintain buildings by reducing the vibrations that harm the structures – some urban changes are more difficult to justify. Even in the case of the hotel project mentioned before, this work by a internationally acclaimed architect was controversial then and remains divisive now.[6] Along these same lines, amongst the residents of Ouro Preto, the question of whether changing road layout (though outside the city centre) equated to destruction or preservation was far from agreed upon. It thus seemed reasonable when the vice-mayor suggested that his policy might find approval in twenty or thirty years. Why would one not give a chance to the future to mediate present disputes over architectural forms? Although the past is central in most citizens' stories in cities such as Ouro Preto, it is the future that offers a prospect for improvements in quality of life, or optimism about increased interactions between tourists and residents. In Ouro Preto, as in Athens, and other cities framed across a hierarchy of time and space, architectural symbolism can often be problematic, and the advantage of the past over present architecture does not always find a space (Faubion 1993: 86). In the disputes between city aesthetics and city uses, the future becomes a ruling alternative.

The headline of the front-page of the prefecture's promotional material reads 'preserving the past, guaranteeing the future', highlighting the controversy between an everyday intervention on streets and the relation with the future (*preservar o passado, garantir o futuro*, Assessoria de Comunicação Social 2013: 1). The transformations in the city – explained through preservation – envisioned a future of better urban mobility, or perhaps simply a future that would understand such transformations. Nevertheless, expectations about the future did not offer answers to present concerns such as water absorption. Asphalt necessitates a previous investment in drainage systems, which became a prominent concern, especially as the use of asphalt was introduced just before the rainy season. In addition, the effect of this intervention on tourists and the residents who depend on the tourism industry was not assessed before transformations begun. Popular reactions to asphalt included perceiving its implementation as a crime.

ASPHALT AS A CRIME AGAINST CULTURAL HERITAGE

One of the most controversial asphalt interventions, initiated in 2013, took place in the Vila Aparecida neighbourhood, located in a hilly area between the city centre and the main university campus. This is a hybrid neighbourhood where students, middle-class, and poor residents live alongside one another. As an area of the city where modern constructions exist and are visible to the eye of those who are in the historic city centre, Vila's skyline is controversial (see Image 1.5b, from the city centre it is possible to see Vila and the museum in the background). Driving the recently paved roads in Vila Aparecida encourages residents to remember how cobblestones (in this case a stone pavement more irregular than cobbles which in Brazil is known as *pé-de-moleque*) would make cars or buses shake, necessitating costly maintenance and increasing the time it took to reach any destination. But others, especially non-residents, complained that the recent asphalt laid by the prefecture altered the historicity of Ouro Preto, chiefly in the proximity of the Museum Casa dos Inconfidentes (see Image 5.1).

The tensions surrounding the use of asphalt in the proximity of the museum are reflected in the readers' comments about the aforementioned regional

Image 5.1. Museum Casa dos Inconfidentes (the use of asphalt stops just at the Museum gate), 2013. *Source*: Personal collection.

newspaper's headline citing the recent use of asphalt. For example, one reader stated:

> Historic cities have to be preserved in their original architecture, as well as the sidewalks, streets and the typical illumination of that time. Asphalt does not suit Ouro Preto or other historic cities. The asphalt already installed should be removed and the mayor should be criminally charged.
>
> (Di Paula 2013: 8, my translation)

However, a prevalent debate in town was whether cobblestones are part of the city's original layout – considering that earlier pavements were not made of stones – and whether certain aspects of authenticity are enough to govern city preservation. I was able to investigate some of these questions with visits to the museum.

Much of Ouro Preto's contemporary history is seen through the lens of Inconfidência Mineira (1789), and as such, there are many streets and monuments named after the plotters, and the houses of those involved in the conspiracy have been preserved. The Museum Casa dos Inconfidentes is a space carefully curated in a way that encourages visitors to imagine how the heroes of Inconfidência Mineira developed their plot. Despite limited evidence, there is a popular belief that the *inconfidentes* met in the house that is today the museum, a house that has a view to the city centre but is difficult to reach from the centre, making it a good location for conspiracy. Though nobody can confirm that the house existed in the eighteenth century, some elements from the construction – for example, the walls made of wattle and daub – indicate this timeframe. The museum, to emphasise the popular imagination of another time, has a selection of furniture and objects that construct a romantic view of the uprising. It evokes the image of what a place where the *inconfidentes* met might have looked like, with a selection of books, clothes, oratories, and other antiques dating back to that era. As the house and the collection of objects within it prompt many questions regarding the origin of each object and the real construction date of the house, the museum is not legally preserved as a heritage site. Even if the structure was recognised as heritage, how the surroundings or road access to a monument should be maintained is debatable (Motta and Thompson 2010). In addition, the museum staff noted to me in our conversations, and it became visibly apparent over the course of my visits, that the street leading to the museum is the only flat ground in that neighbourhood. The members of staff listed a few improvements that came with the introduction of asphalt, such as the disabled could reach the museum using the wheelchair, children could cycle there, and people have used the street for jogging. In the absence of leisure spaces in the city, the new asphalt filled an important gap. In contrast, however, they also expressed concern about the lack of water absorption, one of the characteristics of the new material.

Functionaries were clear about the importance of the house for imagining, rather than representing, another period, and they explained the house as a creative representation of the plot, and for that reason, it is not yet preserved. Not everyone, however, views what the museum offers as a way to spark imagination. In contrast, for some, the museum offers an accurate portrayal of that particular period of time, and as such the introduction of asphalt poses a threat to historicity. One resident of central Ouro Preto demonstrated this line of thought, stating:

> *they can't use asphalt in a street where Tiradentes walked. He did not walk on asphalt. (She took a brief pause and corrected): Well, it is true that he might not have walked on cobblestones either, but a more irregular stone pavement.*

I asked if asphalt could be used if he had not walked on that road, if the street was not related to a historic event and the answer was, 'Yes, of course. Some areas are no problem. But these "small-minded people" (*gentinha*) have no understanding of historic value' (conversation with a downtown resident in Ouro Preto, October 26, 2013).

Although the fact that Tiradentes walked the streets of Ouro Preto remains an inspiration for local and national shared pride, there is no reason to believe he walked the street leading to the museum. In fact, the original route to that house was a green trail through a hill (see Images 5.2a and 5.2b), and the street leading to the museum was created and paved with cobbles only in the 1970s (Santana 2012: 79). My informant, who argued that the street pavement should be maintained and believed people who thought otherwise were inferior, was an upper class resident living in the city centre, not in the museum's neighbourhood or further out. For her and other city centre residents, supporting asphalt was associated with a lack of cultural or historical understanding or appreciation. But for most of the people living in the neighbourhood of Vila Aparecida or those travelling through it to reach the local university, asphalt was a positive intervention, which facilitated transportation and leisure.

When buildings or streets give form to an image of colonial Brazil, not everybody is equally impacted or inspired by the work of imagination and materialization of the past. To begin with, by attaching material forms to romanticised interpretations of the past, there is a risk that these interpretations of events can be detached from their authors as if they were factual representations (Olson 1994: 196), and interpretations may no longer freely change (Brumann 2009: 277). In addition, when narratives of the past are

Image 5.2a. Reaching the museum in the past. ***Source*:** **Fontana (n.d.)**

Image 5.2b. Reaching the museum currently, as of October 25, 2013. ***Source*:** **Personal collection.**

based on attention to details of objects or buildings from the far past, long-term memories are privileged at the cost of denial of more recent events (Reed 2002: 138), 'a simultaneous process of remembering and forgetting'

(Heathcott 2013: 216), and for some people the past becomes an everyday burden.

The route that Tiradentes and other *inconfidentes* symbolically walked now leads to a Museum, which is set in the house they possibly used many years ago. This means that for some people this house and this route no longer simply offer an inspiration for imagination. Instead, they have transformed into a materialization of the past and as such should be maintained in their original form. But by binding together the image of the past with the actual form of a road, not all people are equally given 'the privilege . . . to participate in the work of imagination' (Appadurai 2002: 46). It follows that, despite the importance of national heroes locally and the value of history, its objectification and reference should not be taken for granted and relations with the past, or with representations of the past, can assume negative discourses (Collins 2011: 684) for marginalised people.

In the case of the street leading up to the museum, there was little consensus in the narratives revolving around the introduction of asphalt. Local residents in general value the coup; however, for those living in the proximity of the route to the museum, the road, more than an allegory of the past, is also an everyday route used for leisure or commuting.

Moreover, to understand the value of asphalt in Vila Aparecida, it is important to note that the neighbourhood developed from an informal settlement in the 1960s. Similar to many such settlements in Brazil, it featured dirt roads rather than pavement (Santana 2012: 78). As noted at the beginning of this chapter, dust and mud on the streets that consequently are displayed on residents' feet were and continue to be stigmatising and associated with poverty and grime. Thus it is not surprising that some of Vila's residents support the introduction of asphalt locally as it means an end to dust and the heavy impact it has on residents.

ASPHALT IS THE END OF DUST

Rua Direita is the main street of Ouro Preto (see Image 5.3). A location for work, leisure, passage, and housing, its dynamics change according to the time of day and day of the week. Usually, during the day and weeknights, students, tourists, and workers use it to access museums, hotels, restaurants, shops, and houses. Most of the houses have both commercial and residential uses. It is common, however, to see students or wealthier residents avoiding Rua Direita on Saturday night, as the young people of Ouro Preto like to gather in this central street of the city to listen to music and have some time out. On this one evening out of the week, it becomes the favourite place for the poor, those commuting to the city centre to have some leisure.

Image 5.3. Rua Direita during daytime, July 11, 2013. ***Source*****: Personal collection.**

The people who gather in Rua Direita on a Saturday night are often categorised by wealthier residents of central areas as *pés vermelhos*, 'red feet', or *pés de barro*, 'muddy feet'. When residents from such areas go to the city centre, they are identified by their shoes as coming from underprivileged economic zones. In order to avoid being stigmatised by these assumptions, residents from these areas often cover their footwear with a plastic bag on the way to the town centre to keep their shoes clean. One of the main benefits of introducing asphalt for the underprivileged people of Ouro Preto is that there is no longer unavoidable mud or dust on these paths, and so a person's place of residence can no longer be immediately identified simply from their shoes.

O'Dougherty (2002), looking at Brazil during the 1990s, demonstrated that class statuses are ubiquitous and organised by principles of 'social separateness' (2002: 2). This separation can take different forms in different regions. In Brasília, for example, there are few places that allow for social encounters amongst residents from different economic backgrounds, and classes are spatially distant (Holston 2001: 552–553). In São Paulo, the upper class has moved to condominiums close to locations previously socio-economically disadvantaged. Although they live next to one another, classes are divided by walls (Caldeira 2000). In Ouro Preto, one's appearance – particularly the cleanliness of their shoes – announces one's place of residence and serves to identify and distinguish residents from one another. When different groups of people gather in the city's public spaces (such as during the many cultural festivals the city offers), they do not mix, as Teko explained in chapter 2.

What one sees in the outskirts of Ouro Preto, as in many other Brazilian cities, is that many residential arrangements are born from informal housing settlements. Land occupied for housing is rarely accompanied by the provisions enjoyed in areas that are designed for homes prior to their construction, such as sealed roads, street lights and signs, sewage system, electricity, treated water, postal delivery, and garbage collection, to name a few. Sealing roads is one of the main priorities for residents in Ouro Preto, because asphalt, or the lack of it, can communicate social inclusion or exclusion.

Walking on the muddy streets of Alto do Rosario (see Image 5.4), an informal settlement in the city of Mariana (only 12 km away from Ouro Preto), Andreia, a resident and community leader told me the importance of asphalt amongst other infrastructure provisions. She mentioned that even her children enquire about the absence of urban infrastructure, or in her words:

> *My kids, one is three years old and the other one is five years old, how do I explain to them when they ask me: mum, will my house have a number like grandma's house? Because my mum lives in an urbanised area, you see. . . . Mum, what is the name of that thing there? I find it cute and reply, it is called lamppost, and they ask; will my street have a lamppost? Why is there no lamppost in my street? Then you see, the children also have their impressions, they see the difference. . . . For example, you see here* [in the car] *it is full of boots, the boots stay in the car.*
>
> (Andreia, December 6, 2013)

I certainly understood from her words and the boots in the car that asphalt meant cleanliness, which makes one's place of residence less identifiable by the ubiquitous mud. When one carries the 'mark of dust' (Borges 2003: 121), 'carrying that soft stuff on themselves' (Mrazek 2002: 27, as cited by Larkin 2013: 337) the person not only announces that he or she lives in an occupied land but also is almost automatically stigmatised as poor and violent, as such areas are viewed as impoverished and criminal (Holston 2008: 281). Asphalt, or the 'black carpet' (Borges 2003: 121), apart from allowing buses or private cars to reach places, would also give pedestrians freedom from the dust and from the illegality, poverty, and violence associated with it. Furthermore, infrastructure such as asphalt usually precedes public services. As a result, when roads are paved with asphalt, it generates expectations about a future that entails better transportation, improved public security, or garbage collection. However, asphalt's importance could,

Image 5.4. Streets of mud and dust, 2013. *Source*: Personal collection.

controversially, go as far as stopping other policies, as residents may feel satisfied with asphalt only and stop pressing for public services, explained Andreia. The importance of asphalt in these areas justifies its title, *Senhor Asfalto* (Mr. Asphalt), as some people referred to it in Ouro Preto by the end of 2013. The term *Senhor* preceding the word 'asphalt' pays tribute to the material, sometimes ironically, marking the importance it has for many people in Brazil, especially those confronted with its contrast: dirt roads resulting in muddy and red shoes.

However, in Ouro Preto, *Senhor Asfalto* is not only contrasted with dusty or muddy roads, as is throughout Brazil, but also with cobblestoned streets. Thus in Ouro Preto, streets, which usually serve as connectors between places (Lynch 1960: 41), have, controversially, separated locations through their material: the mark of illegality and poverty that accompanies dirt streets, as well as the boundaries between the 'historic' and the 'modern' areas of the city represented by cobblestone or asphalt. Due to such fundamental biases in the hierarchy of time, class, and materials, decision-makers were wary when entering into discussions about the use of asphalt in town.

GOVERNING WITHOUT RULES

In urban design theory, as depicted by Ellin (1996: 61), there is a movement called townscape, which 'in reaction to modernism's "architectural objects" . . . emphasized the relationship between buildings and all that surrounds them'. The author reminds us, however, that this 'holistic view of the city' (ibid.: 61) could extend disputes about gains and losses in preservation areas to spaces previously not viewed as patrimony. When Ouro Preto's mayor took power in 2013, he tried to diminish the holistic view of cultural heritage by separating the work of cultural preservation from that of urban development (as discussed in chapter 4). However, some other spheres of governance, such as the Council, tried to uphold the encompassing view of the city. To ensure the continued importance of a broad analysis of the city, the Council often used some terms, such as ambience.

In Brazil, ambience is usually articulated as a synonym for the environment or setting of a preserved area, 'the natural or man-made setting which influences the static or dynamic way these [historic] areas are perceived or which is directly linked to them in space or by social, economic or cultural ties' (UNESCO 1976).[7] Though the term is only broadly defined, this concept, together with the idea that a 'historic monument embraces not only the single architectural work but also the urban or rural setting' (Choay 2011: 168, my translation),[8] inspired the expansion of preserved areas in Brazil to encompass areas visible from preserved sites (see Ribeiro 2007: 92).

In Ouro Preto, the above-mentioned ideas, together with the unanticipated growth of the city since the 1950s, encouraged the development of a broader protected perimeter so as to encompass the locales observable from the already preserved site. The perimeter was altered in 1989.[9] Local laws, issued both by the municipality and the local IPHAN office, regulate the preservation of the city. Laws observe concepts such as ambience, encouraging the Council to embrace the city as a whole, and not in terms of a limited perimeter.

Nevertheless, despite embracing maps and legal efforts, asphalt in Rua Engenheiro Correa, leading up to the Museum, was not, in consensual terms, a crime against cultural heritage. Deciding on that area was particularly difficult because of its location in Vila Aparecida, intersecting areas protected under different national and local regulations, which observe both visual and environmental aspects.

When the Council met after asphalt was introduced to discuss the Museum case, Council members highlighted the different laws and decrees that defined preservation perimeters. For example, the museum falls under the perimeter defined nationally and regulated by IPHAN, which authorised the intervention. However, locally the museum was outside the preserved perimeter, which means the Council does not need to discuss the case, but it was inside a location for environmental protection. Members of the Council were then unsure if their analysis was mandatory according to different city zones and maps that do not create a clear mandate for city protection. Despite this uncertainty, above all, the application of asphalt definitely constituted a modification of the cityscape without Council consultation. As I describe in the following, after listing positive and negative aspects of the material itself, the process of decision-making gained centrality in the discussion:

> *'But the community finds it [asphalt] wonderful; it is the end of the dust'. While another member highlighted: 'the modification is a crime against cultural heritage, and fines and prison terms apply'. A third member pointed out: 'asphalt increases the speed of the water, there is no water absorption, and it is an irreversible loss'. When they discussed an area outside a preserved perimeter a member highlighted that 'the idea is to discuss preservation in an embracing procedure and we should write a letter to show we are being disrespected in many ways'.*
>
> (Field notes, October 22, 2013)

Council members spoke about the use of asphalt as a negative intervention due to its impact on the city aesthetics, the inability of roads to absorb rainwater, or the lack of discussions. However, Council members also highlighted the fact that residents may support asphalt because the material meant the end of dust on roads.

The local importance of asphalt was palpable in that October meeting. The Council decided to write a letter addressed to the Public Prosecutor's Office[10] demanding the Council should always be heard before changes such as tarring roads with asphalt take place. However, despite a long morning discussing local urban changes that ignored the Council, signing the letter was far from consensual. Members pointed to the danger in opposing such a key local urban policy for those working directly or indirectly in the prefecture. In the end, only one person – who worked for the municipality – signed the letter, facing professional consequences later (being removed from a managing position) because that was a key municipal project.

According to the local prosecutor's office the use of asphalt in town, was chiefly problematic in Rua Engenheiro Correa because it was not discussed in the Council, the institution that should make decisions such as ones that pertain to the reach of terms like ambience. To fill the void caused by this lack of discussion, the prosecutor's office requested a technical study.

Architects conducted the study for the prosecutor's office,[11] which was used as a precedent in future judicial process to regulate the use of asphalt in town. The study concluded that asphalt was not an acceptable part of the ambience of that particular area of the city. It should not have been used and is appropriate only for the rest of the neighbourhood. Further, the document discussed the lack of studies on water drainage and the lack of public consultation before the intervention. The study suggested, and the prosecutors enforced, amongst other measures, the removal of asphalt on that specific street leading to the museum and the construction of sidewalks to correct aspects of accessibility (Promotoria Estadual de Defesa do Patrimônio Cultural e Turístico 2013: 18–19).

That study viewed asphalt as a negative intervention, impacting the location's ambience, an assessment that did not extend to the creation of sidewalks nor to the use of asphalt in the main road in Vila Aparecida, which was also tarred with the material despite the fact that it leads to Rua Engenheiro Correa. This reinforces the lack of clarity about the term *ambience*, as there are certain elements considered destructive, while others are seen to renovate an area. The asphalt on Rua Engenheiro Correa was problematic not only due to its appearance but also due to the difficulties associated with water absorption and the fact there was little public participation in the decision process as the Prefecture did not consult the Council prior to its introduction.

In the absence of maps detailing preservation boundaries or a clear definition of ambience, the decision-making process was central to halt the use of asphalt in particular spaces in Ouro Preto. Different from the participative resolution of the conflict in this case, in Ghertner's (2010) study in Delhi, an aesthetic order was effective in the absence of secure mapping. The author focused on the slums in Delhi and noted that mapping those areas or knowing residents' profiles through statistics became unmanageable around the 1990s. The Delhi government thus managed this 'increasingly complex and unruly ground situation' (ibid.: 196) through 'the dissemination of aesthetic norms' (ibid.: 187). By *aesthetic norm*, the author means an 'ability to provide a normative dimension to seeing, to cultivate an aesthetic normativity in the population' (ibid.: 208). In other words, in the face of the Commonwealth Games in 2010 and the 'postcolonial anxiety to catch up' (ibid.: 211), the government's vision of a 'world-class city' (ibid.: 199) was opposed to the filthy appearance of the slums. Hence, improving the city was articulated as a necessary improvement not only for the city and the country but also for residents themselves, who were to be relocated (ibid.: 204). In light of these aesthetic norms, ashamed by the visibility of their unkempt homes, residents acknowledged their nuisance for the city and voluntarily moved.

Although aesthetics are also central to the debate in Ouro Preto, a norm, like the one in Delhi, did not offer clarity on determining the boundaries of heritage sites. Unmistakably, preservation measures in town (and in the country) were based on appearance. The basis for Ouro Preto's polygonal perimeter for preservation clears any doubt of this, as the lines are based on viewpoints that offer a panoramic view of the city.[12] Nevertheless, Ouro Preto's residents have built houses across city hills, some of them located within the preserved perimeter and others visible from the preserved area, interrupting that panoramic view.

As discussed across previous chapters, the idealised singularity of city spaces, anchored on parameters of appearance and historic value, presupposes shared values (Canclini 2012: 71). Canclini (ibid.) states that sometimes cultural patrimony meets the expectations of groups of people who feel represented by monuments or preserved practices, calling it a 'social complicity'. However, more often,

> the historic and symbolic prestige of certain goods, almost always, incur a simulation: pretending to ignore that society is not divided into classes, genders, ethnicities and regions, or suggesting that those perceptions are not important in the face of the grandiosity and respect for the protected works.
>
> (ibid.: 71, my translation)

The exclusion of residents from central areas, the perception of social separation during cultural events, the impossibility of eating in expensive restaurants that cater only for 'those from elsewhere', the selectiveness of monuments over-representing Catholic faiths and noblemen, and thus the hopelessness of cultural projects in bridging divides mean that the monumental city of Ouro Preto does not belong to all. More precisely, it belongs less to some residents than to short-term visitors – tourists and students. To shame residents as a visual nuisance or to reaffirm promises of the importance of the city are thus not politically effective. The promises of tourism and historic and cultural values mainly serve to stir up local socio-economic and spatial inequalities. Thus, politically, an aesthetic order is a controversial burden. The Council, having participants with a background in architecture, holds on to a holistic view of cultural heritage in the city, but even in this space, such a view is socially difficult to sustain. In Ouro Preto, as in Salvador's Pelourinho, residents stood up against patrimony not because they built some sort of collective resistance against 'objectified culture' (Collins 2011: 695) but simply because, in these cities, patrimony is where people live.

Therefore, often the prefecture left the preservation task to IPHAN technicians. The technical experts from IPHAN, however, stated that preservation is not a technical but a political action. Many experts have invited local politicians, civil society, and lawmakers – through the Council – to discuss the limits to and processes of heritage. When I talked to the director for historic cities in the IPHAN headquarters in Brasília, Robson explained the organisation's limits in regard to defining what should be preserved and how ideas such as ambience made work at heritage sites contested, the architect clarified that

> *the preserved areas from 1938, when great preservations began . . . were like 'be preserved', and [ever since then] it is very difficult to have institutional or personal control. . . . Later you have delimitations, perimeters, surrounding areas, in the last years, how can I put it, in the last five years or so, you start to see that we need to have more defined norms, a person needs to know when she buys or when she lives in that place what she can do in that place, because we had a lot of that problem in IPHAN . . . every office, every head of an office would think in a different way because the norms were not clear. . . .*
>
> *We have been saying that IPHAN is not there to say no. IPHAN is there to say how to say yes. We have to make comfort, housing, and living possible in these places [heritage sites] so we are there to say yes and if no, then how it could be yes. But that goes through clear norms, norms that we have been working on. Ouro Preto is one of the first cities where we developed a norm that became a municipal law.*[13] *. . . Does it have problems? It does. Does it have to be discussed? It does. . . . What is ambience? It is very subjective. . . . There are studies but not an objective concept . . . that is why there has to be a norm. . . . If I have a house, what is ambience? What can I build? I want to know if I can create another door, build in the entire extension of my property, how many floors I can build, what is the height I can reach. That is what we have to say to citizens and that is what we have been working on at high costs. . . .*
>
> *The decree [25/1937] was very well written. It was very well written because it simply says: if it is not approved by IPHAN then it is wrong. Secondly, it says*

> *that it is wrong if it diminishes how the place looks, mutilates it, which are subjective terms that can be interpreted in various ways. What has been happening for a few years now is that judges began to say 'I find this argument subjective, I think about it differently, so I . . .' and the judges would give the cause to property owners or the interested party and not to the institution. Therefore, it started to press the institution to have clear rules.*
>
> (Robson, November 13, 2013)

Robson brought the importance of defined laws to the fore. He understands laws as a way to diminish the vulnerability and uncertainty of decision-makers. However, on the side of those working to enforce the law, a normative dimension for cultural heritage has its shortcomings. I spoke to the prosecutor working on cultural heritage affairs that appealed in the case of the use of asphalt in Rua Engenheiro Correa. He explained that there were uncertainties in the prevalent judicial understanding in the use of asphalt. To fill legal gaps, he looked for interdisciplinary studies and relied on a team of architects and urban planners. To Marcos Paulo, technical knowledge gathered from different disciplines and the knowledge from civil society needed to be employed when making such a decision. Municipal councils, he highlighted, should be capable of combining the technical knowledge and social meaning in order to inform decision-making for cases such as the use of asphalt. However, he added that the greater the level of subjectivism in the interpretation of law, the lower the judicial reassurance. Besides community discussions, it is important to establish effective laws (as envisioned by Robson). But effective laws, in this case, should come from community councils and technical studies. And in the case of asphalt, effective studies should include geological impacts, based on the principle of precaution, he added.

Combined, these conversations show an understanding that the interpretation of the law and the creation of law are as necessary as they are uncertain. As a result, a decision should involve civil society and draw upon various kinds of knowledge, and the Council's importance was greatly emphasised in this process. The involvement of various areas of knowledge, however, was not part of the asphalt project in Ouro Preto in 2013. The prefecture started the project without further consultation, the Council intervened without assessing residents directly affected, and local geologists, despite concerns about rain and landslides mentioned by the prefecture, the Council, and the prosecutors, did not take up a central position in the decision-making process.

Controversies surrounding asphalt escalated in town during the rainy season in December 2013. Ouro Preto is a city with a tragic history of heavy rainfall followed by disastrous landslides – such as recent ones in 1989, 1992, 1995, 1997, and 1998 (Prefeitura Municipal de Ouro Preto 2012a: 8). Despite recent deaths caused by rain in the above-mentioned years and a general concern about water absorption in town, neither the fire-fighters involved in rescuing people from landslides, nor the geologists, were consulted regarding street materials. Sealed roads on hills give vehicles and pedestrians more grip and diminish the risk of worsening victims' injuries as a result of car accidents, which could justify the change of pavement in some lanes. However, asphalt could also alter the local climate, through an increase in local temperature, for example, and could compromise the city aesthetically. For those reasons, considerations should invite technical studies, as a lieutenant, who had not yet been heard in the process of changing streets, explained to me when I visited the fire brigade. In this same conversation, adding another layer of complexity to the conversation, a local geologist explained the relationship between asphalt and water absorption. According to him, asphalt's lack of water penetrability is not necessarily a negative thing. On the contrary, he clarified the challenge local geologists face in trying to diminish the amount of water absorbed in areas with greater landslide risk. He explained that the problem is that if the water runs over a road covered with asphalt and not cobblestones, there will be a larger volume, and the speed of the water will be greater. He explained that due to this shift other services would need to follow, like a drainage system. That conversation highlighted the need for an interdisciplinary group to examine the positive and negative aspects of asphalt. Once again, the conversation leads to the spheres of a group that can consolidate multiple assessments, such as the Council. However, as discussed, the Council met without sound geological engagement or risk assessments and was absorbed by its own (in)ability to discuss the case.

Obviously, the disagreements over what may or not interfere with the visual appraisal of an area may be endless. For this reason, Canclini (2012: 43) states that 'aesthetics survives not as a normative field, but as an open scope where we look for *forms* not radically detached of all types of functions' (my translation). For example, to the prefecture, asphalt was preservation, to local prosecutors or geologists, it was an invitation for discussion, and to the Council, it was the end of dust, a crime against cultural heritage, a threat regarding landslides, and above of all a necessary topic for discussion. It seems that at this point the Council, the prosecutors, IPHAN, and the prefecture have all realised the inconsistency and the scope for disputes brought by cultural heritage in Ouro Preto. This openness in concepts theoretically privileges the Council in solving conflicts. However, in channels for local input, and the Council in particular, as discussed in chapter 4, only a few individuals are invited to participate. Although members could voice different perspectives, as indeed they can as residents, technical experts, or policy makers, that possibility is hampered by strong pressure – professional misgivings when opposing a key political, social, economic project, for example – which pushes members into an anonymous consensus or unresponsiveness. It follows that the uncertainty of terms and mapping, which invite participation in the first place, is also echoed in the Council's intervention, intimidating members and fragmenting them in a dispute over their role. Everyday routes (of now and before), perceptions of history, aesthetics, and geological aspects remain disputed in such context.

CONCLUSION

Streets made of cobblestones, asphalt, or dirt in Ouro Preto revealed the ambiguity of the senses, oral history, economic and everyday uses of routes, spatial and aesthetic segregation, laws and negotiations of law, and perceptions of landslide risk. Ultimately, the modification of the roads challenged any easy assessment of what preservation or change consists of and divided opinions in town.

Outlining the events surrounding the location where the use of asphalt reached the greatest disagreement in Ouro Preto – Rua Engenheiro Correa – I discussed the controversies involved in defining the historic and aesthetic importance of that area. The museum framed a perception of history and nationalism, which was not equally shared across the city. Some residents valued the imagined footsteps of the Inconfidência and Tiradentes. However, for residents nearby, everyday footsteps also matter. Beyond this, by comparing these asphalt roads to those without pavement, such as those in Alto do Rosário (that has similarities with Vila Aparecida's past and is similar to many other residential areas in Ouro Preto) reinforces the fact that dirt roads are stigmatising for residents. Asphalt is associated with the end of dust, the end of stigmata associated with poverty and violence. This is because Brazil is home to an unequal and segregated society, where poverty is inconsistent with life in city centres; it is as anomalous as it is visible in such areas.

It is not surprising then that many residents in Ouro Preto and beyond, whose shoes have gotten muddy from the unpaved roads, support the use of *Senhor Asphalt*. Nevertheless, the same residents that support such material also fear that its visibility may harm the discussion of less visible aspects, such as water absorption and drainage systems. This is a shared concern, especially because of the heavy rain that falls in Ouro Preto and the occurrences of landslides. Asphalt, however, is not necessarily responsible for unstable terrain and can actually prevent some land instability. This demonstrates that the list of ambiguities in regard to the perception of roads is indeed far-reaching. While the prefecture considered asphalt an aspect of city preservation and social bonding, the Council, prosecutors, and geologists saw the need for greater discussion. In the end, for the local prosecutors who intervened in the project by stopping the use of asphalt in some city areas, it was chiefly the non-observance of the process in decision-making that formed the rationale for their decision.

The discussion of road material demonstrated that the maps and meanings directly related to cultural heritage were uncertain as instruments for making decisions regarding heritage sites. In contrast to the case of the residents of Delhi's slums, in Ouro Preto, residents have not articulated a self-perception of an eyesore. In fact, many residents believe it is inconvenient to have an aesthetic imperative that mainly benefits 'those coming from elsewhere' or a local elite. The ambience was not a key authority for decision. Public participation and an engagement with interdisciplinary studies gained traction as a way forward to decide and implement preservation. However, in the Council, where such discussions have space, participants were unsure of their role.

I conclude that while ambivalences in the work of cultural heritage prompted the creation of municipal councils, the opportunity to participate is not always clear. Secondly, more participants may not mean varied perceptions. This is especially so if the groups do not represent the varied socio-economic realities of the place or if areas of knowledge involved are not broadly represented. The Council in Ouro Preto has a limited range of participants as discussed in chapter 4. Finally, in the case of the use of asphalt, the local controversy certainly discouraged members from assuming a key role as a Council member lost an employment position after interfering with that public policy. Voicing concerns, beyond a representative duty, can become a personal burden, a topic I discuss in greater depth in the next chapter.

Chapter 6

Preservation or Mummification?

Previous analyses in this book have shown that the preservation of Ouro Preto did not lead to shared social meanings and uses of cultural heritage. Political participation in forums such as the Council promises a solution, but as we have seen in the case of modifying streets, the Council is not always invited to share a view. This chapter however examines what happens when the Council indeed is invited in the process of preservation.[1] Grounding cultural heritage in grassroots meetings, rather than in state-centred intellectual solutions, could lead to the shaping of ideas of city preservation according to local demands and hence to the abandonment of the ideal of imposing a meaning on the city (Ellin 1996: 209). In this case, perhaps preservation could connect with varied and conflicting social arrangements (Canclini 2012: 120). This was the expectation in negotiations in Miguel Burnier, one of Ouro Preto's districts.

Miguel Burnier has been falling into a state of decay in recent years. After a population peak in the 1960s (see graph 6.1), the district has lost most of its inhabitants since the middle of the 1990s, when the latest company to operate in the district departed. Those left live in inhospitable conditions, sharing the local streets and landscape with heavy machinery from a mining company that recently arrived. However, the district still faces a shortage of jobs, and the company that settled there is not as labour-intensive as those in the past, and public service delivery is no longer connected with the arrival of industries. However, the same mining company that endangers living conditions also supports the preservation of cultural heritage. Sites and documents have been restored or examined, using preservation as an offset to obtain mining permits.

The relationship between mining and heritage in Ouro Preto (and Minas Gerais in general) is, most of the time, one of reciprocity: previous mining funded the construction of expensive buildings that are now preserved. The maintenance of such structures is expensive, and currently, mining companies operating next to rural districts often negotiate industrial permits by offering the upkeep of urban heritage as compensation.

This chapter will offer an example of a negotiation involving environmental license for mining activities and the preservation of cultural heritage as compensation. The cruelty in this process is that, when history, education, and culture are the compensation for environmental damage, the damage is often here and now but the gain is future-oriented. Additionally, benefits occur far away from damaged places and do not target those whose lives are affected. Complaining about such compensations can however be stigmatising, because of the general appeal of education, history, and art as positive.

Negotiations took place in 2013, when the company, residents, and Council members held several meetings to discuss a future mining expansion. Council meetings discussed preserving the past, solving present infrastructure issues, and allowing for future mining expansion. However, such time appreciations (past, present, and future) impacted participants differently. Mining businesses and the Council, when investing in the preservation of cultural heritage, moved the pendulum 'of nostalgia and longing' (Harms 2011: 91), thus weakening the focus on present problems caused by mining exploration: depopulation, unemployment, pollution, and poor infrastructure. Looking at meetings, I discuss the politics of time negotiations (remembering, imagining, and waiting) and its material consequences for different parties attending Council meetings.

I draw on previous anthropological research that has already discussed the social limits of imagining another time in the face of present decay (Souza 2010). The options for deprived groups have been argued to be 'material and proximate' (Appadurai 2013: 188), because poverty affects the ability to aspire (Dalton, Ghosal and Mani 2014). To put it simply, poverty is time-consuming in commuting, caring, and earning routines. However, other authors have highlighted the use of a future time to transform a distressing present (Nielsen 2014; Baxstrom 2013). In this case, 'the present becomes the effect of the future rather than vice-versa' (Nielsen 2014: 166). Here, I ask whether imagining a different future for Miguel Burnier – through preserved architecture and upcoming urban amenities – may mitigate a troublesome present, characterised by depopulation, a deficit in infrastructure, and industrial pollution. I examine the role of grassroots meetings in expanding and compromising time horizons in this context.

In Miguel Burnier or elsewhere, a 'veneration of memorials or ruins implies a distancing that is usually alien to those who experience those sites as part of their daily lives' (Gordillo 2009: 44). Ordinary residents in Miguel Burnier, however, do praise the past. To them, the industries that operated in the district represent a moment of employment and infrastructure delivery.

Thus remembering the past through materials is connected to remembering a time of jobs related to industries and the infrastructure that came with it. The preservation of monuments alone contrasts with residents' notions of improvements: job creation and service delivery. Moreover, delayed answers for depopulation and noise, water, and air pollution in the District lead to a growing drive amongst residents to leave the location and sell their houses to the company. This alternative could allow for the expansion of mining activities but does not synchronise with cultural investments and the need to maintain the urban nucleus that exists. Mining and residents' interests were mediated by the Council, which had its own interests in preserving buildings in the area.

Government employees, mining company staff, and the affected community have different levels of wealth and power (social networks, secure housing and job, and access to the legal system). Looking ethnographically at participatory meetings is then to look at how cultural heritage exists through public participation and/or for public participants. In what follows I describe Miguel Burnier, its pressing problems of depopulation and pollution, and examine how calculating costs in the process of participating in the present may compromise future outcomes. Miguel Burnier is also an invitation to imagine Ouro Preto's main district in the past: extracting minerals beneath while adding architectonic constructions above.

MIGUEL BURNIER

Miguel Burnier is one of the thirteen districts that compose the municipality of Ouro Preto. It is located 40 km away from Ouro Preto's main region, in the south of an area known as the Iron Quadrangle, one of the most important mineral provinces in the world (Penha 2012: 13) (see map I.1, in the introduction).

Located in a place renowned for its mineral deposits, the area has seen a number of different companies extracting iron ore for steel production since the early nineteenth century. In the beginning of the twentieth century, a train station was opened in the district, and later a road leading to Belo Horizonte crossed Miguel Burnier, thus altering its role from a hub for extractive industries to one of people and product transportation, although mining remained the main economic activity (Penha 2012: 13). The companies that occupied the area challenged the rural to city migration, and residents from Miguel Burnier (mainly workers in local industries) did not move to Belo Horizonte or downtown Ouro Preto. Instead, when companies flourished, the little village attracted new residents.

The companies mining in the village allowed for the growth of the local economy, providing services such as house construction and shops, and

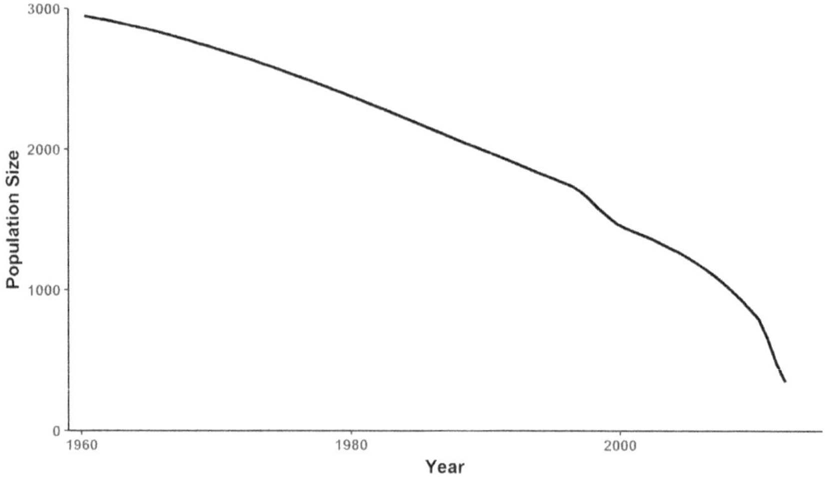

Graph 6.1. Population in Miguel Burnier, graph by the author. In 2013, residents estimated that no more than 380 people lived in the area. ***Sources*****: Batista da Costa 2011: 331; Prefeitura Municipal de Ouro Preto 2007: 27; Portal do Turismo 2014.**

building monumental churches. Miguel Burnier, being a one-company town, unsurprisingly had company-stores, and houses and churches built by the same company. The construction and opening of these various buildings reflect the vigour of the businesses in the area. However, the pattern was different in 2013, because a new mining company had started in the district, but rather than adding structures to the urban nucleus, the new company aimed at demolishing some of the existing ones and mainly hired workers from neighbouring towns rather than amongst the local community (mainly formed by unskilled remaining residents), thus creating a cauldron of frustration and complaints.

Between 1996 and 2004, there was no mining in the area. Train services had been discontinued. Depopulation and deterioration were the result. When a new company acquired the rights to exploit the area in 2004, it was difficult to imagine that this area had once been one of the most important transportation hubs in the region. Marco Antonio, a community leader in the region, active in the district despite not residing there, illustrated in a conversation with me that buildings were falling into ruin, while others, though not yet decaying, belied the role the district once had:

> *At the end of 2006, at the beginning of 2007, I was there in the district and witnessed a mother with her son removing a window from the train station to use it in their wood stove (see Image 6.1).*

Image 6.1. Miguel Burnier's train station. ***Source*****: Almeida Costa 2009.**

This decay moved Marco Antonio to study the area and engage in a project that resulted in the train station's restoration in 2012. That the train station was falling to pieces while a company had just started in the area did not correspond to the trajectory of the district, which had previously experienced progress when companies arrived. According to Marco Antonio, when the company started to work in the area in 2004, the expectations of residents peaked, and when it begun to explore in 2006,

> *I saw an opportunity, a partnership, I saw a big mining company. That means, it will bring progress to the district, employment . . . but it was the contrary. The company arrived really very aggressive . . . they arrived a bit inexperienced, concerned only with exploring. [And the company] continues indifferent to the community, there is no effective compensation. What happens are 'counter negotiations' (negociações de balcão) where a person goes there and asks for a bit of construction material to renovate the house and the company gives them the material. . . . Today the community is at that impasse, will the company remove everybody, reimburse everybody. . . . A lot of people want to leave because it is not easy to live in a place that does not have infrastructure, but a lot of people want to stay because they built their lives there. . . . But if there is infrastructure, a good quality of life, I am sure people would like to remain, but if you walk around, you will see the social reality in the community, the*

unfinished houses that a lot of people do not renovate because they are in that doubt . . . why spend money to then receive an incentive to leave.

(Marco Antonio, July 10, 2013)

Despite Marco Antonio's belief that if infrastructure investments follow, residents would stay and enjoy a better life, he was still very concerned. He explained his misgivings saying that his association mainly looks at cultural investments (music and dance festivals), and some residents criticised his work because the train station, for example, is now looking ageless, after its restoration in 2012, while the houses around remain rundown (Images 6.2a and 6.2b). The station and cultural festivals in Miguel Burnier then contrast with a landscape of deteriorated houses and relegated individuals.

In contrast to Marco Antonio, many residents did not envision a future for themselves in the area and doubted that the cultural investment would lead to higher self-esteem, civic pride, and better services in town, which was then struggling with dust, noise, and depopulation. Marco Antonio also had reservations as he worried about

creat[ing] an illusion for the people of Miguel Burnier while a delusion is created on the backstage, I mean . . . there might be a point when it will not be good to live there, there will be no treated water, the dust will be tremendous, the living conditions will be impossible . . . and I will hear 'everybody moved out and I stayed because I believed you'.

(Marco Antonio, July 10, 2013)

Image 6.2a. Miguel Burnier's train station restored. ***Source*****: Helbert Pereira 2013.**

Image 6.2b. Ruins of the local hotel near Miguel Burnier's train station, 2013. ***Source*****: Personal collection.**

I talked to Marco Antonio just after the topic emerged in the Council. The prefecture had to decide on the company's license to expand mining activities around the town. As part of the municipality's decision about the licence, the Municipal Council for Environmental Development (CODEMA) had to offer an assessment. This institution, however, tied its decision to the one by the Council for the Preservation of Cultural and Natural Patrimony, because the district has preserved buildings and because passing over responsibilities is a way to avoid conflicts (as discussed in chapter 4).[2] Thus, it was up to the Council to decide on the company's future steps in consultation with the community. As already mentioned, residents had diverse expectations and interests (to stay in a better area or to leave the district), and they were invited to voice their concerns. The Council had constructions to protect in the area (in this case, singular buildings and surrounding areas, not a large perimeter like in downtown Ouro Preto); however, the cultural focus was not a daily priority for residents, and the prospect of attracting tourists to visit protected sites in the near future was low (as I will explain in the next section). The second half of 2013 saw great residential, political, cultural, and economic interests playing out in Miguel Burnier, tying together the company, the Council, and the community, all with diversified and often competing interests.

RESIDENTS' DILEMMA

A community-company discussion (*audiência publica*)[3] about the expansion of local mining activities took place on July 12, 2013, in a classroom in Miguel Burnier's only school. Around 7:00 p.m., the classroom was filled with residents on chairs; these were mainly located in the middle of the room. Mixed with residents were members of the Council. The representatives of the prefecture (the vice-mayor among them) took up positions on the side of the room and remained together, while the mining company representatives were standing in front. This positioning in the room not only grouped parties separately but also made visible hierarchies of power.

The company began its presentation, talking about initiatives to improve the quality of life in the community. Representatives outlined the company's offers to the community: renovating the school, improving access to the church, setting a green belt to separate industrial activities from residential activities, creating a football field and renovating the sports centre, improving the facilities at the health centre, and providing some professional courses to train tailors, painters, carpenters, and manicurists. After the presentation of possible upcoming improvements, the vice-mayor said a few words and mentioned he was looking forward to a partnership to improve the community.

The optimistic presentation highlighted various controversies, which were promptly pointed out by the community, mainly represented by its leader, Paulinho: 'There were trees at the back of Teresa's house, they were felled, and you now talk about a green belt?' Additionally, Paulinho and others mentioned that the green belt could please the eye and even diminish dust problems, but it would not suffice to diminish noise. Another controversy was the fact that the community was diminishing in size and having a football field was a reminder of the challenge faced in finding enough adults to play. The improvement of the health centre was also discussed and connected to the lack of people – in this case, local staff. Similarly, the school needed improvements, such as a coat of paint on the walls, but problems ran deeper. For example, new computers had been installed, but there were not enough information technology teachers and the school lacked Internet connection. Regarding the professional courses, the company demanded a minimum number of about twenty people per class, which raised concerns. Also, to whom would the manicurists, painters, or house builders cater in a shrinking community? Lastly, a woman pointed out that though she would like to learn a profession and work, there was no nursery in which to leave her children.

The controversies showed that though some improvements could be made, they were at odds with the district's main problem: population decline. Depopulation became an even greater threat when the company released the results of a census, which amongst other questions asked if residents wanted to leave their homes. The questionnaire found that 64 per cent of residents wanted to leave Miguel Burnier, around 30 per cent wanted to remain, and the others did not know or did not want to respond. Releasing those numbers generated great bewilderment. Paulinho remarked that, when the company announced they would conduct a census, they had declared that if 55 per cent of respondents wanted to leave their houses, the company would try to buy their properties. The company, however, denied this; 'the census was only to get to know the population and their demands'. But Paulinho replied that if the questionnaire was created to get to know the population better, the company could also release other results to understand why people replied they wanted to leave:

> *For example, this was asked at my house: the surveyor asked my mum what bothered her about the company. Before she answered, the surveyor was already ticking nothing, 'right?' Then I said, let me explain to you mum, when the dirty water in the rainy season prevents you from washing the clothes that are mud coloured, the company causes this. When you go out in the middle of the trucks with dust, and mud, and noise, the company also causes those problems . . . if the company wants to release the results, let's release the whole questionnaire to see the reason why people would like to leave.*
>
> (Paulinho, July 12, 2013)

Another resident complemented what Paulinho said by explaining that asking if people would like to go to heaven was different than asking if people would like to die. To him the results were announced just as if people 'wanted to die' (they want to leave the area), when in fact they answered they wanted to go to heaven (they want to live in a better area). But in order 'to go to heaven, they have to die', that is, to live in a better area, they need to leave their houses, as most of them did not feel hopeful that a good life in the middle of mining activities was possible.

The questionnaire, as an instrument of speculation – whether residents would be willing to sell their houses – failed to assess present scarcities, which would explain residents' will. Conflicts about what makes a place worth living in and the ability of policies to mediate current demographic and infrastructure shortages reached a crescendo, and while people reaffirmed their interest in leaving, they made the reasoning behind this interest clear. However, the solution to their complaints offered by the company remained opaque, as improvements were offered, but did not target various inconveniences such as depopulation, heavy vehicle traffic, or issues revolving around air, noise, and water pollution. On the contrary, the company's expansion would potentially further increase such problems.

In addition, the release of the number of people willing to sell their properties affected residents' will to bargain for improvements. The company tried to diminish expectations that it would buy houses but did not deny the possibility of buying a few. It was legally impossible for the company to buy all residents out and destroy homes, as there are protected monuments in the area whose surroundings should be kept (Ribeiro 2007: 40). But some properties were already under negotiation, for example, houses close to a main road.

This context of uncertainty, where conflicting ideas of improvement were affected by the diminishing number of residents and the unpredictability of the impact of mining expansion, may be better understood when viewing the residents' situation in terms of a prisoners' dilemma. The remarkable feature of the prisoners' dilemma (a recurrent instrument in game theory, used to analyse the decision-making of individuals in situations where cooperation would yield the highest outcome for two players but is still avoided), 'is that both sides play their dominant strategy, thus maximiz[ing] their payoff, and yet the outcome is jointly worse than if both followed the strategy of minimising their payoff' (Dixit and Nalebuff 1991: 91). This way, it is possible to identify the conditions that have to be met in a conflict for both sides to give up their individual preferred solution to instead commit themselves to a common agreement with an inferior outcome individually but a better one collectively (ibid.: 91).

Representing the situation for residents in Miguel Burnier through the prisoners' dilemma (see Table 6.1), assuming that residents do not know their neighbours' decisions, we can imagine that: A and B are residents of Miguel Burnier, part of the 64 per cent who would prefer to leave the area; when A or B follow their goal of selling their properties, their risk is to be unable to sell as the company cannot legally buy the district out and spark a mass removal (and it may not be interested, scenario 4). Pursuing one's individual interest could thus lead to missing out chances to negotiate local improvements. The best development would be when residents do not pursue their own best individual interests but rather think collectively of better ways to stay in the area (scenario 1). However, residents are scared of fighting for improvements while their neighbours may be successful in leaving the area (scenario 2 and

Table 6.1: Prisoners' dilemma

	B stays	*B leaves*
A stays	They negotiate improvement (scenario 1)	A stays in an emptier city (scenario 2)
A leaves	B stays in an emptier city (scenario 3)	A and B may both try to sell the house at the same time, but they harm each other's chances as the company may buy some but not all houses, and they miss the opportunity to negotiate improvements to stay (scenario 4)

3), and the amenities (if they come) would be useless in an emptier town; as a result, it is hard to act collectively (scenario 1) and they may end up in the worst scenario (4).

The community leader is a great example of the dilemma faced by the community. Being part of those residents who would like to leave the district, Paulinho is nevertheless negotiating improvements. He explained his torment during the negotiations to me, as he is uncertain about persuading his neighbours to stay while he personally might not and would like to leave (which would make him a traitor). He is equally uncertain about staying and fighting for improvements, as his neighbours may be the ones leaving. Finally, improvements may be delayed or never come (or be insufficient), and he and his fellow residents may feel foolish about false hopes and lost opportunities if they all stay.

The prisoners' dilemma helps in understanding the importance of the Council. One of the solutions for the prisoners' dilemma is 'the emergence of trust' (Dixit and Nalebuff 1991: 102). For example, when residents do not see a future for the district, why would they not try to move out? However, when envisioning a hope (that amenities can be negotiated according to the residents' claim and that improvements will follow), then it might make more sense to stay and negotiate developments. The prefecture could take the role of abridging horizons in negotiations, as the democratic representative of the people; however, the company pays high taxes to the prefecture and, as happens in other development projects in Brazil, residents perceive company and government to be on the same side (Koster and Nuijten 2012: 182). The Council is then the instrument that could increase the likelihood that the company's promises would both meet residents' expectations and take concrete form. The Council carries with it the credential of representing civil society, an endorsed potential as discussed in the previous chapter. The Council could also remedy power asymmetries between the company and residents. However, the Council centres efforts on cultural heritage. Investments in cultural heritage (the restoration of buildings and archival investment in the district) had already been offered by the company to the district to obtain mining licenses in the recent past, and these did not satisfy the community, good reasons for residents' mistrust on a Council dealing with patrimony. But the Council still had the opportunity to balance power inequality in discussions, and moving back to the meeting may help to understand how residents were sceptical about negotiations up to that point.

Many residents (mainly elderly, children, unemployed, and unskilled adults) lacked the knowledge about what was at stake. For example, expanding the mining business was not explained in terms of how many years this activity would last, nor in terms of financial gain for the company (or the municipality in tax collection). This prevented residents from understanding the scope of the negotiations, which would have allowed them to maximise their own outcome. The communication between the company and residents, which had never been praiseworthy, gained a new tool that night, when members of the company announced a call centre, a toll-free number that residents could use to place their complaints and would receive a reply within a few days. Such a scheme was not acclaimed, as it seemed a one-way channel that would tell the company what the main complaints were but would deprive the community leadership from knowing which problems were affecting residents as a whole and if those had been solved, when and how. For example, house removal negotiations could happen behind other residents' backs. In sum, residents faced incomplete information and self-detrimental offers. Nevertheless, during the public hearing, a background noise could be heard throughout, and that was whispers saying: 'it is the time, your chance to negotiate, voice your demands, what do you want?' In other words, the company's desire to expand the business was a good moment for residents to place their demands. The idea of 'this is the time' but the discouragement brought by uncertainties was visible in residents' faces throughout the negotiation.

It did not take long until I heard some people saying: 'Andreza, you should make a point, bargain, you are the only one free here'. Free in that context meant I was not in a fragile situation: such as having a job position that could be threatened by demonstrating an opposing viewpoint to the company (and prefecture). Equally, I would not benefit from the negotiations. However, I was perceived within pre-existing networks, which included Council friends and some members of the community that had opened their views to me. As a researcher my actions had consequences for both my ability to continue working there, and, more importantly, could affect those associated to me. I did ask for more information, especially about the questionnaire, but above of all, this negotiation was a moment where I experienced the intimidation my informants had already described to me (De Souza Santos 2018).

HERE IS THE DEAL: SELF-ESTEEM AND QUALITY OF LIFE

Nearly a month later, a Council meeting followed up on what was discussed at the School in Miguel Burnier. Members of the Council who were unable to attend the meeting learned about the mining expansion and the community's struggle with noise and dust, amongst other industry-related problems. While some members in the Council restated their opinion that it was unacceptable to have to live in a place where one cannot sleep due to truck traffic, to others, the community-company relationship was already addressed through a list of amenities under negotiation between the prefecture and the company (the list the community contested). For them, the Council should stick to observing if expanding activities would affect the main buildings in the village, and members agreed to focus on a narrower mandate.

Other meetings followed on the case of Miguel Burnier, one of them taking place in September had an unusual start as it opened with a last-minute delivery of a correspondence from the local prosecutor's office.[4] This correspondence, read in the meeting, recommended that all Council members should delay a decision on the mining expansion, given that the company's activities would take place very close to the centre of the village and could 'suffocate' the community living there even more. The prosecutor felt that it would be premature to decide at that moment and advised waiting until the company had released its assessment of the cultural and human risks of their expansion and presented a master plan for the area.

The intervention that morning generated mixed feelings amongst those in the meeting. While the representatives of the company expected to finally know the answer about the expansion and were frustrated, for some Council members the recommendation was either unneeded, as they did not feel ready to decide and would discuss longer anyways, or disturbing, as it challenged the autonomy of their sphere of decision. Local prosecutors, however, have a broad legal mandate that includes cultural heritage and environmental conservation, and if the intervention in the Council was surprising at that point, in others, such as in the case of asphalt, the prosecutors' intervention was requested.

In the midst of comments, complaints, and support regarding the recommendation, the company hurried to say that the amenities for the community were a priority and immediately described renovating the sports court, the churches, and the school; the constructing of a new football field; improving health provisions; setting the green belt, and providing courses (sewing, masonry, plumbing, electrical, carpentry, painting). The description of the amenities seemed well established, and a timeframe in which the development was to be executed was also provided with some of them. But some Council members enquired about other amenities also demanded by the community and not considered. 'Should the company provide all public services for the community?' enquired a company representative. Although the controversy about the list of amenities and who should deliver public services in the area gained impulse, another letter, even more controversial, interrupted it.

The content of this other letter, addressing the company, was shared with participants, but it differed from the previous recommendation. This time, the chief administrator for the Secretariat of Culture and Patrimony stated his support to mining expansion.[5] He was however, the direct supervisor of some Council members who were then intimidated to cast their vote that could be opposing to a revealed view of their boss.

That letter was also in contradiction with the assessment by the architect in charge of that project in the Secretariat of Culture and Patrimony. The architect had concluded that the mining expansion was concerning, especially because one of the three mines, if expanded, would reach the edges of the village.[6] That professional (working in the Secretariat and a member in the Council) had initially opposed to the expansion of that mine, which meant the company would need to redesign the proposed expansion. It was clear that, despite technical and Council assessments, other parties were influencing the meeting, and the different forces contradicted each other. These letters, more than a simple interference, meant decisions were far-reaching and would be observed in legal, political, social, and economic spheres.

Being pushed in a decision-making process that would affect all parties, along with having limited information about the project itself, was a shared concern amongst Council participants. Equally challenging was the number of people living in the district and/or the number willing to live there because of the area's changeability. Intimidation and lack of information explains the Council's strategy: delaying decisions and vagueness in offering recommendations, improving the district's quality of life, and recovering the self-esteem of its residents. However open, those terms were repeated by both the Council members and the company.

Some political programmes intended to increase self-esteem of specific groups have been discussed in anthropological literature that focuses on Brazil (Gledhill 2013), because the link between Brazilian public policies and self-esteem is not new. In the case of Ouro Preto (and other cities with cultural appeal, such as Salvador or Olinda), the connection between self-esteem and cultural heritage is strongly fostered in order to create a sense of identity and belonging, as discussed in this book. Standards of culture are, however, top-down. The population in Ouro Preto, for example, did not decide on the themes of museums or local festivities or the sites to be preserved but rather were invited to participate in cultural projects to feel 'integrated' and improve the quality of their lives. The problem with the combination of such normative standards of self-esteem and culture with participative meetings, as Gledhill (2013: 21) states, is that 'rituals of participation have more power than top-down measures alone to create a sense of grassroots "ownership" of policies'. Thus, self-esteem may remain connected to normative cultural standards, and far removed from what participants perceive as necessary for a better life, yet self-esteem may be an accepted result of grassroots meetings.

In Miguel Burnier, the list of improvements in the area, which grew in terms of cultural activities (art projects in the community) to increase residents' quality of life and self-esteem, is at odds with the reality of dust, noise, and depopulation, as Marco Antonio, who advocates for cultural projects as a way to preserve the community, already explained when describing his apprehension. However, along with the company and Council representatives, residents would use the terms 'quality of life' or 'self-esteem' when discussing the area, too.

The use of the terms 'self-esteem' and 'quality of life' by residents to negotiate improvements for the community made it seem at first as if the proposed cultural standards for a better life in Miguel Burnier had gained ground locally. However, to residents, 'quality of life' and 'self-esteem' were often associated with infrastructure and not solely cultural heritage. Hence, the ways participants learn to navigate in the realm of argument and debate and how they may absorb top-down living standards need further examination. When the company listed cultural activities to be implemented, restoring historical documents in Miguel Burnier, introducing 'Community plus Art' (*Comunidade mais Arte*) that would bring art activities to Miguel Burnier, and sponsoring the cultural festival held in the restored train station, they faced a complaint by Paulinho.

As a local community leader he reacted to the list of 'social investments' by saying that more than R$1 million (about £230,000) were spent restoring the train station to improve the 'quality of life' for residents, but the station, though furnished and equipped with books, was closed due to a lack of staff. A Council member added that fragmented actions, such as restoring a train station, making some cultural festivals, or even creating a health centre would lead to nothing because the city was a place to live. One needed places to shop and to meet people; a health system; a sewage system; and ways to move in, out, and around the city. Otherwise, fragmented actions, important as they might be, would not restore the city, she stated. Another Council member pointed out that the investments were principally focussed on the cultural aspects of the city, which was paradoxical, given the data presented by the company that suggested most residents would prefer to leave the area. Would they now stay despite the unfriendly conditions brought by the mining activities for the sake of their pride in being part of that cultural heritage? Or in her words, 'it is very easy to say: look how beautiful your church is, but around the church there is dust and noise and a series of social problems'. The paradox for that Council member was not the cultural and pedagogic actions to change the existing negative outlook but having those 'social investments' while living conditions remained practically the same or chanced to becoming worse if the expansion was approved.

Another meeting finished without concrete ideas of how standards of life quality and self-esteem – in the minds of the company's participants strongly related to cultural projects – could meet residents' daily concern about unemployment, depopulation, and the noise and dust in the area. However, the Council still had a technical visit to make, a one-day trip to Miguel Burnier by a commission formed by three members from different backgrounds:

architecture, community representation, and environmental work. The visit aimed at understanding the location of the mines beyond maps provided by the company. With maps Council members could only see coloured areas, dots, and lines, thus having to imagine the mines, churches, houses, roads, dust, noise, and road traffic. For that reason, questions like: 'Where is the district? Where is the mine? Is that a hill? Will the hill change? Will the climate be affected? Will the direction of the winds change?' were common in Council meetings. Dots and lines on paper representing mines, churches, houses, roads, would however be visited in person and the dust, noise, and road traffic experienced in real life. The visit took place on October 4, 2013, and I accompanied the group.

VISITING THE DISTRICT

Arriving in Miguel Burnier, or at the Mine of Miguel Burnier – as announced by the welcoming billboard when reaching the town – a member of the company greeted us at a security gate. 'Should a gate be installed right at the district's entrance?' 'Can you decide who enters and who leaves the area?', asked the commission member. The controversies about the road, its ownership, and the right to request our identifications at the entrance generated tension right from the start. We had to fill out a registry form, which included our names, documentation, and work affiliation. Only then could we enter the district.

We finally arrived at the centre of Miguel Burnier. Standing out from a landscape of ruins was the train station, a newly restored building looking ageless in the middle of old houses in the city centre. Its restoration in an environment of decay, but also its silence without passengers or trains (Images 6.3a and 6.3b),[7] and its cultural centre that remained closed due to a lack of staff, added to the unreal atmosphere.

Paulinho explained that, to many residents, the restoration of the train station was controversial. Rather than bringing self-esteem, it reminded residents that only some buildings were praiseworthy, granting a sense of worthiness they did not feel in their own lives. He then guided me through the district, showed me some houses, and introduced me to their owners and their stories. It was a cityscape of a few houses and empty streets, some of them recently covered with a coat of painting as a part of art projects (Image 6.4).

Time passed quickly and soon it was lunchtime. We had nearly forgotten the identification event at our arrival when, during lunch, the commission members and I had to identify ourselves to eat at the company's restaurant, the only one in town. An atmosphere of tension pervaded our lunch break, as being controlled and checked in order to then be allowed inside did not feel hospitable, and we became aware of the vigilance in Miguel Burnier. When I left the restaurant to continue my conversation with Paulinho, he also warned me about my camera and how I should be discreet when taking photos.

That community leader explained his agony as we sat down at one of the empty desks in the library (inside the train station). The current negotiation offered scraps to the community, meanwhile the company had already bought eleven houses, and most of the families living in them moved to other cities. Those houses were located near a road used for mining traffic and the safety of the residents had justified the purchase. However, he stated that the company created the risk (the heavy trucks on that road), and safety

Image 6.3a. Children playing on the railway track lacking trains, 2013. *Source*: Personal collection.

Image 6.3b. Children and dogs walking on the railway track. *Source*: Helbert Pereira, 2013.

Image 6.4. Rundown houses, some with a new coat of paint on the wall, 2013. *Source*: Personal collection.

meant removing the people, rather than removing the cause of the danger. In addition, the departure of a few families in a location of only 380 residents brought great uncertainty.

Paulinho explained the local situation by moving back to the past when a previous company occupied the area, which at the time had 1,600 voters (this number excludes those residents fifteen years old and younger who are not eligible to vote). When that company left in 1996, various families left the area too, because they were dependent on the company. Often people's rents along with their grocery, electricity, or pharmacy bills were deducted from their salaries, as the company owned all services in the district. When the company left, there was a community exodus, and even suicides.

The conversation with Paulinho made clear the sense of loss of residents when businesses departed. I wondered if reports like his could clarify residents' expectations of a better life as related to work and the social and economic structure around it, rather than the standard of life quality as cultural heritage. Moreover, although the company is not at the centre of the district's life as it once was and so inhabitants appear not to rely on it as much as they once did, it remains difficult for the inhabitants to argue aggressively with the company for improvements. The institution still provides work for a few residents and holds out the promise of work for a few others. As a result, although the company's offers do not meet the expectations of residents, they have little choice but to take what is offered. Paulinho reported his sense of reservation during the negotiations:

> *They make the community fight and the community fights against itself. Some people want to leave, while others would rather stay. So they give us the rope and with that we hang ourselves. Some do not want to fight because their kids work for the company, some people want to leave the area, some people want to stay and improve the area, the community association works for whose interest?*
> (Paulinho, October 4, 2013)

At this point in the conversation, the rest of the commission, who had been in other parts of the district, joined us, and one mentioned that it was legally impossible to buy all of the residents out, as there were protected monuments in the area whose surroundings should be kept. However, he mentioned the company could let the district come to an end by itself, meaning that residents could leave of their own accord but would not be able to sell their houses to the company as a group.

The statement that the current population could leave of their own accord reminded me of what some of my interview partners told me about downtown Ouro Preto, when the capital was transferred to Belo Horizonte. Residents moved out. There was no sort of financial compensation. However, the emptiness of the city allowed for Ouro Preto's future as a heritage site, and a number of my interviewees said the city would have never been made a cultural heritage site had it remained a capital, growing and changing as capitals do. I wondered if the emptiness of Miguel Burnier could allow for a future made of past, in other words, turning the place into a larger heritage site, as suggested by investments in the restoration of some buildings and documents.

However, despite the correlation I could make with Ouro Preto's downtown area, tourists did not seem interested in Miguel Burnier. To access the district, one had to enter the 'mine of Miguel Burnier', passing through areas of heavy machinery, controlled access, and erosion. Its touristic appeal was minimal. Nevertheless, investments in material and immaterial cultural activities gained ground in that district. I could only wonder why anyone would think it was a good idea to invest in cultural heritage in the area, and I made Paulinho's concern my own. How could a restored train station without a train or passengers be deemed a way to increase people's self-esteem? I found no answer on that tiresome daytrip. However, at the end of the journey and back in downtown Ouro Preto, the commission was both concerned with depopulation and at the same time impressed by the churches and other buildings from the past.

In reflecting on the diverse perspectives concerning Miguel Burnier, or Ouro Preto in general, looking at decay and seeing potential for cultural heritage, tourism, and repopulation is above all the privilege of those who do not live in the area. For ordinary residents, to praise the past may give a sense of worth to buildings and achievements of former inhabitants to the detriment of current ones (Gordillo 2013: 334; Heathcott 2013; Reed 2002: 138). Even if the future could bring a better prospect with renovated buildings, not everyone profits from waiting. If it is true that real estate companies commonly invest in decayed locations such as Miguel Burnier for profit at a future time (Harms 2013), for current residents who are poor, waiting makes them even poorer (2013: 356), as they do not invest in their properties fearing relocation but try to sell their homes despite current low price. The material effects of time (Harms 2011: 93) is also explored in Souza's (2010: 52) work, when he discusses 'the future as a class privilege and not a universal resource' (my translation). When the author talks about the poor in Brazil, he mentions the 'eternised present' and how the poor lack the chance to plan for the future when busy with the everyday tormenting needs (ibid.: 51). Similarly, Appadurai (2013: 188) states that

> the poor, no less than any other group in society, do express horizons in choices made and choices voiced, often in terms of specific goods and outcomes, often material and proximate.

Perhaps it is true that preserving important buildings might grant the district a future. But for residents, the 'less immediate objects of aspiration' (Appadurai 2013: 188) – envisioning Miguel Burnier re-urbanised, perhaps touristic, or certainly culturally equipped – were of less concern. This was not a matter of a lack of the cognitive capacity to see beyond an immediate situation but a question of the residents' need to meet demands for surviving on an everyday basis (ibid.).

However, a body of anthropological literature exists that foregrounds the use of a future time to transform a troublesome present (Nielsen 2014; Baxstrom 2013). In a discussion about house building in the outskirts of Mozambique, Nielsen (2014: 166) contends that

> although prefigured as a failure at the end-point on a linear scale, the future asserts itself by opening up the present moment and establishes temporal differentiations without indicating a progressing trajectory. In a peculiar inversion of conventional linearity, the present becomes the effect of the future rather than vice-versa.

The future may organise the present by giving people a sense of meaningfulness. Meaning in this case is not necessarily related to obtaining success but to the value in trying even when failure is expected (Nielsen 2014: 166). Baxstrom (2013: 151), in his study of Kuala Lumpur, states that 'the creation and use of plans as a vehicle of action in the present remains an effective mode for, at least in part, domesticating this seemingly uncontrolled and uncontrollable present'. Also on house construction, Lea and Pholeros (2010) discuss houses built with pipes that do not connect with any form of sewage. Rather than being a plan for a future, when sewage service is provided, such pipes already offer an illusion of a house that looks 'right' (ibid.: 191).

By grappling with the perspectives presented before, we have some strands of theories to discuss in regard to the case of Miguel Burnier. We have theorists such as Souza (2010) and Appadurai (2013), who associate the ability to plan for the future with socio-economic conditions, and there are also theorists such as Baxstrom (2013) who look at planning, ineffective as a plan might be, as an instrument with which to control conflicts in the present. By combining these theories in relation to Miguel Burnier, I ask whether imagining Miguel Burnier's future or looking at its glorious past is possible not only for those at a distance from the district's dust and noise but also for residents, through participation in the Council. I will suggest an answer to this question by examining reactions to the Council's final decisions.

MAKING DECISIONS, NOT CONFLICTS

It was on December 3, 2013, when the Council finally had to reach a decision on the company's expansion. That morning they had two decisions to make: to decide about the demolition of the houses bought by the company (the houses close to a main road) and the expansion of the three mines. On demolishing houses, a Council member explained that the matter was brought to the Council because sometimes technical experts in the Prefecture did not feel confident about their assessment and wanted the opinion of the Council. This was however discussed as the need to pass on responsibilities, 'a poor reasoning', said another Council member. Defending the importance of the matter, however, a third Council member stated that 'the company bought eleven houses because of the danger imposed to the residents by the heavy vehicles traveling near those houses, instead, it could have offered to shift the traffic away from the families'. Finally, the community representative, supported by another member, pointed out that the community faced a situation of uncertainty: only a few families live in the area, to negotiate house removal with eleven families, thus threatened the existence of all others. The company pushed the legal side of the matter, pointing out that for them the Council was not in a position to approve or deny the demolition of the houses, because the locality was outside the zone of preservation interest. This statement was supported by most Council members. In the end, the Council did not vote on the demolition of the houses but instead on whether it was up to them to decide on the matter. The result was that the Council should not resolve the demolition issue. That decision, despite the previous discussion, had one abstention while all others agreed, and the decision was sent back to the technician in the prefecture.

The agreement, when compared with the discussion about asphalt that had taken place not long before, shows how discretionary assessments revolving around the preservation perimeter and cultural values are. When discussing the use of asphalt, preservation zones lost their relevance, and the discussion about urban changes should have included the Council. In this case, the Council was invited into a discussion outside a preserved perimeter but opted to not offer a position. This point further emphasises that concepts, maps, and perimeters are far from objective or restrictive measures and that Council members have the power and the burden of interpretation.

The unwillingness of the Council to decide on the demolition of the houses and to debate the controversial list of 'improvements' was also connected with members' perception of themselves as being known in the community and possibly labelled a nuisance for the company in its plans for expansion. In final meetings, for example, Council members assumed an apologetic position and postponed decisions. Through personal involvement with the long-running negotiation, Council members accumulated knowledge about the community and its actions, along with awareness of economic and political disputes and interests. This explains why, just as technical experts had hesitated deciding on the demolition of houses and sent the matter to the Council, Council members, despite internal disagreements, forwarded the decision on the house demolition promptly back to technical experts and without their appraisal on the matter.

The company, on the other hand, sent different representatives each time. It was difficult to get to know each representative by name, as they took shifts and always spoke as the company. Speaking as a group or 'as though one's personality were a passive recipient of the bureaucratic functioning' (Sennett 1976: 331), or speaking as a person, had consequences for participants. The company was always addressed as a company (*a empresa*) rather than by the names of the functionaries present, which is the reason I call them 'the company' throughout this chapter. In fact, it was even difficult to remember the faces, names, and functions of each person as they changed frequently. In contrast, towards the end of a semester of meetings, Council members were viewed as individuals (as were members of the community).

There was no possibility, however, to abstain from the mines' expansion decision, and on that issue, the discussion started with two ground-based reports. The first report, shared with Council members, was the result of a technical visit by a sociologist and a historian to the district on September 12, 2013, the result of a request by the local Prosecutor's office. The document described the vulnerability of the community in their relationship with the company by mentioning dust, noise, cracks in house walls, and house removal connected to heavy vehicles on local roads. The study also mentioned a diminished accessibility to some city sites, such as the cemetery. Problems with the quality of the water and communication with the company were also discussed, as well as the uncertainty of the near future of the town, exemplified by the residents' reticence to renovate or make improvements to their houses given their uncertainty about remaining in the area.[8]

The second assessment was the report by the commission formed by three Council members from different areas (architecture, environment, community engagement). The text listed changes in the local topography, deforestation, the ruin of some buildings, the emptiness of some areas, the lack of public services, the consequences of heavy vehicles using the area (noise and dust), and the inappropriate use of public spaces by the company, such as entrance control on the main road giving access to the district. The report also stated a lack of precise information about the planned expansion of the mines. It pointed out the eminent danger of expanding one of them to within only about 500 metres from some residences, an act which could amplify existing noise and dust problems, especially given the direction of the wind in the location as it blows from the mine to the village.[9]

The two reports mainly confirmed on paper what residents had previously exclaimed. However, it was easier for Council members to vote after reading the ground-based summaries, because written reports, above all, made members' decision less personal. All Council members approved the conclusion by the Commission that the mine closer to the urban nucleus should not be expanded and the company did not contest this decision (at least not at that meeting). The meeting finished with joy and a sense of achievement, though discussions on how to improve the quality of life in the community carried on. Council suggestions encompassed making an open contest inviting multidisciplinary groups to offer ideas on how to best revitalise the urban centre of Miguel Burnier.

After that meeting, Miguel Burnier's cityscape still included only a few houses (even fewer, as the Council did not intervene in upcoming demolitions), few residents, a contested list for urban improvement in development, and some protected monuments. Still hovering in the background was the fact that the dust and noise could possibly worsen, given that the mines were to expand (though not as extensively as the company had hoped). These points show that, as much as 'life quality' was valued in Council meetings and in the production of reports, the current living conditions in Miguel Burnier were not fully appreciated and contemplated, as demonstrated in a follow-up meeting that took place in December 2013.

THE AFTERMATH

The list of improvements was communicated to residents in December 2013, together with the Council's decision to approve, with reservation, the expansion of the mines. That follow-up on the Council meetings about Miguel Burnier happened once again in Miguel Burnier's only school. On that day, Paulinho resigned from the community association and organised a social event for residents, some members of the prefecture, and the company. At the event, he announced results of his mandate (mainly some festivities and renewal in key constructions almost invariably supported by the company) and mentioned the compromise reached regarding the company's expansion. Though this was intended to be a cheerful moment, it did not take long before a resident interrupted the celebration to complain about the dirty water around her house. 'I am tired of drinking dirty water', she said. The woman did not get a reply then, and soon we all went for dinner. But while eating at the very same school I visited months before, I was struggling to sense the idea of process and outcomes between the company, the Council, and the community. There certainly was a sense of a job done, Paulinho had completed his mandate, and another leader would start. However, as the woman reminded everyone, the water was still dirty.

Taking into account previous analyses about the ability of a plan, at least minimally, to mediate the present, I am unable to conclude that this was the case in Miguel Burnier. There is little indication to suggest that a list of upcoming 'improvements' created a sense of hope, when the list itself was hardly convincing in terms of its effects for the community facing depopulation. The idea of a future for the town was based on cultural heritage, which for residents did not offer substantial changes in the face of dirty water, noise, and unemployment. Yet, there was a sense of an end, which perhaps was not the end of the district's problems but the end of an intimidating negotiation.

The Council as well as residents were absorbed in the negotiation. My hypothesis, that the Council could remedy power imbalances between a large mining company and a few residents who lacked everything from education to sports opportunities, was not confirmed. Members in the Council worked directly or indirectly for the company or the municipality. Residents, equally, though jeopardised by the results of mining activity, saw in the company possibilities for employment or for small improvements to local buildings and social needs. Residents' (competing) interests featured more in the process than in the outcomes of negotiations, which did not offer flexible solutions for a community with diversified and pressing concerns. In the final meeting, some Council members debated possible improvements for the area that could possibly allow for multiple uses of the city and the maintenance of buildings, by imagining a broad re-urbanisation scheme. The company was allowed to proceed with its expansion (with limitations), but residents were left exactly where they had been at the start of negotiations. To include residents in the work of cultural heritage is not only to include them in the room but also effectively in discussions about the past and future of their place, as well as to open such time horizons by offering first-hand solutions to present concerns. Conceiving one's past and imagining one's own future requires first lessening political constrains. In an environment of socio-economic and political pressure, what I observed in Miguel Burnier was not a social construction of its past and future but the use of grassroots meetings as (a fragile) procedure in local politics.

CONCLUSION

In the case of Miguel Burnier, multi-layered participation was more visible as a procedure than as an outcome. In other words, decisions did not benefit participants, and participants were not necessarily favoured in the process of contributing. The Council's decision assisted the urban nucleus and its monuments disproportionally in relation to grassroots' concerns. To put it differently, mining activities would not advance in the main urbanised area and buildings would be kept, but there was no guarantee that residents would benefit in the short or long term, given the possibility of the continuing or worsening conditions already described as problems. Hence, I provocatively call this the 'mummification' of Miguel Burnier, bearing in mind that the historic urban nucleus offered limited advantages to residents in the present but shall be conserved for the future.

The decision in Miguel Burnier reinforces the mismatch between the value assigned to buildings and the value perceived by people. The train station in the district offers a good opportunity to discuss contradictions involving cultural heritage: restored to enhance self-esteem and attachment to the district amongst residents, it had the opposite effect. To residents, the station represented in material form the fact that some buildings were valued more than them, and this visually reinforced the inequalities they experienced.

Mining and cultural heritage have been connected in Ouro Preto, but the compensation of mining with heritage needs to be discussed through different lenses, and I have offered some. The 'two-timing rhetoric' (Harms 2011: 119) of 'preserving the past for future generations', seen in heritage discussions, may undermine pressing problems caused by mining activities in the present. Residents in Miguel Burnier were unable to capitalise on real estate gains that heritage might bring in the future. In addition, there was little hope that buildings preserved could have local uses and that current residents will be given a future (and past) they feel part of. The future (and past) that residents imagine is one related to employment and offer of public services, not cultural heritage offers. Residents were thus not necessarily trapped in the present in ways of imagination (Souza 2010) but unable to have their dreams of past and future represented in negotiations. A future-oriented development policy thus failed to potentially bring a better quality of life and better self-esteem by organizing a troublesome present (Nielsen 2011, 2014; Baxstrom 2013). In the absence of infrastructure works to ameliorate the damage caused by mining and with imposed views of past and future that had little to do with residents' visions, some inhabitants preferred to sell houses at a cheap price in the present.

Involving local communities in the discussion of defining what would be a proportional compensation for mining activities was, in this case, no guarantee that those involved were able to truly participate and that their views were taken into consideration. Even those who were not living in the area and as such were not affected by extreme internal conditions, such as Council members, failed to stick out their neck for the community during negotiations, as they saw a threat to their employment situation. What I observed in Miguel Burnier was thus not a social construction of its past, present, and future, nor the empowerment of residents. Grassroots meetings, a necessary step to achieve mining permits, on the one hand offered space for residents to publicly voice local needs, and on the other hand, restricted their ability to do so in the face of financial dependency and lack of complete information. Participation could not solve residents' socio-economic problems efficiently, for those same problems affected their (and Council members') ability to voice concerns and negotiate adequate compensations.

What is comprehensive participation remains unclear in Ouro Preto. Delaying decisions and passing on responsibility, rather than 'outright confrontation', were weapons used in the face of clear hierarchical power (Scott 1985: xvi). When delaying decisions, however, the disparate impact of negotiations between parties becomes clear. For residents, while they wait the population shrinks continuously and their houses lose market value. The community cannot afford delays.

So what is the place of cultural heritage in cities such as Miguel Burnier? Considering the work of preservation entails comprehensive participation (Brumann 2009), and that multiple perspectives are not yet secured by creating spheres for popular discussion, cultural heritage works piecemeal and cannot for that reason be disregarded as a failure. Cultural heritage could indeed be an enduring option in cities that are otherwise faced with contested industrial activities. Yet when cultural heritage is a compensation for the same contested industries; when participation is an instrument of limited discussions, and when the images of the past or future remains restricted; then city preservation shapes social segregation in mortar and stone. Heritage in this case recounts an 'energy' of endured socio-economic oppression.

Conclusion

Final Considerations

The year 2013 was a turning point in Brazil. After a decade of economic growth, a recession started to show its devastating face, bringing lasting turmoil to Brazil's political and economic systems. When economics disappoint, democratic governance can be an instrument with which to endow states with legitimacy (Rodrik 2006: 985). The result is, however, a paradox. In Brazil, political participation gained strength at the end of the 1980s, inheriting a system of inequalities where not all citizens had enough education, information about government decisions, or economic independence to take advantage of new mechanisms of governance. Citizens were thus not always 'effective', that is, able to voice priorities or make their demands be heard (Kingstone 2018: 141; Bertorelli et al. 2017: 49). Participation cannot be a value on itself. Which mechanism should then precede participation to reflect participants in the outcomes and not only in the process? This ethnography of Ouro Preto is an attempt to answer this question.

Ouro Preto is a city like no other in Brazil to investigate mechanisms that can create political resilience amidst economic and demographic shocks. Through architecture and design 'offer[ing] a substantial material and symbolic assistance for identity construction' (Aykan 2013: 384), the 'architects of memory' (Chuva 2009) hoped to re-signify the nation. Brazilian Baroque became the material manifestation of a national past of heroes. National unity through architecture addressed a narrative of 'us vs. them', or, 'Brazilians vs. colonisers', without, however, addressing racial, social, economic, regional, educational, and gender inequalities within the so-called in-group. In addition, it was due to the depopulation of historic cities, and not a shared value in preserving buildings, that houses lingered unchanged before they were preserved. Preservation hoped to offer these places new economic meanings, especially through tourism and investments in higher education.

Whereas heritage did succeed in attracting tourists and students, it created a system where permanent residents have a servile relationship in relation to 'those coming from elsewhere', and perceptions of colonial continuity remain despite a narrative of national independence.

Belonging to a place, as addressed throughout the book, requires more than representational inclusion. Participatory spaces for contestation were created to channel complains, listen to diversified voices about values and uses of heritage sites, and define how to manage preservation, thus making the city more inclusive. However, having meetings is not the same as participating, and voicing opinions during negotiations is no guarantee of related outcomes. Looking at the preservation and its contestation of Brazil's most emblematic, historic, and artistic urban heritage site, what we see is that neither monuments nor increased participation offers an easy pathway for political and national inclusion in a context of economic and social exclusion. Yet, not only participation but also preservation values are of growing importance in contemporary Brazil.

Brazilian inner cities are marked by segregation and violence. Large metropolises in the country have witnessed the emigration of middle-class families from central urban areas to gated condominium complexes in the suburbs. This phenomenon, more pronounced since the 1980s, is clearly visible in cities like São Paulo. Wealthier families prefer fortified enclaves, while the urban poor occupy central areas (Caldeira 2000). Poverty, irregular housing, drug abuse, and crime mark the city centre of São Paulo (De Souza Santos 2018). Such visible destitution defies local urban programmes. City centres defined by crime, poverty, and squalor lead many Brazilians to feel nostalgic towards an idealised past (Holston 2008: 283). This phenomenon of nostalgia in the face of violence, crime, or abrupt city transformations is not restricted to Brazil. Ellin (1996: 124) describes the obsession with the past as a 'larger search for meaning and security in a world that appears increasingly meaningless and scary'. The same author states that the past could 'compensate for the sense of estrangement in an increasingly mechanized and segmented world' (ibid.: 124). Projects aimed at designing a new appearance for city centres, based on an image of a past of harmony between different classes and races, abounded in Brazilian major cities in the 2000s. This expectation set cities such as Ouro Preto at the forefront. Thus, when studying the disputes surrounding the preservation of Ouro Preto's cultural heritage, it is the Brazilian national imagery of social harmony, nostalgia, and hope for a culturally democratic society that I address.

Ouro Preto is a city that has a cultural city centre, where residents of varied backgrounds gather at open events, and the centre is a hub for housing, commerce, tourism, education, and transportation. What first meets the eye in Ouro Preto is an urban utopia in a Brazilian contemporary context. As discussed throughout this book, however, Ouro Preto's cultural city centre, at the time of preservation and in the present, represents a social hierarchy of what is considered cultural, historic, and worth preserving.

Heritage and participation, avenues for the development of identity and democratic inclusion, are also opportunities for the unequal amalgam of Brazilian society to resurface. When fluid city perceptions, impacted by diverse ways of being in the city, meet a stationary urban structure, the result cannot be simple adaptation. Participation is indeed a meaningful way to listen to those more affected, and for that reason, I offered an assessment of historic, social, economic, and political conditions that affect participation in heritage governance. By chronicling perceptions and practices of city preservation in Ouro Preto, this book contributes to the anthropological knowledge of the politics of cultural heritage, locating meanings of monuments and sites in everyday disputes of city use, with findings I summarise in the following.

CITY IMAGE AND SOCIAL MEANING

The image of Brazil as represented in Ouro Preto, of heroism and nationalism in a cultural and educational city centre, was my starting point to examine heritage policies in the city. In a country constantly changing and growing, I enquired about the process of maintaining a cityscape despite the discontent of many users. Local disputes regarding the maintenance of Ouro Preto's preserved areas were summarised in a main guiding research question: In preserving the form of a place, which symbolic meanings are maintained and which others are produced? I answered this question with ethnographic material, looking both at existing diverse meanings attributed to preserved areas (which are not always accounted for in official documents) and at existing coping mechanisms to uphold or change locations, such as public participation.

As chapter 1 showed, the expectations held for Ouro Preto's city centre when preservation practices were first established were strongly connected to a narrative of the past that highlighted national heroes, especially those who conspired against Portuguese rule during the colonial years. Nevertheless, other interpretations than that of heroism also exist for that rebellion, a movement led by and for a Brazilian-born elite (Maxwell 1973). The past has varied narratives, but to privilege one over others was part of a political movement of nationalism expressed through selective city forms. From Ouro Preto to Brasília, Aleijadinho to Niemeyer, Baroque architecture or modernist façades were intended to promote Brazilian sovereignty and national pride through city design. Nevertheless, selecting forms to promote experiences does not only establish ideas of national independence. Authors such as

Rama (1996), who looked at Latin American cities at the time of colonialism and during independence movements, saw that in colonial and in some postcolonial cities, locations were first imagined on paper before construction. Between plan and uses of these locations in Latin American cities, there was a gap, as the expectations of the local users were not accounted for. The preservation of Ouro Preto, for example, privileged higher education, hotel constructions, and fine arts, looking at new publics for the city, while local residents (mainly migrants from rural districts) found little space in the monumental city. This gap between plan and reality is often mediated through the plan itself, the promises (in this case, of inclusion and identity) still being made (Rama 1996). However, how long can the outcome of the promises underlying city preservation be delayed before the effect of the promises wears off? Ouro Preto's permanent residents did not find sufficient economic opportunities in tourism, or a place in higher education institutions. The well-kept city centre mainly hosts short-term visitors – tourists and students. From a city dynamic that privileges some publics – especially those not born in the city – follows perceptions of enduring social segregation. Instead of a town of national heroism, many local residents see in the city the enduring interplay of power and powerlessness that has prevailed throughout the colonial and postcolonial years.

Chapter 2 confirmed new interpretations of the city that arise when official ones are unable to mend city divides. Observing spaces and events in Ouro Preto, it is clear that colonial perpetuity, rather than independence, is at the centre of local narratives. Most permanent residents hold that the city privileges mainly students and tourists, the *forasteiros*, the people from outside, who have priority in central housing and do not sympathise with the local population. Students are often epitomised as the main group of *forasteiros*, associated with breaking existing norms for noise and enjoying privileged housing. However, when listening to the narratives of students and permanent residents, the relationship between the two perceived main groups in town is not simply one of dichotomous rivalry. There are conflicts within groups and cooperation between. Permanent residents look to each other for job opportunities – mainly through informal employment – and at the same time compete against each other in provisory means of earning money. Students also cooperate in their residence halls and organise their own hierarchy amongst house members. However, students who live in other types of accommodation feel alienated or scared of a prevalent student system associated with outlandish rules and parties. Relationships in Ouro Preto are complex, irregular, and temporary. Looking at the past, social relationships in Ouro Preto have always been complex and multi-layered. Authors such as Romeiro (2008) write about the complexity of the War of the Emboabas, looking at a similar interest between Brazilian-born men and the invaders from the coast (Portuguese, *emboabas*) in the search for gold. Others such as Maxwell (1973) look at the Inconfidência, depicting a Brazilian movement aimed at changing the political, not the social, system. Certainly, Ouro Preto is inviting the study of religious syncretism, inter- and intra-class/race relationships that existed, and, currently, the mechanism of disputes and cooperation between residents, students, and tourists. Nevertheless, the past, represented through national heroes against Portuguese invaders, contrary to official expectations, favours a narrative of enduring negative 'energy' of the city, a city that never changes in excluding its own offspring.

With residents seeing local events or higher education opportunities as excluding natives and privileging *forasteiros*, narratives focus on the preserved cityscape as a continuation of a relationship of powerful 'others' and a powerless majority. Tour guides often have a positive relationship with tourists and the city. However, they are excluded from housing and study opportunities. They usually demonstrate such ambiguities in tours that praise the city, but epitomise the location as a 'good stepmother but an awful mother', catering mainly for those who are not directly its progeny. While maintaining the cityscape, local preservation policies have therefore attempted to change residents' perceptions of exclusion through pedagogic projects aimed at mending the divide between residents and 'others', the topic of chapter 3.

The projects I presented in chapter 3 centred on both students and poor permanent residents, groups that for different reasons are mainly perceived as not enjoying what the city has to offer. Students were invited to have city walks; permanent residents joined galleries or looked for locations to be preserved in their own surroundings in the city's outskirts. In investigating those projects, it became clear that one of the projects' main limitations is that the cultural opportunities they offer do not relate to existing ways of living and perceiving the city. Projects tried to change city perceptions without addressing the underlying conditions, such as the situation of students in their houses or the socio-economic exclusion of permanent residents. Finally, I looked at gold mines as historic sites and as a possible alternative in mediating the narratives of exclusion. Gold mines breach the centre/periphery dualism, as they show the city centre as a result of mining activities taking place elsewhere. Tours through mines present the biographies of local non-elite heroes, such as Chico Rei, and religions other than Catholicism. Finally, ideas of power and powerlessness gain a new contour in spiritualistic narratives, when oppressed slave spirits are powerful in mining territories. The metaphysical power-space relations of mines differ from main local narratives in including the majority rather than the elite. However, as mainly tourists, and especially foreign tourists, visit mines, I concluded that sightseeing in the city and instruction did not alter perceptions of 'negative energy of the city'.

The discussion in the first half of the book shows conflicts in the city previous to cultural heritage practices but also deriving from those. In the second part of this book, I investigated public participation in cultural heritage as a means to resolve local disputes. When pedagogic instruments to smooth city perceptions could not efficiently mediate city disputes, spheres for popular participation gained importance in the city.

POLITICAL PARTICIPATION AS A VALUE IN ITSELF

In chapter 4, I looked at countries like Brazil and South Africa and discussed the challenge to move away from state-central policies for housing or security, mainly after the 1980s and 1990s. In the case of Brazil, state-centred planning and preservation strategies pursued from the 1930s until the 1960s subsequently lost impetus. Especially after the 1988 Constitution and the 2001 City Statute, Brazilian urban policies have looked at new methods for popular participation in urban governance. This was also a period of neoliberal economic policies in Latin America to stabilise economies threatened by high inflation. Diminished state spending capacity was accompanied by participatory mechanisms. However, local participation has various challenges, and I discussed some in the context of grassroots meetings to address cultural heritage in Ouro Preto. The Council, a policy group responsible with upholding cultural heritage, consists mainly of residents: representatives of housing associations, technical experts, and politicians. Residents, though being directly affected by heritage decisions in their everyday life (housing, employment, entertainment), do not often debate with those in power: 'those who command do so because they can; those who obey do so because they are sensible'. Social relationships in town are far from anonymous, as they tend to be in larger cities. To disagree with local policies is to disagree with local politicians, possibly directly affecting one's personal or professional contacts. Thus, the number of people willing to, or able to, participate in Council meetings is limited; and those who participate cannot broadly share all possible perspectives involved in the negotiation. Discussions may reach minimalist solutions to avoid conflicts. It follows that given social restrictions, cultural heritage may be established as a participative process, yet it may not offer even-handed solutions. The following chapters looked at case studies of this.

In chapter 5, I examined the modification of road material in Ouro Preto and nearby areas. Changing roads exemplified the limits in defining terms and areas associated with cultural heritage. Strictly defined perimeters of a preserved area were challenged by words such as 'ambience', the environment where a monument is located. Looking at preserved areas, one could also include access roads as part of a cultural experience. Adding to the complexity of mapping sites of historic and aesthetic interest, the discussion of materials themselves proved to be complex. Asphalt could at the same time preserve Baroque buildings by diminishing the vibration caused by vehicles, or diminish the aesthetic and historic appreciation of the city by modernising a colonial layout. In terms of water absorption, road material is important, inviting studies about how and where roads should become less permeable through the use of asphalt to protect buildings and people. In terms of functions, road material was ambiguous. Roads may be locations of permanence that already enhance aspects of history, such as a road a hero potentially walked on (favouring a cobblestone pavement). On the other hand, roads may be locations for leisure or commuting (supporting asphalt). In Ouro Preto, road materials were employed to define the edges of historic and non-historic, cultural and non-cultural spaces. Moreover, asphalt in Brazil is an important element in urban policies, as it diminishes the association of poor locations with illegality and dirt. When walking a street tarred with asphalt, the poor clean up the mud they carry on their shoes, making social distinction less visible and peripheral places accessible. In Ouro Preto, asphalt contrasts with dirt as well as stone material. Roads, therefore, made visible class differentiation and cultural heritage's segregating function, already present in narratives in the city. When governing without rules in the face of great social impact, the controversies around roads were solved privileging the importance of policy process: participation. The use of asphalt was judged irregular because the prefecture implemented it, but the Council did not discuss it. However, the same lack of clear rules, which cast doubt on when the consideration of the Council should be invited, also meant that decisions in the Council are based on subjective assessments of members. But the people deciding on blurred legal terms are not anonymous but rather are known to everyone. As residents and professionals who work in the city, interfering in such a controversial public policy created tension for individual Council members. Cultural heritage's open terms and boundless impact invite discussions of the limits and benefits of patrimony, but local discussions are harmed by the openness of terms in a context of pronounced (political and economic) impact.

The reservations of participants in grassroots meetings were a central aspect discussed in chapter 6. I offered an analysis of disputes between a mining company, residents directly affected by mining activities, and Council members who had to decide on the mines' possible expansion. In discussions about mining, it became clear that some residents worked for the company, others hoped to do so in the future, and in general, the company provided some improvements for local residents when requested. The picture was not very different in the Council. The company paid taxes to the prefecture, where many Council members worked. Directly or indirectly, mining activities pervaded economic and professional ties in town, and all interested parties observed the work of Council members. Participating in meetings with multiple goals goes hand in hand with the misgivings associated with operating in a context of political, economic, and technical imbalances. The future of Miguel Burnier was broadly discussed but limited in catering to all discussants, mainly ignoring the residents, who finished the negotiations not far from where they started.

I concluded the second half of this book with an understanding that participants are a means in the process of preservation, rather than contemplated as part of heritage outcomes. Participation lends an air of legitimacy to the process, but its influence might be limited. To wrap up my argument, and discuss the future of cultural heritage and participation in Ouro Preto and beyond, I ask, as Berlant (2011) does in her introduction to *Cruel Optimism*: 'What happens when those fantasies [of cultural heritage and political participation] start to fray? – Depression, dissociation, pragmatism, cynicism, optimism, activism, or an incoherent mash?' (Berlant 2011: 2).

THE FUTURE OF HERITAGE PRACTICES IN BRAZIL

I started my investigation with a lived and perhaps common sense understanding that Ouro Preto differs from other Brazilian cities in the use and maintenance of central public spaces. I was wrong in my first assumptions in many ways. The city centre of Ouro Preto, though maintained and not run-down like that of São Paulo or many other large Brazilian cities, is not a city centre of hybrid and harmonious conviviality. People who use the city centre have varied (and often frustrated) expectations regarding its uses. Preserved buildings in the area usually foster permanent residents' negative interpretations of the past. Ideas of national and local belonging are far from the reality of residents who communicate everyday inequalities in the city. While social dynamics challenge preserved spaces, citizens are invited to voice their varied experiences in participatory meetings for city preservation. My second assumption then, and a guiding research question, was that the Council was a location for residents to discuss the existing variety of meanings and city uses, which could explain why the city centre of Ouro Preto remains unchanged. The function of buildings might change while the form of the city remains the same. However, while city dwellers differ in their understanding of city spaces and events, the process of directing city preservation is restrictive both in the number of participants and in partakers' perspectives towards cultural heritage. In Ouro Preto, the centre is not preserved through the contemplation of different and often conflicting uses in the present and images of the past. Rather, it remains mainly associated with a standard historical account and the middle-class public in search of refined arts or educational opportunities. This association flies in the face of local residents, their everyday claims, and narratives. Thus, this approach to cultural heritage is ineffective. Even though all over the world cultural heritage is often a means of expressing a particular history, not one but various pasts can gain expression. Heritage can attract and speak to tourists, but if the majority of permanent residents share a sense of exclusion, politicians may profit from such perception by pandering to residents and passing laws that are detrimental to cultural heritage. More interesting would be an approach that allows cultural heritage to evoke varied and often conflicting meanings, uses, and experiences. These could then lead to the engagement of residents with the city in multiple ways.

The practical failures in the approach of cultural heritage should then not lead to a simplistic dismissal of preserved locations as sketches of dystopia. What needs to be addressed is the fact that patrimony on one hand evokes a variety of local meanings but on the other hand does not overcome a political agenda looking for a shared meaning. Both through national policies, anxious to anchor Brazilians with a material past and normative ways of urban living, and through local participation, unable to equally present coexisting perspectives and backgrounds, cultural heritage falls short in its multiple meanings and uses. It is thus politics that needs consideration when discussing some of the immediate shortcomings of cultural heritage. In the following, I offer suggestions on how to take the discussion of this book further on a theoretical level and in local public policies, to avoid the idealisations of both heritage and political participation and instead recognise their real faults and possibilities.

Cities such as Ouro Preto, facing a fluctuating population and complex and temporary uses of preserved areas, cannot homogenise notions of national history, a key premise associated with cultural heritage. The cityscape and monuments necessarily exclude many versions of history and living forms in such locations. Urban preservation thus cannot, on its own, anticipate individuals' perceptions, experiences, memories, or forgetfulness; these are associated with individual experiences in the city with all that these entail (gender, class, day or night uses, etc.). Pedagogically instructing people how to use or understand the city denies such everyday intricacies. Ultimately, if people who feel excluded from their monuments and museums preserve them because they are instructed to do so, this may ignore the main image associated with Ouro Preto, that of defiance against injustice and colonialism. Other scholars have addressed expectations about national belonging in relation to cities in other developing economies, such as South Africa. Simone (2004), when writing about Johannesburg, discusses the importance of studies and government policies that allow for understanding relationships amongst residents, and between residents and the city, as irregular. Most of the time, complexities and temporalities in everyday relationships in the city are considered to be a failure. Looking at individuals as infrastructure, the author suggests that often people – in their everyday flows – are the core of the city; they cooperate, improvise, and make life possible (ibid.: 407). Urban ethnographies in countries such as Brazil and South Africa have to allow for a discussion of cultural heritage as diverse in both storytelling and uses. In such countries, the city structure – streets, houses, and monuments – and the human element – how houses are built, streets used, and monuments narrated – are always changing in a context of informal employment, uncertain housing conditions, and growing families.

A more feasible discussion for the preservation of cultural heritage in Ouro Preto is one that allows monuments and sites to convey imageries of dissent, thus keeping the material heritage but also its multiple meanings. Canclini (2012: 132) suggests that cultural heritage, in its manifold interpretations, invites flexible compromises regarding the use of preserved sites. The city could then reinvent itself as the stage, the background before which life plays out, not the other way round. The editors of history would then need to engage at the same time with provisional city narratives, uses, and pasts, as well as physical and metaphysical spaces and official and imagined biographies, to maintain a steady cityscape. Gold mines in Ouro Preto could provide a lesson in this respect. Appadurai (2013: 183) adds that cultural heritage, rather than offering a view of the past, could 'bring the future back in'. The author states that often culture (patrimony among other cultural expressions) remains associated with the past, thus often dissociated from future-oriented developments (ibid.: 180). In the context of Ouro Preto, however, the idea of heritage was developed not only with history in mind but also tourism and education as economic strategies. But the promised results (economic boost and population growth) were delayed and subsequently came to fruition through other industrial means; the financial and social gains of tourism and education proved disputable. Cultural heritage then lost its future-oriented spark and (inefficiently) maintained mainly the narrative of heroism and national memory to keep up its forms. Bringing the future back into Ouro Preto means discussing a city ever re-interpreted and as such renewed, both in meanings and uses.

Nonetheless, to account for fast-changing meanings and uses (economic and social) and suggest more flexible compromises, we need to discuss possibilities for civilian participation in preservation policies. But participation in Ouro Preto often proved detrimental for the participants. The final point in this discussion looks at how to make participation and heritage policies more encompassing.

As discussed in the second part of this book, the participation of individuals in Council meetings was constrained, and looking at the conditions underlying restriction (and suggesting new possibilities) is one of the contributions of this work. Likewise in the discussion about racial inclusion in Brazil, obtaining freedom from slavery did not suffice to breach with race relations developed during slavery (Fernandes 1969). Liberty did not remove inequities (ibid.). Correspondingly, participatory opportunities do not mean effective participation if socio-economic inequalities persist. The blame often falls on the inadequacy of participants instead of epitomising the incompleteness of Brazil's democratic inclusion. Commonplace in political discussions of Brazil is the association of shortcomings in Brazilian democracy with a denigrating reading of Brazilian political culture. Classic theoretical analyses about Brazilian politics often echo Holanda (2006), who portrays the 'cordial Brazilian man' as a man moulded by the family, applying personal relationships to all spheres of public life. Or DaMatta (1991a: 133), who exposes Brazilian 'practices of "bending" legal codes and the impersonal norms of public life'.[1] However, there is more to Ouro Preto's local political problems than a mere system of residents who are preoccupied with their own personal relationships, bending the law subjectively. Non-participation in public meetings or, for those who participate, silence in meetings, retreat from city events, the violation of public rules for city preservation, amongst other social practices in town, are all part of the ways ordinary people have to cope with the struggle for housing and employment in a small town of known individuals. Retreating from political participation is not a simple disdain – people reflect about the city and their position on it tirelessly – but socio-economic and demographic dynamics also force people to withdraw because 'those who command do so because they can; those who obey do so because they are sensible'. Understanding retreat, in this case, addresses the rationale of residents with competing interests and in socio-economically unequal positions in relation to other participants. The assumption that compromises that arise in grassroots meetings are inclusive and democratic is therefore naive. More realistic is the view that, as discussed in chapter 6, people receive a 'rope to hang themselves'. Meetings are participative but restricted in the number of participants and in the possibilities to reveal multiple views in a context of established power hierarchies. There is little opportunity for the development of inclusive compromises, yet participation give legitimacy to unrepresentative decisions. The Council, as a participative political space, needs to confront this perception of being inefficient if it is to be a centre for political participation and make heritage a popular endeavour. One way to do so is to understand aspects of everyday cooperation, silence, and non-compliance to local rules, which often take place in neighbourhoods, rather than voiced discussions in public meetings. This reinforces the importance of urban ethnographies in bringing everyday accounts into a political and social sphere. Borne out of this study is also the strategy of sharing participatory mandates. Council members experienced intimidation during mining negotiations as discussed in chapter 6. However, in the same meetings, representatives of the company took turns, thus diminishing their personal involvement and recognisability. Taking turns in meetings would require not only a change in current legislation that ties mandates to individuals but also greater use of written practices, such as minutes. Reports and minutes could inform new participants taking over from previous ones. A greater reliance on written, rather than verbal, means of participation is already in course. However, with written practices, participants deprived of a bureaucratic culture (Cornwall and Shankland 2013; Abram 2017: 39) may shy away, and the use of such new strategies needs to be followed by new studies.

Finally, Ouro Preto and other preserved cities are inviting for broad comparative analysis. Many heritage sites recreate old industries using their former vocation (like pottery or porcelain in Meissen, Germany, or lacemaking in Bruges, Belgium) to improve the economic opportunities of their residents. Revitalising cities through their pasts bring us back to the beginning of this conclusion. In heritage cities around the world, images of the past shape hopes to remedy rundown or depopulated urban areas. Images of the past, however, can also speak about the legacies of environmental and social abuses. Which factors influence the success of such policies in terms of preservation, popular acceptance, and economic survival are still unclear. Historic factors, national idiosyncrasies, socio-economic dynamics, legal aspects, and political goodwill all are bound to change the perception and experience of a heritage site by its inhabitants.

What we know is that a dominant narrative based on 'exceptional value', suppressing all other understandings, cannot sustain heritage sites in the long run (Canclini 2012: 70). Public participation cannot be the end goal but a method to reach optimal compromises for everyone involved. At the same time, the people involved in the participation process cannot remain a means to gain legitimacy. The improvement of their lives has to become the goal of participatory discussions if cultural heritage is to become more accepted by residents. Unless heritage is locally valuable (diverse, useful, future-oriented), a presumed universal significance is insufficient. Not only are monuments in danger if it is politically more efficient to bring them down, but the positive messages they represent (e.g., of human creativity) may become overshadowed if their standard interpretation suppresses, rather than includes, citizens. If mainly reinforcing unfairness, ultimately, such cultural heritage sites may be locally meaningless or show that inequality and colonialism persist in new ways, leaving little space for new imaginations of citizenship, contrary to what was hoped in the case of Brazil.

Notes

INTRODUCTION

1. Considering the patrilineal Western norms grounded in the concept of heritage, I use the terms 'heritage' and 'patrimony' as interchangeable in this book, as does Collins (2009).

2. Secretariat of Tourism of Ouro Preto, visited on September 25, 2013. Though the functionaries presented some details of the number of visitors, the number of tourists who visit the city is only calculated through the number of guests visiting museums, usually 500,000 every year. However, they explained that not all tourists go to museums and that the real number of tourists may be much higher.

CHAPTER 1

1. The Council is the Municipal Council for the Preservation of Natural and Cultural Patrimony, a collegiate group formed by politicians, technicians, and community leaders to discuss local heritage policies; decisions by the Council may be suggestive or binding. I will discuss how it was formed and its current work in chapter 4.

2. The first settlements in Ouro Preto (*arraiais*), dating from June 1696 to 1698, grew to the category of Vila in 1711, and the city was named Vila Rica (Rich Village). After Independence (1822), the city was named The Imperial City of Ouro Preto (Ouro Preto means black gold in Portuguese, referring to the black mineral evolving into the gold found in town). After 1889, when Brazil became a Republic, the city was called Ouro Preto (Martins de Araújo 2013: 14–17). Nowadays some people in town still refer to Ouro Preto as Vila Rica.

3. Lei 3, passed on September 25, 1891, can be found in the *Coleção das Leis de Minas Gerais – 1891, Imprensa Official do Estado de Minas Gerais, Ouro Preto.* I had access to the collection in a visit to the Municipal Archive of Ouro Preto on December 4, 2013.

4. *Registro de Atas de Sessões da Câmara 1901 a 1905*; from a visit to the Municipal Archive of Ouro Preto, on December 12, 2013.

5. Foi aqui, nestas altas penedias,
Que parecem romper o firmamento,
Que raiou fulgente o pensamento
Da liberdade que pregou o Messias
Foi aqui! – Diz a voz das ventanias;
Foi aqui! – Diz o velho monumento;
Foi aqui! – Tudo diz com sentimento,
Contando a historia dos passados dias.
Salve! Cidade legendaria e ilesa!
Se hoje a moderna geração despreza
Teu Passado de glorias e de soes,
Minha alma ajoelha comovida e em pranto
Beija teu seio generoso e santo
Onde pulsaram corações de heróis (This is the original version in Portuguese)

6. The idea of preserving monuments and objects of 'national interest' is mainly attributed to France, a country that has been classifying national monuments since 1830. Brazil began to legislate in the area, together with other countries that also followed a nationalist impulse in monumental preservation (such as Mexico and the United States), only in the early twentieth century. However while most countries mainly selected isolated buildings and objects, in Brazil large city perimeters were protected, supported by an encompassing law: Decree 25 from 1937 (Chuva 2009: 50–54), which endorsed the capacity of places and materials to narrate facts of a past.

7. See The Athens Charter for the restoration of historic monuments 1931.

8. The current acronym is IPHAN: Institute for Historic and Artistic Patrimony. In the beginning of preservation practices, the acronym was SPHAN (as it was a secretariat and not an institute). To avoid confusion, I refer to the organ as IPHAN throughout the book.

9. Document accessed on September 13, 2013 through official request. It collects detailed information about the hotel construction.

10. Brasília is today preserved, and Portaria 314, passed on October 8, 1992, establishes the definitions and criteria for the preservation of the city, focussing on the maintenance of the urban conception of the city in its four main scales: monumental, residential, gregarious, and bucolic.

11. The Director of Pro-Memoria, Italo Campofiorito, wrote to Lucio Costa on November 24, 1989, asking for a letter to support the preservation of the urban setting of Brasília. The letter in reply was written on January 1, 1990, and both the documents are the first pages of the process of 'tombamento' N. 1.305-T-90 Vol. 1 "Conjunto Urbanistico (Plano Piloto), Brasília/Distrito Federal. Accessed in visit to Noronha Santos Archive, Rio de Janeiro, on April 24, 2013.

12. Decree 25, September 3, 1932 and Decree 13, September 19, 1931 can be found in the book *Livro de Transcrição Decretos e Leis 1931–1942* at the Municipal Archive of Ouro Preto, which I visited on November 28, 2013.

13. Decree 13, September 19, 1931 (see also Decree 25, September 3, 1932). Accessed during a visit to the Municipal Archive of Ouro Preto on November 28, 2013.

14. Ouro Preto was inscribed in the Brazilian heritage book as a Fine Art in Brazil (*Livro do tombo 3, de Belas Artes*) on April 20, 1938, later on September 15, 1986, it was also inscribed for its archaeological, ethnographic and landscaping values (*Livro do tombo 1, Arqueológico, Etnográfico e Paisagístico*) and historical values (*Livro do tombo 2, Histórico*). Information obtained at the Noronha Santos Archive, Rio de Janeiro, on April 24, 2013.

15. Included in the UNESCO World Heritage List in September 1980.

16. Even though São Francisco's churchyard shows the maintenance of main architectural lines, some authors, such as Castriota (2009) highlight the change in the use of its frontal area from a local grocery trade area to a touristic one focussing on art craft. This is not the only change that occurred, from that churchyard it is possible to see some new housing areas emerge on the slope of hills (ibid.: 144–45). Nevertheless, the preservation of one of the most important Baroque churches in Brazil exemplifies preservation efforts in the city to maintain central constructions.

17. A local law, *Lei Complementar 93*, January 20, 2001, establishes norms and conditions to use and subdivide Ouro Preto's urban area. The law regulates construction parameters for protected areas in detail and for other areas, rather than defining conditions, it sets a decision-making process.

18. Number of students detailed during conversation with the university principal, Professor Dr Marcone Souza on September 30, 2013.

19. Monumenta was a national project led by the Brazilian Ministry of Culture in association with Inter-American Development Bank that contemplated twenty-six cities to finance maintenance and restoration of preserved areas, aiming at boosting the commercial and touristic appeal of those areas (Batista da Costa 2011: 269, 272).

20. PAC is an acronym for Programme to Accelerate Growth; national development policies targeted historic cities in PAC's two versions in 2009 and 2013.

21. Speech by Brazil's President Dilma Rousseff, in the city of São João-del-Rei, in the state of Minas Gerais, on August 20, 2013.

CHAPTER 2

1. There are different types of student accommodation in Ouro Preto. In Repúblicas students select colleagues to be part of the house; they have flags, rituals, and a hierarchy amongst house members. There are Federal Repúblicas, the university owning the houses and charging no accommodation fees and Private Repúblicas, where students rent a house and share the costs. In both cases, students, rather than the university, manage the houses, making it different from other university accommodations. Repúblicas are divided by gender. The system of rituals found in Repúblicas in Ouro Preto is similar to what other universities call societies or fraternities. This is mainly inspired by the University of Coimbra, as Ouro Preto has sent its students there since the eighteenth century; Maxwell (1973) details that 'between 1772 and 1785 300 Brazilian-born students had matriculated at the University of Coimbra' (ibid.: 82).

2. Silence Law; *Lei Complementar* 16, passed on July 17, 2006, and modified in 2011 by *Lei Complementar* 111, passed on December 23, 2011.

3. Feld (1984) writes about sound structure as social structure. Though the author examines another region of the world and is more focussed on socio-musicology, a lesson I learned from Feld when looking at Ouro Preto was to hear social structures when listening to the soundscape.

4. In short, the public university system in Brazil is as follows: state schools that focus on the three final years preceding university (*Ensino Médio*) often lack material and human resources, and students coming from those schools have a lower chance of entering the federal universities (accessible through a very competitive entrance exam). This is a perverse inversion; free of charge, federal universities often select students who could afford the best and most expensive schools. However, recent national policies (offering differentiated allocation to unprivileged students) have made change possible. In Ouro Preto, the university has welcomed more local residents (about 30 per cent, according to the principal) but remains viewed as a university for students from outside the local area.

5. According to Dr Marcone, the university has 11,087 students on-campus and 4,421 off-campus, and for students it offers: 2,815 on-campus meal programmes and 2,447 maintenance bursaries (varying from full or partial). Another 784 students receive a transportation bursary. He also detailed salaries paid to students who are tutors and those in university extension projects and research projects. In addition, there are 900 accommodation opportunities in Federal Repúblicas that charge no accommodation fees, and the university restaurant offers subsidised meals at R$2 (£0.49) per person (for those who pay for it).

6. Although numbers varied in interviews, recent data show that in 2010 nearly 70 per cent of undergraduate students did not come from the regions where UFOP has a campus. They make up the main population that look for accommodation in town. Repúblicas host 52 per cent of students, which is the preferred type of residency (Universidade Federal de Ouro Preto 2010: 14–15).

7. More recently, Repúblicas in Ouro Preto were targeted in the media regarding accommodation and student performance (Simões 2013), hosting visitors during carnival (Do Vale 2013b), and regarding rape incidents at student parties (Faria 2014).

8. Student representatives have mentioned some small-scale charity projects to change negative perceptions about student life in town, and the university too has a series of cooperation programmes, as detailed by Professor Rogerio on October 1, 2013. Staff and students of the university lead programmes that focus on the community in eight main areas: communication, culture, human rights, education, environment, health, technology, and employment. These programmes include, for example, teaching English to the community or offering pharmaceutical consultation. Aimed at integrating the community and the university, Professor Rogerio explains that such programmes still lack publicity and the possibility of being initiated by the community and continued beyond the university calendar.

9. Marcelo explained on August 28, 2013, that Bauxita started as an industrial neighbourhood in the 1930s and hosted approximately 3,500 employees. In 1983, another 169 houses were built through the BNH (National Bank for Residential Policies), and in 1989, some residents moved to the area after a strong rain that destroyed parts of the city. However, after 2006, when the university expanded, the

neighbourhood begun to grow at a fast pace, and he lost track of residential numbers. Marcelo, however, estimates that 10,000 people live in Bauxita nowadays, and about 60 per cent of them are students. The number of houses did not grow proportionally, indicating high density within houses.

10. Various articles in the local press addressed real estate speculation in Ouro Preto during the time of my fieldwork, such as in the article by Moreira (2013: 12–5), which indicated the rise in the number of students as a key factor in rental prices' ascending curve.

11. Conversation held in September 30, 2013.

12. Despite the separations during the Jazz Festival, having the event in an open space charging no entrance fee was already a positive shift, as a resident remarked soon after the event. That festival used to be indoors and charged for entrance.

13. MIMO is an acronym for *Mostra Internacional de Musica de Olinda*, a music festival that started in the city of Olinda, Brazil, in 2004 and extended to other preserved towns in Brazil, such as Paraty and Ouro Preto. The festival also encompasses cinema exhibition, visual arts, and educational activities; all of the activities are free of charge (MIMO Festival 2019).

14. Extracted from Prefeitura Municipal de Ouro Preto (2019), accessed through official request in 2019. The emblem – showcasing three hills – originally represents three main housing settlements in Ouro Preto during the eighteenth century. Each government slightly modified the emblem, and the version here presented refers to the mandate of the Mayor Julio Ernesto Grammont Machado de Araujo.

15. My interview partners in Ouro Preto often repeated this expression, which in Portuguese is *manda quem pode, obedece quem tem juízo*. There are probably different ways one could translate this expression to English. In my ethnography I use the translation that Goldman (2013: 54) uses in his book about politics in Brazil. Though I do not quote the book every time I use this common saying, I am using the same translation throughout this book.

16. Interview with Marcia and Fabiana at the Secretariat of Tourism in Ouro Preto, held on September 25, 2013.

17. Because of low salaries paid in the tourism industry, many people prefer jobs in mining companies than in hospitality. However, the number of placements in mining businesses has diminished, and companies usually hire people from neighbouring cities (Ouro Preto's territory is very comprehensive, and neighbouring cities may have a geographic advantage in commuting to mining areas), as I will discuss in chapter 6.

18. In Ouro Preto's outskirts, like elsewhere in Brazil, houses are designed and built by the owners, without a certified architect or engineer. These houses show 'concrete embodiment and imaginary representations of people's relations to their conditions of existence' (Holston 1991: 456), such as capacity for improvising and persistence.

19. Millions of protesters occupied streets in Brazil in June 2013 against expensive and inefficient transport services. What started in the city of São Paulo soon spread to different cities in Brazil, a movement known as *June Protests*. The complexities of *June Protests*, such as the different agendas, and the format of protests across different cities surely call for a case-by-case analysis rather than generalisations. Here I focus on attendance at some of the protests in Ouro Preto.

CHAPTER 3

1. In his volume *Distinction: A Social Critique of the Judgment of Taste*, Bourdieu (2010) discusses the illusion of personal preferences and explains 'taste' based on socio-economic determinants (ibid.: 93–95).

2. In Ouro Preto, narratives about Aleijadinho idealise his Brazilian creativity, reminding the listener of Gilberto Freyre's sociology of a hybrid and unique Brazilian culture that goes beyond its racial roots (Souza 2000: 79). In *The Mansions and the Shanties* (1963), Freyre presents the *mulato*, the 'type' that had access to culture and was capable of rising socially (Souza 2000: 91). Freyre's work could consecrate miscegenation as a positive value, and his theory was valuable in the construction of Brazilian nationality (Nascimento 2003: 44). Aleijadinho, both in his biography and artistic work, expresses ideals of Brazilian nationalism – miscegenation and values associated to work and education towards economic ascension. However, as discussed in this book, there are negative aspects on what became discussed as a myth of racial democracy in Brazil, such as silences and metaphors in the discussion of racism (Sheriff 2001: 218).

3. Aleijadinho's Medal was created in 1974 of up to twenty-five nominees to recognise the work and dedication to the city. The medals are given on November 18, the death anniversary of Aleijadinho, at São Francisco Church (Decree 27/1974). Nationally, Aleijadinho was declared the patron of art in Brazil on December 12, 1973 (Law 5984/1973).

4. Maxwell (1973) describes the production of the artist as 'some of the world's finest rococo churches' and the design of São Francisco Church as 'where the extraordinary development of the Minas Baroque was most clearly demonstrated. . . [as it] proposed new solutions of plan and façade and produced a unified whole which Germain Bazin has numbered among "the most perfect monuments of Luso-Brazilian art"' (ibid.: 94).

5. Writing in 1964, at the time of the 150th anniversary of Aleijadinho's death, Rezende (1965) comments on a week of celebrations for the artist who left sculptures and temples erected in the cities of Ouro Preto, Congonhas, Mariana, and other towns in Minas Gerais. The author refers to a newspaper article that compares Aleijadinho to Shakespeare, in the sense that there has been doubt about both Shakespeare and Aleijadinho's list of works. Doubts about Aleijadinho's work remain in Ouro Preto today and controversy surrounds the artist regarding his portfolio, the disease that afflicted him, and how he could create without hands but tools strapped to him. His art, however, is celebrated regardless.

6. A robbery of seventeen sacred pieces in Pilar Church in 1973 led to restrictions being imposed in main temples across the city, and photographs can now be taken only when authorised in advance. During the year 2013, a newspaper article recalled the fortieth anniversary of the robbery and the various rumours of a case that remains unsolved (Werneck 2013).

7. The term 'façade' has a negative connotation in Brazil when employed to describe someone; 'a person of façade' means someone that has an exterior attitude different from his or her interior intention. When tour guides say that many tourists

prefer to see the city only in its façade, they mean people are not interested in accounts of the meaning or process of an artwork but only in its main visual aspects. Therefore, those guides explain that many house owners have rebuilt the interior of their houses (demolishing walls, floor, ceiling, and repainting the interior) and have maintained only the façade for tourists' photographs.

8. I analyse projects on patrimonial education mainly through brochures, official reports, and interviews with coordinators and not recipients of such projects. Amongst those on the receiving side there were many children, and my ethnographic training and ethical approval did not include research with children.

9. Proposition 02/2001 suggested changing the motto in Latin on Ouro Preto's flag because of its racist connotation, and this became law in 2005, as reported in the Brazilian newspaper *Folha de São Paulo*, November 18, 2005 (Guimarães 2005).

10. More information available in printed brochures: Fundação de Arte de Ouro Preto 2009: *Sentidos Urbanos Patrimônio e Cidadania.*

11. I assessed results from the Programme *Sou do morro e também sou patrimônio* in December 2012 through the Secretaria Municipal de Cultura e Patrimônio, September 4, 2013. The conclusion of the document indicates that though pupils could engage with the project and enjoy activities, pupils remain geographically distant from the city centre, their main cultural reference.

12. Parts of this chapter appeared in 'Cultural Marginality and Urban Place Making: The Case of Leicester and Ouro Preto', Cupples, J. and Slater, T. (eds.) (2019, forthcoming) *Producing and Contesting Urban Marginality: Interdisciplinary and Comparative Dialogues* (London: Rowman & Littlefield International, Transforming Capitalism Series).

13. Some studies about slavery gained prominence during the time of my fieldwork. Marcia Valadares, member of the Forum for Racial Equality of Ouro Preto, explained her research in town to me, which was about the alternative literacies of slaves. Projects such as hers have been minimal in Brazil, where the issue of racism is silenced or intermingled in discussions about class, education, and culture (Souza 2010: 188). It is then not surprising that residents in Ouro Preto refer to city groups in terms of house location and education and rarely refer to race as an indicator of divisions, despite the local history of slavery, as discussed in chapter 2.

14. For a record about local narratives about spiritual haunting in Ouro Preto, see Xavier (2009).

15. The black population in Ouro Preto in 1776 was four times larger than that of whites (Maxwell 1973: 263). As a result, it is common to hear people ponder the lack of rebellion from slaves in Ouro Preto. In mine tours, explanations abound, focussing on the violence and oppression of the masters as well as language barriers and internal disputes amongst slaves.

CHAPTER 4

1. Brazil held several constitutions since its independence in 1822. Under monarchist or republican (democratic or dictatorial) administrations, citizens had

restricted rights to elect representatives (in terms of gender, income, literacy), and elections were known for corruption (see Holston 2008: 92,103). The 1988 Constitution is considered a citizens' constitution because suffrage rights were unrestricted, municipalities gained more political autonomy in relation to the national government, the politics of urban development (detailed in Article 182) looked for the social function of the city (properties and land could not be underused or misused), and cities with more than 20,000 inhabitants needed to write a master plan to determine their urban development. Those elements about citizens and citizens' rights in the city later culminated with the creation of the City Statute (2001) that regulated civilian participation in the democratic making of the city (see Andrade dos Passos 2010: 85).

2. 1988 Constitution (Constituição da Republica Federativa do Brasil 1988) Articles 182 and 216.

3. Holston (2008) discusses 'rights as privilege' in Brazil (ibid.: 254). The author explains that 'people desist pursuing their rights . . . in the context of differentiated citizenship, the poor often get the phrase "go find your rights" thrown in their faces as a cynical threat when they accuse others of violating or neglecting their rights. The message is clear: the search for rights will be in vain; therefore don't bother and either accept what happened or try an extra-legal resolution' (ibid.: 257).

4. Parts of this section 'Avoiding Confrontations' appeared in De Souza Santos (2018).

5. I am thankful to the functionaries in *Casa dos Conselhos* (the local institution that administers municipal councils), with whom I spoke various times, including during a long visit on November 8, 2013, when I obtained consolidated numbers on the functioning of councils in town in 2013.

6. The 1988 Constitution establishes that a percentage of taxes collected through the circulation of goods and services should be transferred to municipalities. In Minas Gerais, municipalities need to attend to their obligations regarding the preservation of cultural heritage in order to receive their share. Projects on patrimonial education and having a council on cultural heritage are amongst practices that municipalities should follow (see 1988 Federal Constitution Articles 158, 159, and 161; Minas Gerais State Law 18.030, passed on January 12, 2009).

7. Livro de Atas do Conselho Consultivo Municipal – Registro de Atas de Sessões 1931–1948, and Atas do Conselho Consultivo 1971. Visit to the Arquivo Municipal de Ouro Preto, November 28 and 29, 2013.

8. Lei Orgânica Municipal, March 28, 1990, which organises the local administration, mentioned twenty-two councils in town, including one on patrimonial preservation. Law 17, April 26, 2002, regulated the attributions of the Council, which is presently structured by Law 708, September 27, 2011, and by the Council's internal statute passed on June 23, 2010 that details procedures for meetings, voting process, among others.

9. Law 708, September 27, 2011 – that organises the Municipal Council for the Preservation of Cultural and Natural Patrimony.

10. Law 17, April 26, 2002, which regulates the preservation of cultural heritage, and Law 708, September 27, 2011, which organises the Municipal Council for the Preservation of Cultural and Natural Patrimony.

11. Law 17, April 26, 2002.

12. Projeto de Lei Complementar 01/2013, which structured the municipal administration of Ouro Preto by listing all secretariats that would exist from then on.

13. Letter (Oficio Gab 007 2013) sent on February 1, 2013, by Ouro Preto's Mayor, Jose Leandro Filho, to the President of the House of Representatives, Vereador Leonardo Edson Barbosa. Accessed at the House of Representatives of Ouro Preto.

14. Livro de Atas 2 do Conselho Municipal de Preservação do Patrimonio Cultural e Natural de Ouro Preto, accessed at the Secretariat of Culture and Patrimony on 29 November 2013.

15. The then-current structure of the Secretariat had received the *Rodrigo Melo Franco Award*, a distinction given by the Brazilian Ministry of Culture to municipalities since 1987 in recognition to preservation actions. In October 2011, Ouro Preto was awarded R$20,000 in recognition to the model of administration launched in 2005, when the Secretariat of Patrimony and Urban Development augmented its structure in order to analyse more restoration or construction projects, and to register patrimonial objects and sites for potential preservation both within the city centre and in the surrounding districts (Prefeitura Municipal de Ouro Preto 2011 – accessed in April 2013 at Secretariat of Culture and Patrimony).

16. In Ouro Preto, as discussed in chapter 1, there is strong pressure to govern in favour of *Ouropretanos*, as opposed to students and tourists. This dichotomous view does not always prevail, for there is also the position that what is good for tourists is good for *Ouropretanos* because tourism generates jobs. In 2013, the prevailing political view was that opposing permanent residents to 'others'.

17. This is an argument similar to the one used by the local prosecutor. According to Dr Domingos, who worked on various cases regarding cultural heritage in town, the advantage of discussing controversial cases in the Council, rather than through norms, is because a norm may be open to whatever it does not strictly forbid, but a decision process allows for projects to be decided on a case-by-case basis. Throughout several conversations with the local prosecutor, the approach towards a solid process, rather than a well-defined law, was repeatedly emphasised, as I exemplify on chapter 5.

CHAPTER 5

1. PROMOVA (*Programa Gestor das Ações de Revitalização de Ouro Preto* or in English Administrative Programme of Actions to Revitalise Ouro Preto) is a local key public policy originated in 2013. It focuses on urban mobility, infrastructure, health, and education and became pivotal in local discussions when street layouts were changed.

2. Stoller (1997) argues that 'in anthropology, for example, it is especially important to incorporate into ethnographic works the sensuous body – its smells, tastes, textures, and sensations' (ibid.: xv). Smells, textures, and sensations affecting the body in the city have to do with street material in Ouro Preto. Stone, dust, and asphalt were materials easily noticed throughout my fieldwork and especially when road changes began to take shape.

3. There are different types of routes in Ouro Preto. Local Law 93 (passed on January 20, 2001) distinguishes regional, arterial, collector, and local roads according to their functions. In this chapter my main concern is the lanes of local use (streets used for public and private transportation within Ouro Preto's main residential areas), and I refer to them as either streets or roads interchangeably.

4. Oficio Mensagem 61, from September 10, 2013, collected at House of Representatives for the city of Ouro Preto, on November 6, 2013.

5. In the first municipal decrees to preserve the city, the idea was to maintain the façades (portals, sills, columns) of buildings according to the prevalent colonial architecture (Decree 25, September 3, 1932). In 1938, the attention to buildings extended to include the architectural urban setting of Ouro Preto, and the city was included in the National Heritage Book of Fine Arts. In 1949, a blueprint of the area to be maintained was added to the process (*Conjunto Arquitetonico e Urbanistico da Cidade de Ouro Preto*, Volume 1).

6. Castriota (2009) states that in 1938, there were 1,000 buildings in the area urbanised in the eighteenth century, and from 1938 to 1985 another 2,000 buildings were erected in the area (Castriota 2009: 146, discussed in Santana 2012: 34). Though constructions altered the availability of empty spaces in the preserved area, because most of them followed the colonial layout, not all projects were controversial. However, interventions that did not follow colonial form were in some cases destroyed and in other cases remain divisive (e.g., the Grande Hotel by Oscar Niemeyer).

7. This definition of the 'environment' of a preserved area was translated in Brazil as 'ambience' (Ribeiro 2007: 40).

8. The author comments on the *Venice Charter 1964* (International charter for the conservation and restoration of monuments and sites), published by the International Council on Monuments and Sites.

9. From a visit to IPHAN, Noronha Santos, in Rio de Janeiro, on April 24, 2013 (SPHAN n.d. *Processo de Tombamento Conjunto Arquitetônico e urbanístico da cidade de Ouro Preto*).

10. The Public Prosecutor's Office (Ministério Publico), according to the 1988 Constitution Article 127, is an organisation in charge of 'the defence of judicial order, of the democratic regime and of social and individual interests'. As such, it works autonomously in relation to the three traditional spheres of power: judicial, legislative, and executive. The prosecutor's office has branches in states and municipalities. In this case, the Council sent the letter to the office in Ouro Preto, which acts, in addition to other areas, in the defence of the environment and the cultural and historical patrimony.

11. Laudo de Vistoria 78, from October 2, 2013. The document from the Ministério Publico do Estado de Minas Gerais – Promotoria Estadual de Defesa do Patrimônio Cultural e Turístico, was written by an architect and offers considerations about the use of asphalt near the Museum Casa dos Inconfidentes. I obtained the document through electronic communication with Dr Domingos, on November 1, 2013.

12. See SPHAN (n.d.) *Processo de Tombamento Conjunto arquitetônico e urbanístico da cidade de Ouro Preto*. From a visit to IPHAN Noronha Santos, in Rio de Janeiro on April 24, 2013.

13. The laws and decrees that Robson refers to, which coordinate the preservation in Ouro Preto are the local IPHAN guidance (Portaria 312, October 20, 2010); law that establishes norms and conditions to use and subdivide the urban area (Lei Complementar 93, January 20, 2001); the local Master Plan (Lei Complementar 29, December 28, 2006); and the Decree 25, November 30, 1937 (mentioned in chapter 1). Together these are the main urban norms guiding the work of city conservation in Ouro Preto. More specifically about the term ambiance, though the word is mentioned, for example, in Portaria 312, it is not defined and is mainly associated with the maintenance of the appearance of the urban and architectural cityscape of Ouro Preto and the immediate area around chapels.

CHAPTER 6

1. Parts of this chapter appeared in my article: De Souza Santos, Andreza Aruska. "Trading time and space: Grassroots negotiations in a Brazilian mining district." *Ethnography* (2019).

2. Report CODEMA (*Conselho Municipal de Desenvolvimento Ambiental*, in English: Municipal Council for Environmental Development), 01/2013, passed on June 19, 2013, tied the approval of the company's expansion to a favourable assessment by the Municipal Secretariat of Culture and Patrimony. That Secretariat analysed the matter through the Council for the Preservation of Cultural and Natural Patrimony. This document was distributed electronically to all participants in Council meetings on September 26, 2013.

3. Public audience is an instrument described in the City Statute (Law 10257/2001). The law states that, amongst other methods, debates, audiences, and public consultations should be used to generate the democratic management of cities (Art. 43).

4. Recomendação 10 (2013), Oficio 800/2013 – Promotoria de Justiça da Comarca de Ouro Preto, September 23, 2013. This document was read in the meeting and distributed electronically to all participants in Council meetings on September 26, 2013.

5. Letter communication by the *Secretario Municipal de Cultura e patrimônio*, September 23, 2013. This document was read in the meeting and distributed electronically to all participants in Council meetings on September 26, 2013.

6. Parecer técnico 001/2013, September 24, 2013. This document was read in the meeting and distributed electronically to all participants in Council meetings on September 26, 2013.

7. The emptiness of Burnier's train station is especially concerning as the station names the district. The District of Miguel Burnier was first known as Rodeio, later São Julião, and became Miguel Burnier in 1948, a name inspired by the Station's engineer and rail director Miguel Noel Nascentes Burnier (Prefeitura Municipal de Ouro Preto 2007: 15, 23).

8. Technical report by CIMOS (2013) – Coordenadoria de Inclusão e Mobilização Sociais do Ministério Publico de Minas Gerais (Minas Gerais Public Prosecutors' Coordination of inclusion and social mobilization) – referring to a technical visit to

Miguel Burnier on September 12, 2013, motivated by the Prosecutor of Ouro Preto (Ofício 0650/2013/PJOP). Documents accessed in a visit to the Coordenadoria de inclusão e mobilização sociais, Belo Horizonte, October 23, 2013.

9. Commission formed on September 24, 2013, and they visited the District on October 4, 2013.

CONCLUSION

1. See Souza 2011: 415; see also Souza 2001, for a broader discussion on DaMatta.

Bibliography

Abram, Simone. 'Contradiction in Contemporary Political Life: Meeting Bureaucracy in Norwegian Municipal Government'. *Journal of the Royal Anthropological Institute* 23, no. S1 (2017): 27–44.

Abram, Simone, and Gisa Weszkalnys. 'Elusive Promises: Planning in the Contemporary World: An Introduction', in *Elusive Promises: Planning in the Contemporary World*, eds. S. Abram & G. Weszkalnys. New York: Berghahn Books, 2013, 1–34.

Albert, Victor Attila. *The Limits to Citizen Power: Participatory Democracy and the Entanglements of the State*. London: Pluto Press, 2016.

Almeida Costa, Marco Antonio. 'Miguel Burnier Train Station'. Personal Archive, 2009.

Altbeker, Antony. *A Country at War with Itself: South Africa's Crisis of Crime*. Cape Town: Jonathan Ball Pub, 2007.

Andrade dos Passos, Luciana. *Planejamento urbano e participação da população: labirinto democrático?* Unpublished PhD Thesis. Brasília: Department of Architecture and Urbanism, University of Brasília, 2010.

Appadurai, Arjun. 'The Right to Participate in the Work of the Imagination (Interview with Arjen Mulder)'. *TransUrbanism* (2002): 33–46.

Appadurai, Arjun. *The Future as Cultural Fact: Essays on the Global Condition*. London: Verso, 2013.

Assessoria de Comunicação Social. *Realização da Prefeitura Municipal de Ouro Preto no ano de 2013*. Ouro Preto: Prefeitura Municipal de Ouro Preto, 2013.

Avila, Affonso. 'The Baroque Culture of Brazil', in *Brazil Body & Soul*, ed. E. J. Sullivan. New York: Guggenheim Museum, 2001, 114–127.

Avritzer, Leonardo. 'New Public Spheres in Brazil: Local Democracy and Deliberative Politics'. *International Journal of Urban and Regional Research* 30, no. 3 (2006): 623–637.

Avritzer, Leonardo. 'O Estatuto da Cidade e a democratização das políticas urbanas no Brasil'. *Revista Crítica de Ciências Sociais* 91 (2010): 205–221.

Avritzer, Leonardo. 'The Different Designs of Public Participation in Brazil: Deliberation, Power Sharing and Public Ratification'. *Critical Policy Studies* 6, no. 2 (2012a): 113–127.

Avritzer, Leonardo. 'Sociedade civil e Estado no Brasil: da autonomia à interdependência política'. *Opinião Pública* 18, no. 2 (2012b): 383–398.

Aykan, Bahar. 'How participatory is participatory heritage management? The politics of safeguarding the Alevi Semah ritual as intangible heritage'. *International Journal of Cultural Property* 20, no. 4 (2013): 381–405.

Batista da Costa, Everaldo. *Totalidade Urbana e Totalidade Mundo: As Cidades Coloniais Barrocas Face a Patrimonializacao Global*. Unpublished PhD thesis. São Paulo: University of São Paulo, 2011.

Baxstrom, Richard. 'Even Governmentality Begins as an Image: Institutional Planning in Kuala Lumpur', in *Elusive Promises: Planning in the Contemporary World*, eds. S. Abram & G. Weszkalnys. New York: Berghahn Books, 2013, 117–136.

Berlant, Lauren. *Cruel Optimism*. Durham, NC, and London: Duke University Press, 2011.

Bertorelli, Ebony, Patrick Heller, Siddharth Swaminathan, and Ashutosh Varshney. 'Does Citizenship Abate Class?' *Economic & Political Weekly* 52, no. 32 (2017): 47.

Borges, Antonadia. *Tempo de Brasília: Etnografando Lugares Eventos da Política*. Rio de Janeiro: Dumara Distribuidora, 2003.

Borneman, John. *Belonging in the Two Berlins: Kin, State, Nation*. Cambridge: Cambridge University Press, 1992.

Bourdieu, Pierre. *Distinction: A Social Critique of the Judgment of Taste*. London and New York: Routledge, 2010.

Brumann, Christoph. 'Outside the Glass Case: The Social Life of Urban Heritage in Kyoto'. *American Ethnologist* 36 (2009): 276–299.

Caldeira, Teresa P. R. *City of Walls: Crime, Segregation and Citizenship in São Paulo*. Berkeley: University of California Press, 2000.

Caldeira, Teresa P. R., and James Holston. 'State and Urban Space in Brazil: From Modernist Planning to Democratic Interventions', in *Global Assemblages: Technology, Governmentality, Ethics*, eds. A. Ong & S. Collier. London: Blackwell, 2005, 393–416.

Caldeira, Teresa P. R., and James Holston. 'Participatory Urban Planning in Brazil'. *Urban Studies* 52, no. 11 (2015): 2001–2017.

Canclini, Nestor G. *A Sociedade sem Relato: Antropologia e Estética da Iminência*. São Paulo: Editora da Universidade de São Paulo, 2012.

Carvalho, Bruno. *Porous City: A Cultural History of Rio de Janeiro*. Liverpool: Liverpool University Press, 2013.

Castriota, Leonardo B. *Patrimônio Cultural: Conceitos, Politicas, Instrumentos*. Belo Horizonte: IEDS, 2009.

Chasteen, John C. 'Introduction: Beyond Imagined Communities', in *Beyond Imagined Communities: Reading and Writing in Nineteenth-Century Latin America*, eds. S. Castro-Klarén & J. C. Chasteen. Washington, D.C.: Woodrow Wilson Center Press, 2003, ix–xxv.

Choay, Francoise. *O Patrimônio em Questão: Antologia Para um Combate*. Belo Horizonte, Brazil: Fino Traço Editora, 2011.

Chuva, Márcia. 'Fundando a Nação: A Representação de um Brasil Barroco, Moderno e Civilizado'. *Revista Topoi* 4, no. 7 (2003): 313–333.

Chuva, Márcia. *Os Arquitetos da Memoria: Sociogênese das Praticas de Preservação do Patrimônio Cultural no Brasil (Anos 1930–1940)*. Rio de Janeiro: Editora UFRJ, 2009.

Collins, John F. 'Historical and Cultural Patrimony in Brazil: Recent Work in Portuguese'. *Latin American Research Review* 44 (2009): 291–301.

Collins, John F. 'Melted Gold and National Bodies: The Hermeneutics of Depth and the Value of History in Brazilian Racial Politics'. *American Ethnologist* 38 (2011): 683–700.

Conley, Tom, and Marc Augé. *In the Metro*. Minneapolis: University of Minnesota Press, 2002.

Connerton, Paul. *How Societies Remember*. Cambridge University Press, 1989.

Cornwall, Andrea. 'Deliberating Democracy: Scenes from a Brazilian Municipal Health Council'. *Politics and Society* 36, no. 4 (2008): 508–531.

Cornwall, Andrea, and Alex Shankland. 'Cultures of Politics, Spaces of Power: Contextualizing Brazilian Experiences of Participation'. *Journal of Political Power* 6, no. 2 (2013): 309–333.

Costa, Lucio. 'Letter', in *Instituto do Patrimônio Histórico e Artístico Nacional*, IPHAN, Tombamento N. 1.305-T-90 Vol. 1 Conjunto Urbanístico (Plano Piloto). *Brasília/Distrito Federal*, 1990, 1–4.

Da Gama Cerqueira, Adriano S. Lopes. *Mapa da Exclusão Social em Ouro Preto*. Mariana: NEASPOC, 2003.

Dalsgaard, Anne L. *Matters of Life and Longing*. Copenhagen: Museum Tusculanum Press, University of Copenhagen, 2004.

Dalton, Patricio S., Sayantan Ghosal, and Anandi Mani. 'Poverty and Aspirations Failure'. *The Economic Journal* 126, no. 590 (2015): 165–188.

DaMatta, Roberto. *Carnivals, Rogues and Heroes: An Interpretation of the Brazilian Dilemma*. Notre Dame: University of Notre Dame Press, 1991a.

DaMatta, Roberto. *A Casa e a Rua: Espaço, Cidadania, Mulher e Morte no Brasil*. Rio de Janeiro: Editora Guanabara Koogan S.A., 1991b.

De Souza Santos, Andreza Aruska. 'Chandigarh and Brasília: Utopias or Dystopias?' in *Analyzing Globalization in the 21st Century*, eds. G. Fulquet, C. Janz & A. Kumar. New Delhi: Palm Leaf Publications, 2013, 163–175.

De Souza Santos, Andreza Aruska. 'Risky Closeness and Distance in Two Fieldwork Sites in Brazil'. *Contemporary Social Science* 13, no. 3–4 (2018): 429–443.

De Souza Santos, Andreza Aruska. 'Trading time and space: Grassroots negotiations in a Brazilian mining district'. *Ethnography* (2019). https://doi.org/10.1177/1466138119848456.

De Souza Santos, Andreza Aruska, and Tom Hulme. 'Cultural marginality and urban place making: The case of Leicester and Ouro Preto', in *Producing and Contesting Urban Marginality: Interdisciplinary and Comparative Dialogues*, eds. Julie Cupples & Tom Slater. London: Rowman & Littlefield International, 2019.

Di Paula, Sebastião. 'Asfaltamento de Area Histórica Esta Suspenso em Ouro Preto'. *Jornal Estado de Minas* 8 (2013).

Dixit, Avinash K., and Barry J. Nalebuff. *Thinking Strategically: The Competitive Edge in Business, Politics, and Everyday Life*. New York: Norton, 1991.

Do Vale, João. H. 'Justiça Mantem Suspenção de Asfaltamento de Area Historica de Ouro Preto'. *Jornal Estado de Minas* (2013a). Available online: http://www.em.com.br/app/noticia/gerais/2013/11/05/interna_gerais,467402/justica-mantem-suspensao-de-asfaltamento-de-area-historica-em-ouro-preto.shtml, accessed October 7, 2015.

Do Vale, João. H. 'Repúblicas Federais de Ouro Preto São Proibidas de Cobrar Estadia no Carnaval de 2014'. *Jornal Estado de Minas* (2013b). Available online: http://www.em.com.br/app/noticia/gerais/2013/12/19/interna_gerais,480961/republicas-federais-de-ouro-preto-sao-proibidas-de-cobrar-estadia-no-carnaval-de-2014.shtml, accessed November 12, 2015.

Ellin, Nan. *Postmodern Urbanism*. Oxford: Blackwell, 1996.

Faria, Lucas. 'Mulher Relata Abuso em 1998'. *Jornal O Tempo* (2014). Accessible online: http://www.otempo.com.br/cidades/mulher-relata-abuso-em-1998-1.898831, accessed November 12, 2015.

Faubion, James D. *Modern Greek Lessons: A Primer in Historical Constructivism*. Princeton, NJ: Princeton University Press, 1993.

Fausto, Boris. *A Concise History of Brazil*. Cambridge: Cambridge University Press, 1999.

Feld, Steven. 'Sound Structure as Social Structure'. *Ethnomusicology* 28, no. 3 (1984): 383–409.

Fernandes, Florestan. *The negro in Brazilian Society*. New York and London: Columbia University Press, 1969.

Ferrez, Marc. *O Mercado e a Igreja de São Francisco, Obra de Aleijadinho*. São Paulo, Brazil: Instituto Moreira Salles, 1880.

Fontana, Luiz. *Pilar*. Acervo do fotografo Luiz Fontana: Arquivo Fotografico Jose Goes Do Instituto de Filosofia, Artes e Cultura da Universidade Federal de Ouro Preto, 1936.

Fontana, Luiz. n.d. *Ponte Xavier, no Fundo Casa Onde se Reuniram os Inconfidentes*. Arquivo Fotografico Jose Goes Do Instituto de Filosofia, Artes e Cultura da Universidade Federal de Ouro Preto.

Freyre, Gilberto. *The Mansions and the Shanties: The Making of Modern Brazil*. London: Weidenfeld and Nicolson, 1963.

Fundação de Arte de Ouro Preto. *Sentidos Urbanos Patrimônio e Cidadania*. Ouro Preto: FAOP, 2009.

Ghertner, D. Asher. 'Calculating without Numbers: Aesthetic Governmentality in Delhi's Slums'. *Economy and Society* 39, no. 2 (2010): 185–217.

Gledhill, J. 'Redeeming the Promise of Inclusion in the Neo-Liberal City: Grassroots Contention in Salvador, Bahia, Brazil', in *Elusive Promises: Planning in the Contemporary World*, eds. S. Abram & G. Weszkalnys. New York: Berghahn Books, 2013, 117–136.

Goldman, Marcio. *How Democracy Works: An Ethnographic Theory of Politics*. Herefordshire, UK: Sean Kingston Publishing, 2013.

Gordillo, Gastón. 'The Ruins of Ruins: On the Preservation and Destruction of Historical Sites in Northern Argentina'. *Archaeologies and Ethnographies: Iterations of the Past* (2009): 30–54.
Gordillo, Gastón. 'Bringing a place in ruins back to life', in *Reclaiming Archaeology: Beyond the Tropes of Modernity*, ed. Alfredo González-Ruibal. London and New York: Routledge, 2013: 323–336.
Guareschi, Pedrinho A., and Sandra Jovchelovitch. 'Participation, Health and the Development of Community Resources in Southern Brazil'. *Journal of Health Psychology* 9, no. 2 (2004): 311–322.
Guimarães, Thiago. 'Texto da Bandeira de Ouro Preto Considerado Racista e Alterado'. *Folha de São Paulo* (2005). Available online: http://www1.folha.uol.com.br/folha/cotidiano/ult95u115415.shtml, accessed May 5, 2015.
Halbwachs, Maurice. *On Collective Memory.* University of Chicago Press, 1992.
Hale, Lindsay L. 'Preto Velho: Resistance, Redemption, and Engendered Representations of Slavery in a Brazilian Possession-Trance Religion'. *American Ethnologist* 24 (1997): 392–414.
Harms, Erik. *Saigon's Edge: On the Margins of Ho Chi Minh City*. Minneapolis: University of Minnesota Press, 2011.
Harms, Erik. 'Eviction Time in the New Saigon: Temporalities of Displacement in the Rubble of Development'. *Cultural Anthropology* 28, no. 2 (2013): 344–368.
Harris, Mark. 'Ways of Knowing', in *Ways of Knowing: New Approaches in the Anthropology of Experience and Learning*, ed. M. Harris. Oxford: Berghahn Books, 2007, 1–26.
Heathcott, Joseph. 'Heritage in the Dynamic City: The Politics and Practice of Urban Conservation on the Swahili Coast'. *International Journal of Urban and Regional Research* 37, no. 1 (2013): 215–237.
Helbert Pereira, Fernando. 'Miguel Burnier Train Station Restored'. Personal Archive, 2013.
Helbert Pereira, Fernando. 'Children and dogs walking on the railway track lacking trains'. Personal Archive, 2013.
Hellman, Judith. 'Structural Adjustment in Mexico and the Dog that Didn't Bark'. *Center for Research on Latin America and the Caribbean Working Paper Series*. North York, Ontario, Canada: York University, 1997.
Herzfeld, Michael. 'Engagement, Gentrification, and the Neoliberal Hijacking of History'. *Current Anthropology* 51 (2010): S259–S267.
Holanda, Sergio B. *Raízes do Brasil*. São Paulo, Brazil: Companhia das Letras, 2006.
Holston, James. 'Autoconstruction in Working-Class Brazil'. *Cultural Anthropology* 6, no. 4 (1991): 447–465.
Holston, James. 'The Spirit of Brasília: Modernity as Experiment and Risk', in *Brazil Body & Soul*, ed. E. J. Sullivan. New York: Guggenheim Museum, 2001, 540–557.
Holston, James. *Insurgent Citizenship: Disjunctions of Democracy and Modernity in Brazil*. Princeton, NJ: Princeton University Press, 2008.
Holston, James. *A Cidade Modernista: Uma Crítica de Brasília e sua Utopia*. São Paulo, Brazil: Companhia das Letras, 2010.
Holston, James, and Arjun Appadurai. 'Cities and Citizenship'. *Public Culture* 8 (1996): 187–204.

Hughes, Gordon. *Understanding Crime Prevention, Social Control, Risk and Late Modernity*. Buckingham, PA: Open University Press, 1998.

Imprensa Universitária da UFOP Ouro Preto. *UFOP Informativo*. Ouro Preto, 1982.

Instituto Brasileiro de Geografia e Estatística (IBGE). *Cidades: Ouro Preto* (2010). Available on-line: https://cidades.ibge.gov.br/brasil/mg/ouro-preto/panorama, accessed March 15, 2019.

Instituto Brasileiro de Geografia e Estatística (IBGE). *Perfil dos Municipios Brasileiros* (2012). Available online ftp://ftp.ibge.gov.br/Perfil_Municipios/2012/munic2012.pdf, accessed October 1, 2015.

Instituto do Patrimônio Histórico e Artístico Nacional (IPHAN). *Portaria 312, Anexo 1 Planta de Macro-Setorização* (2010). Available online: http://portal.iphan.gov.br/uploads/legislacao/Portaria_n_312_de_20_de_outubro_de_2010.pdf, accessed October 23, 2015.

Instituto do Patrimônio Histórico e Artístico Nacional (IPHAN). *Conjuntos Urbanos tombados (cidades históricas)* (2015). Available on-line: http://portal.iphan.gov.br/pagina/detalhes/123, accessed August 5, 2015.

Instituto do Patrimônio Histórico e Artístico Nacional (IPHAN). n.d. '*Revista e Boletins do Instituto do Patrimônio Histórico e Artístico Nacional* (1937–1947)'. Electronic Collection. Available online: http://www.docvirt.com/WI/RevIPHAN/RevIPHAN.htm, accessed October 23, 2019.

Jornal do Brasil. 'Mudanca da Capital'. (Rio de Janeiro), December 13, 1897.

Jornal Minas Geraes. 'O Tiradentes'. (Ouro Preto), April 21, 1892, 4.

Jornal Voz de Ouro Preto. 'Grande Hotel Villa Rica'. (Ouro Preto), November 10, 1935, 2.

Jovchelovitch, Sandra. 'Narrative, memory and social representations: A conversation between history and social psychology'. *Integrative Psychological and Behavioral Science* 46, no. 4 (2012): 440–456.

Kingstone, Peter. *The Political Economy of Latin America: Reflections on Neoliberalism and Development after the Commodity Boom*. New York: Routledge, 2018.

Knox, Hannah, and Penny Harvey. 'Anticipating Harm: Regulation and Irregularity on a Road Construction Project in the Peruvian Andes'. *Theory, Culture & Society* 28, no. 6 (2011): 142–163.

Koster, Martijn, and Monique Nuijten. 'From Preamble to Post-Project Frustrations: The Shaping of a Slum Upgrading Project in Recife, Brazil'. *Antipode* 44, no. 1 (2012): 175–196.

Kubitschek, Juscelino. *Por que construí Brasília*. Brasília: Senado Federal, 2010.

Larkin, Brian. 'The Politics and Poetics of Infrastructure'. *Annual Review of Anthropology* 42 (2013): 327–343.

Latour, Bruno, and Albena Yaneva. 'Give Me a Gun and I Will Make All Buildings Move: An ANT's View of Architecture'. *Explorations in Architecture: Teaching, Design, Research* (2008): 80–89.

Lea, Tess, and Paul Pholeros. 'This Is Not a Pipe: The Treacheries of Indigenous Housing'. *Public Culture* 22, no. 1 (2010): 187–209.

Leonidio, Otavio. *Carradas de Razoes: Lucio Costa e a Arquitetura Moderna Brasileira 1924–1951*. Rio de Janeiro, Brazil: Editora PUC-Rio, 2007.

Lombard, Melanie. 'Citizen Participation in Urban Governance in the Context of Democratization: Evidence from Low-Income Neighbourhoods in Mexico'. *International Journal of Urban and Regional Research* 37, no. 1 (2013): 135–150.

Lynch, Kevin. *The Image of the City*. Cambridge, MA: MIT Press, 1960.

Macdonald, Sharon. 'Is "Difficult Heritage" Still "Difficult"? Why Public Acknowledgment of Past Perpetration May No Longer Be So Unsettling to Collective Identities'. *Museum International* 67, no. 1–4 (2015): 6–22.

Marques, Ronaldo. 'Novas vizinhanças com a transferência da Capital', in *A historia da Escola de Minas 1876–2013*, ed. P. Lemos. Ouro Preto, Brazil: Editora Graphar, 2013, 251–258.

Marks, Monique, and Debby Bonnin. 'Generating Safety from Below: Community Safety Groups and the Policing Nexus in Durban'. *South African Review of Sociology* 41 (2010): 56–77.

Martins de Araujo, Eurico. *Republicas de Estudantes: Elo de Ouro Entre Antigos Alunos e a Escola de Minas*. Goiania, Brazil: Editora Kelps, 2013.

Maxwell, Kenneth. *Conflicts and Conspiracies: Brazil and Portugal, 1750–1808*. Cambridge, UK: Cambridge University Press, 1973.

McGranahan, Carole. 'Narrative Dispossession: Tibet and the Gendered Logics of Historical Possibility'. *Comparative Studies in Society and History* 52 (2010): 768–797.

Meira, Ana L. G. *O passado no futuro da cidade: Politicas públicas e participação dos cidadãos na preservação do patrimônio cultural de Porto Alegre*. Porto Alegre, Brazil: Editora da Universidade Federal do Rio Grande do Sul, 2004.

Metcalf, Thomas R. *An Imperial Vision: Indian Architecture and Britain's Raj*. New Delhi and New York: Oxford University Press, 1989.

'MIMO Festival'. https://mimofestival.com/brasil/mimo-festival/. Accessed March 12, 2019.

Mitchell, Timothy. *Colonising Egypt*. London: University of California Press, 1991.

Moreira, Adriana. 'Imoveis Valiosos'. *Revista em Minas* (2013): 12–15.

Moreira, Paulo. *Modernismo Localista das Américas: Os Contos de Faulkner, Guimaraes Rosa e Rulfo*. Belo Horizonte, Brazil: Editora UFMG, 2012.

Motta, Lia, and Analucia Thompson. *Entorno de Bens Tombados*. Rio de Janeiro, Brazil: IPHAN, 2010.

Mrázek, Rudolf. *Engineers of Happy Land: Technology and Nationalism in a Colony*. NJ: Princeton University Press, 2018.

Nascimento, Paulo C. 'Dilemas do Nacionalismo'. *Revista Brasileira de Informação Bibliográfica em Ciências Sociais* 56 (2003): 33–53.

Nielsen, Morten. 'Futures Within: Reversible Time and House-Building in Maputo, Mozambique'. *Anthropological Theory* 11, no. 4 (2011): 397–423.

Nielsen, Morten. 'A Wedge of Time: Futures in the Present and Presents without Futures in Maputo, Mozambique'. *Journal of the Royal Anthropological Institute* 20 (2014): 166–182.

O'Dougherty, Maureen. *Consumption Intensified: The Politics of Middle-Class Life in Brazil*. Durham, NC: Duke University Press, 2002.

Olson, David R. *The World on Paper: The Conceptual and Cognitive Implications of Writing and Reading*. New York: Cambridge University Press, 1994.

Owensby, Brian P. *Intimate Ironies: Modernity and the Making of Middle-Class Lives in Brazil*. Palo Alto, CA: Stanford University Press, 1999.

Penha, Ulisses Cyrino. 'Miguel Burnier: Geologia e Paisagens', in *Miguel Burnier: Marcas Históricas*, eds. A. Baeta & H. Pilo, 13–27. Belo Horizonte, Brazil: Gerdau, 2012.

Pires. Aurea. 'A Cidade'. (Ouro Preto), June 30, 1902, 4.

Portal do Turismo de Ouro Preto. *Dados geográficos* (2014). Available online: http://www.ouropreto.mg.gov.br/portal_do_turismo_2014/dados-geograficos, accessed October 18, 2015.

Prefeitura Municipal de Ouro Preto. *Invetario do Distrito de Miguel Burnier*. Ouro Preto, Brazil: Prefeitura Municipal de Ouro Preto, 2007.

Prefeitura Municipal de Ouro Preto. *Um Novo Modelo de Gestão de Cidades Históricas; O Acervo Cultural do Município de Ouro Preto: Conhecimento, Proteção e Difusão através do Inventario*. Ouro Preto, Brazil: Prefeitura Municipal de Ouro Preto, 2011.

Prefeitura Municipal de Ouro Preto. *Dossiê de Risco Geológico: Programa Municipal de Analise Geotécnica e Diagnostico de Risco de Ouro Preto*. Ouro Preto, Brazil: Prefeitura Municipal de Ouro Preto, 2012a.

Prefeitura Municipal de Ouro Preto. *Inventario de Proteção ao Acervo Cultural*. Ouro Preto, Brazil: Prefeitura Municipal de Ouro Preto, 2012b.

Prefeitura Municipal de Ouro Preto. *Mapa Ouro Preto*. n.d. Available online: http://www.ouropreto.mg.gov.br/patrimonio/imagens/mapaop.png, accessed December 8, 2015.

Prefeitura Municipal de Ouro Preto. *Ouro Preto's Emblem*. Ouro Preto, Brazil, 2019.

Promotoria Estadual de Defesa do Patrimônio Cultural e Turístico. Ministério Publico do Estado de Minas Gerais: Laudo de Vistoria Numero 78, 2013.

Rabinow, Paul. *French Modern*. Cambridge, MA: MIT Press, 1989.

Rama, Angel. *The Lettered City*. Durham, NC, and London: Duke University Press, 1996.

Rebhun, Linda-Anne. *The Heart Is Unknown Country: Love in the Changing Economy of Northeast Brazil*. Palo Alto, CA: Stanford University Press, 1999.

Reed, Adam D. E. 'City of Details: Interpreting the Personality of London'. *Journal of the Royal Anthropological Institute* 8 (2002): 127–141.

Rezende, Angelica de. 1965. *Lembrando Ouro Preto e o Aleijadinho*. Belo Horizonte, Brazil: Imprensa Oficial do estado de Minas Gerais, 1965.

Ribeiro, Darcy. *The Brazilian People: The Formation and Meaning of Brazil*. Gainesville: University Press of Florida, 2000.

Ribeiro, Rafael W. *Paisagem Cultural e Patrimônio*. Rio de Janeiro, Brazil: IPHAN, 2007.

Riedel, Augusto. *Cadeia de Ouro Preto*. Rio de Janeiro, Brazil: Biblioteca Nacional do Brasil, 1868–1869.

Rodrik, Dani. 'Goodbye Washington Consensus, Hello Washington Confusion? A Review of the World Bank's Economic Growth in the 1990s: Learning from a Decade of Reform'. *Journal of Economic literature* 44, no. 4 (2006): 973–987.

Romeiro, Adriana. *Paulistas e Emboabas no Coração das Minas: Ideias, Praticas e Imaginário Politico no Século XVIII*. Belo Horizonte, Brazil: Editora UFMG, 2008.

Rousseff, Dilma. *Discurso da Presidenta da República, Dilma Rousseff, na cerimônia de anúncio da seleção de obras do PAC Cidades Históricas* (2013). Available online: http://www2.planalto.gov.br/acompanhe-o-planalto/discursos/discursos-da-presidenta/discurso-da-presidenta-da-republica-dilma-rousseff-na-cerimonia-de-anuncio-da-selecao-de-obras-do-pac-cidades-historicas, accessed April 17, 2015.

Routon, Kenneth. 'Conjuring the Past: Slavery and the Historical Imagination in Cuba'. *American Ethnologist* 35, no. 4 (2008): 632–649.

Santana, Marcel M. *As Bordas Da Cidade Colonial: Um Estudo da Paisagem Tombada de Ouro Preto-MG*. Master Dissertation. Universidade Federal de Viçosa, 2012.

Schofield, P., J. Das-Munshi, L. Bécares, C. Morgan, V. Bhavsar, M. Hotopf, and S. L. Hatch. 'Minority Status and Mental Distress: A Comparison of Group Density Effects'. *Psychological Medicine* 46, no. 14 (2016): 3051–3059.

Scott, James C. *Weapons of the Weak: Everyday Forms of Peasant Resistance*. New Haven, CT: Yale University Press, 1985.

Secretaria Municipal de Patrimônio e Desenvolvimento Urbano. *Quadro V Volume Único Educação Patrimonial Sou do Morro e Também Sou Patrimônio*. Ouro Preto, Brazil: Prefeitura Municipal de Ouro Preto, 2012.

Sennett, Richard. *The Fall of Public Man*. Cambridge, UK: Cambridge University Press, 1976.

Sennett, Richard. *Flesh and Stone: The Body and the City in Western Civilization*. London: Clays Ltd., 1996.

Serviço do Patrimônio Histórico e Artístico Nacional Seção de história (SPHAN), n.d. *Conjunto Arquitetônico e urbanístico da cidade de Ouro Preto*. Processo de tombamento. Processo N. 70-T-38, 1. Book.

Sheriff, Robin E. *Dreaming Equality: Color, Race and Racism in Urban Brazil*. New Brunswick, NJ: Rutgers University Press, 2001.

Silverman, Helaine. 'Touring Ancient Times: The Present and Presented Past in Contemporary Peru'. *American Anthropologist* 104, no. 3 (2002): 881–902.

Simões, Lucas. 'Aluno Ruim não Terá Republica'. *Jornal O Tempo* (Ouro Preto), November 1, 2013: 27.

Simone, AbdouMaliq. 'People as Infrastructure: Intersecting Fragments in Johannesburg'. *Public Culture* 16 (2004): 407–429.

Slater, Tom. 'Your Life Chances Affect Where You Live: A Critique of the "Cottage Industry" of Neighbourhood Effects Research'. *International Journal of Urban and Regional Research* 37, no. 2 (2013): 367–387.

Souza, Jesse. 'Gilberto Freyre e a Singularidade da Cultura Brasileira'. *Tempo Social* 12 (2000): 69–100.

Souza, Jesse. 'A Sociologia Dual de Roberto da Matta: Descobrindo Nossos Mistérios ou Sistematizando Nossos Auto-Enganos?' *Revista Brasileira de Ciências Sociais* 16 (2001): 47–67.

Souza, Jesse. *Os Batalhadores Brasileiros: Nova Classe Media ou Nova Classe Trabalhadora?* Belo Horizonte, Brazil: Editora UFMG, 2010.

Souza, Jesse. *A Ralé Brasileira: Quem é e Como Vive*. Belo Horizonte, Brazil: Editora UFMG, 2011.

Stiglitz, Joseph. 'From Yellow Vests to the Green New Deal'. *Project Syndicate* (January 7, 2019). https://www.project-syndicate.org/commentary/yellow-vests-green-new-deal-by-joseph-e-stiglitz-2019-01.

Stoller, Paul. 'Embodying Colonial Memories'. *American Anthropologist* 96 (1994): 634–648.

Stoller, Paul. *Sensuous Scholarship*. Philadelphia: University of Pennsylvania Press, 1997.

Tropia, Eduardo. 'The Ceiling in São Francisco de Assis Church'. Personal Archive, 1980.

Ulturgasheva, Olga. 'Ghosts of the Gulag in the Eveny World of the Dead'. *The Polar Journal* 7, no. 1 (2017): 26–45.

Underwood, David K. 'Toward a Phenomenology of Brazil's Baroque Modernism', in *Brazil: Body & Soul*, ed. E. J. Sullivan. New York: Guggenheim Museum, 2001, 526–538.

UNESCO. *Recommendation Concerning the Safeguarding and Contemporary Role of Historic Areas* (1976). Available online: http://portal.unesco.org/en/ev.php-URL_ID=13133&URL_DO=DO_TOPIC&URL_SECTION=201.html, accessed October 23, 2015.

UNESCO. *Convention Concerning the Protection of the World Cultural and Natural Heritage* (1980). Available online: http://whc.unesco.org/archive/repcom80.htm, accessed May 7, 2015.

UNESCO. *State of Conservation: Historic Town of Ouro Preto* (1990). Available online: http://whc.unesco.org/en/soc/1614, accessed May 7, 2015.

UNESCO. *State of Conservation: Historic Town of Ouro Preto* (1993). Available online: http://whc.unesco.org/en/soc/1752, accessed May 7, 2015.

UNESCO. *State of Conservation: Historic Town of Ouro Preto* (2003). Available online: http://whc.unesco.org/en/soc/2779, accessed May 7, 2015.

UNESCO. *State of Conservation: Historic Town of Ouro Preto* (2004). Available online: http://whc.unesco.org/en/soc/1504, accessed May 7, 2015.

Universidade Federal de Ouro Preto. *Perfil Socioeconomico e Cultural dos Estudantes da Graduação* (2010). Available online: http://www.prace.ufop.br/Perfil%20do%20Aluno%20UFOP%20-%202010.pdf, accessed October 8, 2013.

Velho, Gilberto. 'Patrimonio, Negociação e Conflito'. *Mana Estudos de Antropologia Social* 12 (2006): 237–248.

Xavier, Angela L. *Tesouros, Fantasmas e Lendas de Ouro Preto*. Ouro Preto, Brazil: Edição do autor, 2009.

Werneck, Gustavo. Roubo de Peças Sacras da Basílica em Ouro Preto Completa 40 Anos de Impunidade. *Estado de Minas* (2013). Available online: http://www.em.com.br/app/noticia/gerais/2013/09/01/interna_gerais442837/roubo-de-pecas-sacras-de-basilica-em-ouro-preto-completa-40-anos-de-impunidade.shtml, accessed September 15, 2015.

Zweig, Stefan. *Brazil, Land of the Future*. London: Cassel and Company Ltd., 1942.

Index

Page references for figures are italicized and page references for tables are bold.

About the Author

Dr Andreza Aruska de Souza Santos is Director of the Brazilian Studies Programme and Lecturer at the Latin American Centre, University of Oxford. Her work focuses on urban ethnography, political participation, informal economies, mining towns, and social memory. She completed her PhD in social anthropology at the University of St. Andrews.

www.ingramcontent.com/pod-product-compliance
Lightning Source LLC
Chambersburg PA
CBHW031132270326
41929CB00011B/1598